C-2104   CAREER EXAMINATION SERIES

This is your
PASSBOOK for...

Professional Level Exam (PLE)

Test Preparation Study Guide
Questions & Answers

COPYRIGHT NOTICE

This book is SOLELY intended for, is sold ONLY to, and its use is RESTRICTED to individual, bona fide applicants or candidates who qualify by virtue of having seriously filed applications for appropriate license, certificate, professional and/or promotional advancement, higher school matriculation, scholarship, or other legitimate requirements of education and/or governmental authorities.

This book is NOT intended for use, class instruction, tutoring, training, duplication, copying, reprinting, excerption, or adaptation, etc., by:

1) Other publishers
2) Proprietors and/or Instructors of "Coaching" and/or Preparatory Courses
3) Personnel and/or Training Divisions of commercial, industrial, and governmental organizations
4) Schools, colleges, or universities and/or their departments and staffs, including teachers and other personnel
5) Testing Agencies or Bureaus
6) Study groups which seek by the purchase of a single volume to copy and/or duplicate and/or adapt this material for use by the group as a whole without having purchased individual volumes for each of the members of the group
7) Et al.

Such persons would be in violation of appropriate Federal and State statutes.

PROVISION OF LICENSING AGREEMENTS – Recognized educational, commercial, industrial, and governmental institutions and organizations, and others legitimately engaged in educational pursuits, including training, testing, and measurement activities, may address request for a licensing agreement to the copyright owners, who will determine whether, and under what conditions, including fees and charges, the materials in this book may be used them. In other words, a licensing facility exists for the legitimate use of the material in this book on other than an individual basis. However, it is asseverated and affirmed here that the material in this book CANNOT be used without the receipt of the express permission of such a licensing agreement from the Publishers. Inquiries re licensing should be addressed to the company, attention rights and permissions department.

All rights reserved, including the right of reproduction in whole or in part, in any form or by any means, electronic or mechanical, including photocopying, recording, or by any information storage and retrieval system, without permission in writing from the Publisher.

Copyright © 2024 by
National Learning Corporation

212 Michael Drive, Syosset, NY 11791
(516) 921-8888 • www.passbooks.com
E-mail: info@passbooks.com

PUBLISHED IN THE UNITED STATES OF AMERICA

PASSBOOK® SERIES

THE *PASSBOOK® SERIES* has been created to prepare applicants and candidates for the ultimate academic battlefield – the examination room.

At some time in our lives, each and every one of us may be required to take an examination – for validation, matriculation, admission, qualification, registration, certification, or licensure.

Based on the assumption that every applicant or candidate has met the basic formal educational standards, has taken the required number of courses, and read the necessary texts, the *PASSBOOK® SERIES* furnishes the one special preparation which may assure passing with confidence, instead of failing with insecurity. Examination questions – together with answers – are furnished as the basic vehicle for study so that the mysteries of the examination and its compounding difficulties may be eliminated or diminished by a sure method.

This book is meant to help you pass your examination provided that you qualify and are serious in your objective.

The entire field is reviewed through the huge store of content information which is succinctly presented through a provocative and challenging approach – the question-and-answer method.

A climate of success is established by furnishing the correct answers at the end of each test.

You soon learn to recognize types of questions, forms of questions, and patterns of questioning. You may even begin to anticipate expected outcomes.

You perceive that many questions are repeated or adapted so that you can gain acute insights, which may enable you to score many sure points.

You learn how to confront new questions, or types of questions, and to attack them confidently and work out the correct answers.

You note objectives and emphases, and recognize pitfalls and dangers, so that you may make positive educational adjustments.

Moreover, you are kept fully informed in relation to new concepts, methods, practices, and directions in the field.

You discover that you are actually taking the examination all the time: you are preparing for the examination by "taking" an examination, not by reading extraneous and/or supererogatory textbooks.

In short, this PASSBOOK®, used directedly, should be an important factor in helping you to pass your test.

PROFESSIONAL LEVEL EXAM (PLE)

INTRODUCTION

This test makes it possible for an applicant to be considered for several different professional entry level jobs through a single examination by measuring basic abilities that are common to these jobs.

Taking the test: Applicants should prepare for taking the test by following the practices and techniques suggested below:

1. Study the sample questions included in this document carefully. Also, the instructions included in the actual test booklet should be read carefully.

2. Use the clock or your watch as an aid in keeping track of the time during the examination.

3. In order to avoid running the risk of arriving too late to be admitted to the examination, allow extra time for traveling to the testing center.

How to answer the questions: Read each question carefully. Then read all of the answer choices to each question before deciding which answer is correct. If you are having difficulty determining the correct answer to a question, skip that one and come back to it later if you have time. It is to your advantage to answer each question even if you must guess at the answer. The final grade will be based only on the number of correct answers. There is no penalty for guessing.

Make no marks in the test booklet: All answers will be marked on a separate answer sheet. A mark on the answer sheet may be erased; however, care should be taken to make sure the erasure is complete. Any stray marks on the answer sheet may count against you. Scratch paper will be provided for making calculations. (Note: You will NOT be allowed to use calculators on the test.)

Additional Suggestions: Oral directions by the monitor and written directions in the test booklet are given to help the examinee and should be followed very closely. Pay close attention to the instructions given by the monitor at the beginning of the test session.

Test Contents (not necessarily in the order listed below on the actual test)

Problem Solving   (25 Questions)
Communication and Interaction with Others (25 questions)
Written Communication   (35 Questions)
Interpreting Written Material   (20 Questions)

Total = 105 Questions

PROBLEM SOLVING

Many jobs require the ability to conceptualize work requirements, accurately project resource needs, and coordinate activities. This requires skill in evaluating circumstances, identifying concerns and information needs, making computations and analyzing data, and considering alternatives. The test questions designed to assess these skills will be based on information in a chart or table that you must review, interpret, and in some cases, manipulate. The key to answering these types of questions is to make sure that you thoroughly review the information and consider the larger context or objective to which the information relates.

Sample Question 1

Session 3 Program Summary

	Attendees at Orientation	Program Registrants	Participants Completing Program
Program A	88	72	61
Program B	45	39	30
Program C	58	52	46

1. Which of the programs has the greatest success in getting orientation attendees to register for the program?

   A. Program A.
   B. Program B.
   C. Program C.

The correct answer is response option C. This is determined by computing the ratio of attendees to registrants for each of the three programs which is done by dividing the number of program registrants by the number of attendees. In this case, Program A would be 72/88 which rounds to .82 or 82% success, Program B would be 39/45 which rounds to .86 or 86% success, and Program C would be 52/58 which rounds to .90 or 90% success.

The best approach for these types of questions is to first review the entire table to get a good idea what information is being depicted. Next, carefully read each question and pay special attention to key words such as "greatest" or "least" to be certain what the question is asking you to determine. Then, consider the mathematical operations necessary to interpret the information presented. In this case, it was necessary to compute a ratio or percentage. In other problems, you might need to compute sums, averages, or similar basic arithmetic calculations. The key is to remember that this type of information represents relationships between things and you must accurately determine the relationship that is the subject of the problem and then select the correct approach.

Sample Question 2

Orientation Meeting Planning:
You must plan orientation meetings for new participants in a State program. You will be traveling to different locations and want to fit as many meetings into a single day as possible at each location. You have the information shown below to assist you in planning.

Time to allow for each meeting:	45 minutes
Time to allow after each meeting to organize enrollment forms:	10 minutes
Start time:	8:15 a.m.
Breaks:	20 minutes mid-morning
	20 minutes mid-afternoon
Lunch:	1 hour as close to noon as possible
End time:	No later than 5:00 p.m.

2. What is the maximum number of meetings that can be scheduled in a single day?

   A. 5
   B. 6
   C. 7
   D. 8

The answer is option C, 7 meetings. To determine the answer, you must plan out a complete schedule using the information provided.

By allocating the required time to each step you should see that since the 7th meeting ends at 4:20 p.m. and each meeting requires a total of 55 minutes, there is not enough time available in the day to schedule any more meetings.

Sample Question 3

Background: You work for a unit that provides administrative support to other State departments. Your supervisor asked you to have a meeting with your peers to discuss how to get client departments to turn in service requests in a more timely manner. The goal is to provide your unit with enough time to respond appropriately rather than just react to situations which have been delayed to the point that they are considered emergencies. When the group met, you summarized some of the main ideas and created the list shown below. You now intend to categorize the ideas based on a model of problem solving that identifies a problem's causes, symptoms, solutions, and relationship or correlation with other variables.

Task: Review the statements to familiarize yourself with the idea statements. Then, for each idea statement, determine if the idea is best categorized as a cause, symptom, solution, or relationship.

Initial Task Force Meeting

A	There is nothing on the request form that indicates how far in advance it should be turned in.
B	More than two-thirds of service requests are received at a point that requires expedited or emergency processing to meet the department's needs.
C	Requests that have been handled outside of the standard process have twice the likelihood of having errors.
D	An education briefing could be prepared for department representatives to provide information on the correct procedure and time requirements.

3. Statement A is best categorized as a:

   A. cause.
   B. solution.
   C. symptom.
   D. relationship.

The answer is response option A. The statement indicates that the request form does not indicate time requirements and this is a possible cause of the problem. To arrive at this answer, you must do two things. First, determine what the problem actually is. In this case, the problem has been defined as requests not being made in a timely manner. Next, look at each response option and decide how it relates to the problem. Statement A provides a reason why forms might be turned in late, making it a possible cause and, therefore, the correct answer. Statement B gives information that indicates the amount of requests that are late, making it a symptom. Statement C gives information related to the outcome associated with late requests, making it a relationship. Statement D offers an approach for making others more aware of time requirements, making it a solution.

COMMUNICATION AND INTERACTION WITH OTHERS

Professional jobs require skill in communicating directly with others by working cooperatively, attempting to understand other people's needs, actively listening, and clearly conveying one's own ideas to minimize conflict, resolve disagreements, and effectively influence or persuade. Test questions in this area require the application of basic communication and interpersonal concepts within the context of the work environment. To successfully answer the questions, you should imagine yourself in the role of a State employee in the situation presented and select the answer that is most likely to achieve the desired objective and reflect appropriate behavior and professionalism for a State employee.

Sample Question 4

4. If you are engaged in conversation with another person, the communication technique that is most likely to ensure that you understand what the other person is attempting to communicate is to:

   A. make continued eye contact.
   B. ask the person to speak slowly.
   C. nod your head in agreement while the person speaks.
   D. repeat back to the person what you believe they are saying.

The answer is option D. Making eye contact and nodding are aspects of communication, however, they are meant to show engagement and do not necessarily ensure understanding. Similarly, speaking slowly does not ensure that the message is accurately received. Only option D, repeating back the information is recognized as an effective technique for ensuring understanding.

Sample Question 5

5. If a person with whom you are interacting is frustrated about a situation and wants to vent by talking it out before moving on to productive conversation, it is best to:

   A. offer the person suggestions on how to calm down.
   B. politely excuse yourself, but do not explain the reason.
   C. point out to the person that the current behavior is unproductive.
   D. recognize that this is an important part of moving past the emotion and allow them to express their feelings.

The answer is option D. The other three response options do not allow the person to work past their frustration and may antagonize the person more. Cutting the person off in the midst of this process may make the person feel that their feelings are not viewed as important or reasonable. Most people just want the opportunity to be heard.

WRITTEN COMMUNICATION

Professional jobs require written communication through various types of correspondence and reports. This requires skill in expressing ideas clearly and concisely with correct English usage. The types of questions that you will encounter in the test to assess these skills include identifying the best choice for completing a sentence, identifying errors in sentences, and determining the best organization of sentences to form a paragraph.

Sample Questions 6 and 7

Some questions will require you to identify the best choice for completing a sentence. For these questions, you will be provided with a written passage which is identified as a piece of correspondence that you must edit. The sentence will have numbered blanks for which you must select the best alternative for completing the sentence. The alternatives will provide one correct option while the remaining response options are incorrect in some way. Incorrect options will involve errors in punctuation, grammar, or word usage.

Below is a sample piece of text and the corresponding questions:

I wanted to __1__ you that I have encountered some problems when using the client data base. Only one of my last five queries __2__ accurate.

6. Which of the following is the most appropriate to place in space number 1?

    A. note
    B. advice
    C. advise
    D. instruct

7. Which of the following is most appropriate to place in space number 2?

    A. is
    B. are
    C. has been
    D. have been

The correct answer for question 6 is response option C (advise). Advise means to give information and is the most appropriate word for the context of the sentence. Options A and B are grammatically incorrect. Option D does not convey the intended meaning since the word used means to teach.

The correct answer for question 7 is response option C (has been). That option is the only verb form that is grammatically correct given the beginning of the sentence and the intent to reflect something that has occurred in the past. Viewing the sentence without the preposition "of my last five queries" makes this clearer. The sentence then reads "Only one has been accurate."

Sample Questions 8 and 9

Some questions will require you to identify errors in sentences. The errors you must identify will involve errors in punctuation, grammar, and word usage. To respond to the questions you will only need to specify if the sentence is correct or incorrect. You will not need to specifically identify the errors.

Use the key below to answer the two questions that follow.

Key
A = The sentence is correct.
B = The sentence is incorrect.

8. Evaluating circumstances and recommending appropriate actions.

9. All client's records can be found in the master file.

The correct answer to question 8 is option B. The sentence is grammatically incorrect because it is a sentence fragment that does not contain both a subject and a verb. The correct answer to question 9 is also B. In this case, the sentence is incorrect because the punctuation of the word "client's" reflects a singular possessive. Since the sentence begins with the word "All", the word clients should be a plural possessive with the apostrophe after the "s" rather than before it.

Sample Question 10

Some questions will require you to organize sentences into the most appropriate order to form a logical and cohesive paragraph. To do this, you will need to identify which role each sentence should play including a topic sentence, the body of the paragraph, and the closing sentence. You must also determine if there are sentences that are inessential for conveying the paragraph's meaning in a clear and concise manner and could be eliminated.

Instructions: The sentences below comprise a paragraph about client information. Review the sentences and then answer the five questions that follow regarding how the sentences should be organized to form a logical and cohesive paragraph.

Sentence ID	Sentence Text
A	Such information is considered confidential and can only be released if specific procedures are followed.
B	Clients have a right to request information contained in their files.
C	Client files will be audited on an annual basis.
D	Once received, written requests will be responded to by a client services representative within five work days.
E	Requests for file information must be made on the forms provided in service offices and on the department's website.

10. Which sentence is the best sentence to use as a topic sentence to begin the paragraph?

    A. Sentence A.
    B. Sentence B.
    C. Sentience C.
    D. Sentence E.

The correct answer to the question is response option B. The combined theme of the sentences is client information requests and how they are processed. Therefore, starting the paragraph with the statement that clients have a right to receive the information is the most logical and useful sentence placement. For logical development, sentences A and E should serve as the body of the paragraph. Sentence D reflects how the information release process is completed and, as such, is the best sentence to conclude the paragraph. Sentence C relates to the separate topic of auditing files and can be eliminated.

INTERPRETING WRITTEN MATERIAL

Professional jobs often require referencing written information to determine appropriate actions. Such information may be found in a wide range of documents such as policies, procedures, correspondence, reports, and regulations. This requires skill in interpreting and evaluating written information. Questions of this type will be based upon reading passages provided in the test.

Sample Question 11

Instructions: Use the information below to answer the question that follows.

Helping Young Children Handle Stress

Many circumstances may cause a child to experience stress. These circumstances usually arise from things that are out of the child's control such as family changes or discord, abuse, a change in residence, natural disasters, or tragic events. A child's thinking is not developed enough to fully consider options or the results of actions and this can increase stress levels. Those who work with young children can help them to better handle these circumstances by being supportive and engaging in activities that will help the children develop coping strategies. Activities that encourage and develop social skills, problem-solving skills, the ability to focus attention, and the ability to act independently will all help children cope better by increasing their resiliency. This resilience will promote the attitude and enhance the skills necessary for handling stressful situations successfully.

11. According to the reading passage, a person who works with children can best assist them in handling stress by helping them to develop skills that enable them to:

    A. avoid stress.
    B. control circumstances.
    C. become more resilient.
    D. consider options more effectively.

The correct answer to the question is response option C. By reading the entire passage, the reader can follow the progression of thought and determine that the paragraph essentially states that children can learn to handle stress better if the adults who work with them engage them in activities which make them more resilient. This is clearly summarized in the paragraph's concluding sentence.

The best way to approach this type of question is to read the entire passage before reading the questions to familiarize yourself with its content. Then, read the question and go back to the paragraph to read specifically for the information requested by the question. Make sure to eliminate response options from your consideration that are clearly in error or those which are true statements, but not the answer to the question.

HOW TO TAKE A TEST

I. YOU MUST PASS AN EXAMINATION

A. *WHAT EVERY CANDIDATE SHOULD KNOW*

Examination applicants often ask us for help in preparing for the written test. What can I study in advance? What kinds of questions will be asked? How will the test be given? How will the papers be graded?

As an applicant for a civil service examination, you may be wondering about some of these things. Our purpose here is to suggest effective methods of advance study and to describe civil service examinations.

Your chances for success on this examination can be increased if you know how to prepare. Those "pre-examination jitters" can be reduced if you know what to expect. You can even experience an adventure in good citizenship if you know why civil service exams are given.

B. *WHY ARE CIVIL SERVICE EXAMINATIONS GIVEN?*

Civil service examinations are important to you in two ways. As a citizen, you want public jobs filled by employees who know how to do their work. As a job seeker, you want a fair chance to compete for that job on an equal footing with other candidates. The best-known means of accomplishing this two-fold goal is the competitive examination.

Exams are widely publicized throughout the nation. They may be administered for jobs in federal, state, city, municipal, town or village governments or agencies.

Any citizen may apply, with some limitations, such as the age or residence of applicants. Your experience and education may be reviewed to see whether you meet the requirements for the particular examination. When these requirements exist, they are reasonable and applied consistently to all applicants. Thus, a competitive examination may cause you some uneasiness now, but it is your privilege and safeguard.

C. *HOW ARE CIVIL SERVICE EXAMS DEVELOPED?*

Examinations are carefully written by trained technicians who are specialists in the field known as "psychological measurement," in consultation with recognized authorities in the field of work that the test will cover. These experts recommend the subject matter areas or skills to be tested; only those knowledges or skills important to your success on the job are included. The most reliable books and source materials available are used as references. Together, the experts and technicians judge the difficulty level of the questions.

Test technicians know how to phrase questions so that the problem is clearly stated. Their ethics do not permit "trick" or "catch" questions. Questions may have been tried out on sample groups, or subjected to statistical analysis, to determine their usefulness.

Written tests are often used in combination with performance tests, ratings of training and experience, and oral interviews. All of these measures combine to form the best-known means of finding the right person for the right job.

II. HOW TO PASS THE WRITTEN TEST

A. NATURE OF THE EXAMINATION

To prepare intelligently for civil service examinations, you should know how they differ from school examinations you have taken. In school you were assigned certain definite pages to read or subjects to cover. The examination questions were quite detailed and usually emphasized memory. Civil service exams, on the other hand, try to discover your present ability to perform the duties of a position, plus your potentiality to learn these duties. In other words, a civil service exam attempts to predict how successful you will be. Questions cover such a broad area that they cannot be as minute and detailed as school exam questions.

In the public service similar kinds of work, or positions, are grouped together in one "class." This process is known as *position-classification*. All the positions in a class are paid according to the salary range for that class. One class title covers all of these positions, and they are all tested by the same examination.

B. FOUR BASIC STEPS

1) Study the announcement

How, then, can you know what subjects to study? Our best answer is: "Learn as much as possible about the class of positions for which you've applied." The exam will test the knowledge, skills and abilities needed to do the work.

Your most valuable source of information about the position you want is the official exam announcement. This announcement lists the training and experience qualifications. Check these standards and apply only if you come reasonably close to meeting them.

The brief description of the position in the examination announcement offers some clues to the subjects which will be tested. Think about the job itself. Review the duties in your mind. Can you perform them, or are there some in which you are rusty? Fill in the blank spots in your preparation.

Many jurisdictions preview the written test in the exam announcement by including a section called "Knowledge and Abilities Required," "Scope of the Examination," or some similar heading. Here you will find out specifically what fields will be tested.

2) Review your own background

Once you learn in general what the position is all about, and what you need to know to do the work, ask yourself which subjects you already know fairly well and which need improvement. You may wonder whether to concentrate on improving your strong areas or on building some background in your fields of weakness. When the announcement has specified "some knowledge" or "considerable knowledge," or has used adjectives like "beginning principles of..." or "advanced ... methods," you can get a clue as to the number and difficulty of questions to be asked in any given field. More questions, and hence broader coverage, would be included for those subjects which are more important in the work. Now weigh your strengths and weaknesses against the job requirements and prepare accordingly.

3) Determine the level of the position

Another way to tell how intensively you should prepare is to understand the level of the job for which you are applying. Is it the entering level? In other words, is this the position in which beginners in a field of work are hired? Or is it an intermediate or advanced level? Sometimes this is indicated by such words as "Junior" or "Senior" in the class title. Other jurisdictions use Roman numerals to designate the level – Clerk I, Clerk II, for example. The word "Supervisor" sometimes appears in the title. If the level is not indicated by the title, check the description of duties. Will you be working under very close supervision, or will you have responsibility for independent decisions in this work?

4) Choose appropriate study materials

Now that you know the subjects to be examined and the relative amount of each subject to be covered, you can choose suitable study materials. For beginning level jobs, or even advanced ones, if you have a pronounced weakness in some aspect of your training, read a modern, standard textbook in that field. Be sure it is up to date and has general coverage. Such books are normally available at your library, and the librarian will be glad to help you locate one. For entry-level positions, questions of appropriate difficulty are chosen -- neither highly advanced questions, nor those too simple. Such questions require careful thought but not advanced training.

If the position for which you are applying is technical or advanced, you will read more advanced, specialized material. If you are already familiar with the basic principles of your field, elementary textbooks would waste your time. Concentrate on advanced textbooks and technical periodicals. Think through the concepts and review difficult problems in your field.

These are all general sources. You can get more ideas on your own initiative, following these leads. For example, training manuals and publications of the government agency which employs workers in your field can be useful, particularly for technical and professional positions. A letter or visit to the government department involved may result in more specific study suggestions, and certainly will provide you with a more definite idea of the exact nature of the position you are seeking.

III. KINDS OF TESTS

Tests are used for purposes other than measuring knowledge and ability to perform specified duties. For some positions, it is equally important to test ability to make adjustments to new situations or to profit from training. In others, basic mental abilities not dependent on information are essential. Questions which test these things may not appear as pertinent to the duties of the position as those which test for knowledge and information. Yet they are often highly important parts of a fair examination. For very general questions, it is almost impossible to help you direct your study efforts. What we can do is to point out some of the more common of these general abilities needed in public service positions and describe some typical questions.

1) General information

Broad, general information has been found useful for predicting job success in some kinds of work. This is tested in a variety of ways, from vocabulary lists to questions about current events. Basic background in some field of work, such as sociology or economics, may be sampled in a group of questions. Often these are principles which have become familiar to most persons through exposure rather than through formal training. It is difficult to advise you how to study for these questions; being alert to the world around you is our best suggestion.

2) Verbal ability

An example of an ability needed in many positions is verbal or language ability. Verbal ability is, in brief, the ability to use and understand words. Vocabulary and grammar tests are typical measures of this ability. Reading comprehension or paragraph interpretation questions are common in many kinds of civil service tests. You are given a paragraph of written material and asked to find its central meaning.

3) Numerical ability

Number skills can be tested by the familiar arithmetic problem, by checking paired lists of numbers to see which are alike and which are different, or by interpreting charts and graphs. In the latter test, a graph may be printed in the test booklet which you are asked to use as the basis for answering questions.

4) Observation

A popular test for law-enforcement positions is the observation test. A picture is shown to you for several minutes, then taken away. Questions about the picture test your ability to observe both details and larger elements.

5) Following directions

In many positions in the public service, the employee must be able to carry out written instructions dependably and accurately. You may be given a chart with several columns, each column listing a variety of information. The questions require you to carry out directions involving the information given in the chart.

6) Skills and aptitudes

Performance tests effectively measure some manual skills and aptitudes. When the skill is one in which you are trained, such as typing or shorthand, you can practice. These tests are often very much like those given in business school or high school courses. For many of the other skills and aptitudes, however, no short-time preparation can be made. Skills and abilities natural to you or that you have developed throughout your lifetime are being tested.

Many of the general questions just described provide all the data needed to answer the questions and ask you to use your reasoning ability to find the answers. Your best preparation for these tests, as well as for tests of facts and ideas, is to be at your physical and mental best. You, no doubt, have your own methods of getting into an exam-taking mood and keeping "in shape." The next section lists some ideas on this subject.

IV. KINDS OF QUESTIONS

Only rarely is the "essay" question, which you answer in narrative form, used in civil service tests. Civil service tests are usually of the short-answer type. Full instructions for answering these questions will be given to you at the examination. But in case this is your first experience with short-answer questions and separate answer sheets, here is what you need to know:

1) Multiple-choice Questions

Most popular of the short-answer questions is the "multiple choice" or "best answer" question. It can be used, for example, to test for factual knowledge, ability to solve problems or judgment in meeting situations found at work.

A multiple-choice question is normally one of three types—
- It can begin with an incomplete statement followed by several possible endings. You are to find the one ending which *best* completes the statement, although some of the others may not be entirely wrong.
- It can also be a complete statement in the form of a question which is answered by choosing one of the statements listed.

- It can be in the form of a problem – again you select the best answer.

Here is an example of a multiple-choice question with a discussion which should give you some clues as to the method for choosing the right answer:

When an employee has a complaint about his assignment, the action which will *best* help him overcome his difficulty is to
  A. discuss his difficulty with his coworkers
  B. take the problem to the head of the organization
  C. take the problem to the person who gave him the assignment
  D. say nothing to anyone about his complaint

In answering this question, you should study each of the choices to find which is best. Consider choice "A" – Certainly an employee may discuss his complaint with fellow employees, but no change or improvement can result, and the complaint remains unresolved. Choice "B" is a poor choice since the head of the organization probably does not know what assignment you have been given, and taking your problem to him is known as "going over the head" of the supervisor. The supervisor, or person who made the assignment, is the person who can clarify it or correct any injustice. Choice "C" is, therefore, correct. To say nothing, as in choice "D," is unwise. Supervisors have and interest in knowing the problems employees are facing, and the employee is seeking a solution to his problem.

2) True/False Questions

The "true/false" or "right/wrong" form of question is sometimes used. Here a complete statement is given. Your job is to decide whether the statement is right or wrong.

SAMPLE: A roaming cell-phone call to a nearby city costs less than a non-roaming call to a distant city.

This statement is wrong, or false, since roaming calls are more expensive.

This is not a complete list of all possible question forms, although most of the others are variations of these common types. You will always get complete directions for answering questions. Be sure you understand *how* to mark your answers – ask questions until you do.

V. RECORDING YOUR ANSWERS

Computer terminals are used more and more today for many different kinds of exams.

For an examination with very few applicants, you may be told to record your answers in the test booklet itself. Separate answer sheets are much more common. If this separate answer sheet is to be scored by machine – and this is often the case – it is highly important that you mark your answers correctly in order to get credit.

An electronic scoring machine is often used in civil service offices because of the speed with which papers can be scored. Machine-scored answer sheets must be marked with a pencil, which will be given to you. This pencil has a high graphite content which responds to the electronic scoring machine. As a matter of fact, stray dots may register as answers, so do not let your pencil rest on the answer sheet while you are pondering the correct answer. Also, if your pencil lead breaks or is otherwise defective, ask for another.

Since the answer sheet will be dropped in a slot in the scoring machine, be careful not to bend the corners or get the paper crumpled.

The answer sheet normally has five vertical columns of numbers, with 30 numbers to a column. These numbers correspond to the question numbers in your test booklet. After each number, going across the page are four or five pairs of dotted lines. These short dotted lines have small letters or numbers above them. The first two pairs may also have a "T" or "F" above the letters. This indicates that the first two pairs only are to be used if the questions are of the true-false type. If the questions are multiple choice, disregard the "T" and "F" and pay attention only to the small letters or numbers.

Answer your questions in the manner of the sample that follows:

32. The largest city in the United States is
    A. Washington, D.C.
    B. New York City
    C. Chicago
    D. Detroit
    E. San Francisco

1) Choose the answer you think is best. (New York City is the largest, so "B" is correct.)
2) Find the row of dotted lines numbered the same as the question you are answering. (Find row number 32)
3) Find the pair of dotted lines corresponding to the answer. (Find the pair of lines under the mark "B.")
4) Make a solid black mark between the dotted lines.

VI. BEFORE THE TEST

Common sense will help you find procedures to follow to get ready for an examination. Too many of us, however, overlook these sensible measures. Indeed, nervousness and fatigue have been found to be the most serious reasons why applicants fail to do their best on civil service tests. Here is a list of reminders:

- Begin your preparation early – Don't wait until the last minute to go scurrying around for books and materials or to find out what the position is all about.
- Prepare continuously – An hour a night for a week is better than an all-night cram session. This has been definitely established. What is more, a night a week for a month will return better dividends than crowding your study into a shorter period of time.
- Locate the place of the exam – You have been sent a notice telling you when and where to report for the examination. If the location is in a different town or otherwise unfamiliar to you, it would be well to inquire the best route and learn something about the building.
- Relax the night before the test – Allow your mind to rest. Do not study at all that night. Plan some mild recreation or diversion; then go to bed early and get a good night's sleep.
- Get up early enough to make a leisurely trip to the place for the test – This way unforeseen events, traffic snarls, unfamiliar buildings, etc. will not upset you.
- Dress comfortably – A written test is not a fashion show. You will be known by number and not by name, so wear something comfortable.

- Leave excess paraphernalia at home – Shopping bags and odd bundles will get in your way. You need bring only the items mentioned in the official notice you received; usually everything you need is provided. Do not bring reference books to the exam. They will only confuse those last minutes and be taken away from you when in the test room.
- Arrive somewhat ahead of time – If because of transportation schedules you must get there very early, bring a newspaper or magazine to take your mind off yourself while waiting.
- Locate the examination room – When you have found the proper room, you will be directed to the seat or part of the room where you will sit. Sometimes you are given a sheet of instructions to read while you are waiting. Do not fill out any forms until you are told to do so; just read them and be prepared.
- Relax and prepare to listen to the instructions
- If you have any physical problem that may keep you from doing your best, be sure to tell the test administrator. If you are sick or in poor health, you really cannot do your best on the exam. You can come back and take the test some other time.

VII. AT THE TEST

The day of the test is here and you have the test booklet in your hand. The temptation to get going is very strong. Caution! There is more to success than knowing the right answers. You must know how to identify your papers and understand variations in the type of short-answer question used in this particular examination. Follow these suggestions for maximum results from your efforts:

1) Cooperate with the monitor

The test administrator has a duty to create a situation in which you can be as much at ease as possible. He will give instructions, tell you when to begin, check to see that you are marking your answer sheet correctly, and so on. He is not there to guard you, although he will see that your competitors do not take unfair advantage. He wants to help you do your best.

2) Listen to all instructions

Don't jump the gun! Wait until you understand all directions. In most civil service tests you get more time than you need to answer the questions. So don't be in a hurry. Read each word of instructions until you clearly understand the meaning. Study the examples, listen to all announcements and follow directions. Ask questions if you do not understand what to do.

3) Identify your papers

Civil service exams are usually identified by number only. You will be assigned a number; you must not put your name on your test papers. Be sure to copy your number correctly. Since more than one exam may be given, copy your exact examination title.

4) Plan your time

Unless you are told that a test is a "speed" or "rate of work" test, speed itself is usually not important. Time enough to answer all the questions will be provided, but this does not mean that you have all day. An overall time limit has been set. Divide the total time (in minutes) by the number of questions to determine the approximate time you have for each question.

5) Do not linger over difficult questions

If you come across a difficult question, mark it with a paper clip (useful to have along) and come back to it when you have been through the booklet. One caution if you do this – be sure to skip a number on your answer sheet as well. Check often to be sure that you have not lost your place and that you are marking in the row numbered the same as the question you are answering.

6) Read the questions

Be sure you know what the question asks! Many capable people are unsuccessful because they failed to *read* the questions correctly.

7) Answer all questions

Unless you have been instructed that a penalty will be deducted for incorrect answers, it is better to guess than to omit a question.

8) Speed tests

It is often better NOT to guess on speed tests. It has been found that on timed tests people are tempted to spend the last few seconds before time is called in marking answers at random – without even reading them – in the hope of picking up a few extra points. To discourage this practice, the instructions may warn you that your score will be "corrected" for guessing. That is, a penalty will be applied. The incorrect answers will be deducted from the correct ones, or some other penalty formula will be used.

9) Review your answers

If you finish before time is called, go back to the questions you guessed or omitted to give them further thought. Review other answers if you have time.

10) Return your test materials

If you are ready to leave before others have finished or time is called, take ALL your materials to the monitor and leave quietly. Never take any test material with you. The monitor can discover whose papers are not complete, and taking a test booklet may be grounds for disqualification.

VIII. EXAMINATION TECHNIQUES

1) Read the general instructions carefully. These are usually printed on the first page of the exam booklet. As a rule, these instructions refer to the timing of the examination; the fact that you should not start work until the signal and must stop work at a signal, etc. If there are any *special* instructions, such as a choice of questions to be answered, make sure that you note this instruction carefully.

2) When you are ready to start work on the examination, that is as soon as the signal has been given, read the instructions to each question booklet, underline any key words or phrases, such as *least, best, outline, describe* and the like. In this way you will tend to answer as requested rather than discover on reviewing your paper that you *listed without describing*, that you selected the *worst* choice rather than the *best* choice, etc.

3) If the examination is of the objective or multiple-choice type – that is, each question will also give a series of possible answers: A, B, C or D, and you are called upon to select the best answer and write the letter next to that answer on your answer paper – it is advisable to start answering each question in turn. There may be anywhere from 50 to 100 such questions in the three or four hours allotted and you can see how much time would be taken if you read through all the questions before beginning to answer any. Furthermore, if you come across a question or group of questions which you know would be difficult to answer, it would undoubtedly affect your handling of all the other questions.

4) If the examination is of the essay type and contains but a few questions, it is a moot point as to whether you should read all the questions before starting to answer any one. Of course, if you are given a choice – say five out of seven and the like – then it is essential to read all the questions so you can eliminate the two that are most difficult. If, however, you are asked to answer all the questions, there may be danger in trying to answer the easiest one first because you may find that you will spend too much time on it. The best technique is to answer the first question, then proceed to the second, etc.

5) Time your answers. Before the exam begins, write down the time it started, then add the time allowed for the examination and write down the time it must be completed, then divide the time available somewhat as follows:
    - If 3-1/2 hours are allowed, that would be 210 minutes. If you have 80 objective-type questions, that would be an average of 2-1/2 minutes per question. Allow yourself no more than 2 minutes per question, or a total of 160 minutes, which will permit about 50 minutes to review.
    - If for the time allotment of 210 minutes there are 7 essay questions to answer, that would average about 30 minutes a question. Give yourself only 25 minutes per question so that you have about 35 minutes to review.

6) The most important instruction is to *read each question* and make sure you know what is wanted. The second most important instruction is to *time yourself properly* so that you answer every question. The third most important instruction is to *answer every question*. Guess if you have to but include something for each question. Remember that you will receive no credit for a blank and will probably receive some credit if you write something in answer to an essay question. If you guess a letter – say "B" for a multiple-choice question – you may have guessed right. If you leave a blank as an answer to a multiple-choice question, the examiners may respect your feelings but it will not add a point to your score. Some exams may penalize you for wrong answers, so in such cases *only*, you may not want to guess unless you have some basis for your answer.

7) Suggestions
    a. Objective-type questions
        1. Examine the question booklet for proper sequence of pages and questions
        2. Read all instructions carefully
        3. Skip any question which seems too difficult; return to it after all other questions have been answered
        4. Apportion your time properly; do not spend too much time on any single question or group of questions

5. Note and underline key words – *all, most, fewest, least, best, worst, same, opposite*, etc.
6. Pay particular attention to negatives
7. Note unusual option, e.g., unduly long, short, complex, different or similar in content to the body of the question
8. Observe the use of "hedging" words – *probably, may, most likely*, etc.
9. Make sure that your answer is put next to the same number as the question
10. Do not second-guess unless you have good reason to believe the second answer is definitely more correct
11. Cross out original answer if you decide another answer is more accurate; do not erase until you are ready to hand your paper in
12. Answer all questions; guess unless instructed otherwise
13. Leave time for review

b. Essay questions
1. Read each question carefully
2. Determine exactly what is wanted. Underline key words or phrases.
3. Decide on outline or paragraph answer
4. Include many different points and elements unless asked to develop any one or two points or elements
5. Show impartiality by giving pros and cons unless directed to select one side only
6. Make and write down any assumptions you find necessary to answer the questions
7. Watch your English, grammar, punctuation and choice of words
8. Time your answers; don't crowd material

8) Answering the essay question

Most essay questions can be answered by framing the specific response around several key words or ideas. Here are a few such key words or ideas:

M's: manpower, materials, methods, money, management
P's: purpose, program, policy, plan, procedure, practice, problems, pitfalls, personnel, public relations

   a. Six basic steps in handling problems:
      1. Preliminary plan and background development
      2. Collect information, data and facts
      3. Analyze and interpret information, data and facts
      4. Analyze and develop solutions as well as make recommendations
      5. Prepare report and sell recommendations
      6. Install recommendations and follow up effectiveness

   b. Pitfalls to avoid
      1. *Taking things for granted* – A statement of the situation does not necessarily imply that each of the elements is necessarily true; for example, a complaint may be invalid and biased so that all that can be taken for granted is that a complaint has been registered

2. *Considering only one side of a situation* – Wherever possible, indicate several alternatives and then point out the reasons you selected the best one
3. *Failing to indicate follow up* – Whenever your answer indicates action on your part, make certain that you will take proper follow-up action to see how successful your recommendations, procedures or actions turn out to be
4. *Taking too long in answering any single question* – Remember to time your answers properly

IX. AFTER THE TEST

Scoring procedures differ in detail among civil service jurisdictions although the general principles are the same. Whether the papers are hand-scored or graded by machine we have described, they are nearly always graded by number. That is, the person who marks the paper knows only the number – never the name – of the applicant. Not until all the papers have been graded will they be matched with names. If other tests, such as training and experience or oral interview ratings have been given, scores will be combined. Different parts of the examination usually have different weights. For example, the written test might count 60 percent of the final grade, and a rating of training and experience 40 percent. In many jurisdictions, veterans will have a certain number of points added to their grades.

After the final grade has been determined, the names are placed in grade order and an eligible list is established. There are various methods for resolving ties between those who get the same final grade – probably the most common is to place first the name of the person whose application was received first. Job offers are made from the eligible list in the order the names appear on it. You will be notified of your grade and your rank as soon as all these computations have been made. This will be done as rapidly as possible.

People who are found to meet the requirements in the announcement are called "eligibles." Their names are put on a list of eligible candidates. An eligible's chances of getting a job depend on how high he stands on this list and how fast agencies are filling jobs from the list.

When a job is to be filled from a list of eligibles, the agency asks for the names of people on the list of eligibles for that job. When the civil service commission receives this request, it sends to the agency the names of the three people highest on this list. Or, if the job to be filled has specialized requirements, the office sends the agency the names of the top three persons who meet these requirements from the general list.

The appointing officer makes a choice from among the three people whose names were sent to him. If the selected person accepts the appointment, the names of the others are put back on the list to be considered for future openings.

That is the rule in hiring from all kinds of eligible lists, whether they are for typist, carpenter, chemist, or something else. For every vacancy, the appointing officer has his choice of any one of the top three eligibles on the list. This explains why the person whose name is on top of the list sometimes does not get an appointment when some of the persons lower on the list do. If the appointing officer chooses the second or third eligible, the No. 1 eligible does not get a job at once, but stays on the list until he is appointed or the list is terminated.

X. HOW TO PASS THE INTERVIEW TEST

The examination for which you applied requires an oral interview test. You have already taken the written test and you are now being called for the interview test – the final part of the formal examination.

You may think that it is not possible to prepare for an interview test and that there are no procedures to follow during an interview. Our purpose is to point out some things you can do in advance that will help you and some good rules to follow and pitfalls to avoid while you are being interviewed.

What is an interview supposed to test?

The written examination is designed to test the technical knowledge and competence of the candidate; the oral is designed to evaluate intangible qualities, not readily measured otherwise, and to establish a list showing the relative fitness of each candidate – as measured against his competitors – for the position sought. Scoring is not on the basis of "right" and "wrong," but on a sliding scale of values ranging from "not passable" to "outstanding." As a matter of fact, it is possible to achieve a relatively low score without a single "incorrect" answer because of evident weakness in the qualities being measured.

Occasionally, an examination may consist entirely of an oral test – either an individual or a group oral. In such cases, information is sought concerning the technical knowledges and abilities of the candidate, since there has been no written examination for this purpose. More commonly, however, an oral test is used to supplement a written examination.

Who conducts interviews?

The composition of oral boards varies among different jurisdictions. In nearly all, a representative of the personnel department serves as chairman. One of the members of the board may be a representative of the department in which the candidate would work. In some cases, "outside experts" are used, and, frequently, a businessman or some other representative of the general public is asked to serve. Labor and management or other special groups may be represented. The aim is to secure the services of experts in the appropriate field.

However the board is composed, it is a good idea (and not at all improper or unethical) to ascertain in advance of the interview who the members are and what groups they represent. When you are introduced to them, you will have some idea of their backgrounds and interests, and at least you will not stutter and stammer over their names.

What should be done before the interview?

While knowledge about the board members is useful and takes some of the surprise element out of the interview, there is other preparation which is more substantive. It *is* possible to prepare for an oral interview – in several ways:

1) Keep a copy of your application and review it carefully before the interview

This may be the only document before the oral board, and the starting point of the interview. Know what education and experience you have listed there, and the sequence and dates of all of it. Sometimes the board will ask you to review the highlights of your experience for them; you should not have to hem and haw doing it.

2) Study the class specification and the examination announcement

Usually, the oral board has one or both of these to guide them. The qualities, characteristics or knowledges required by the position sought are stated in these documents. They offer valuable clues as to the nature of the oral interview. For example, if the job involves supervisory responsibilities, the announcement will usually indicate that knowledge of modern supervisory methods and the qualifications of the candidate as a supervisor will be tested. If so, you can expect such questions, frequently in the form of a hypothetical situation which you are expected to solve. NEVER go into an oral without knowledge of the duties and responsibilities of the job you seek.

3) Think through each qualification required

Try to visualize the kind of questions you would ask if you were a board member. How well could you answer them? Try especially to appraise your own knowledge and background in each area, *measured against the job sought*, and identify any areas in which you are weak. Be critical and realistic – do not flatter yourself.

4) Do some general reading in areas in which you feel you may be weak

For example, if the job involves supervision and your past experience has NOT, some general reading in supervisory methods and practices, particularly in the field of human relations, might be useful. Do NOT study agency procedures or detailed manuals. The oral board will be testing your understanding and capacity, not your memory.

5) Get a good night's sleep and watch your general health and mental attitude

You will want a clear head at the interview. Take care of a cold or any other minor ailment, and of course, no hangovers.

What should be done on the day of the interview?

Now comes the day of the interview itself. Give yourself plenty of time to get there. Plan to arrive somewhat ahead of the scheduled time, particularly if your appointment is in the fore part of the day. If a previous candidate fails to appear, the board might be ready for you a bit early. By early afternoon an oral board is almost invariably behind schedule if there are many candidates, and you may have to wait. Take along a book or magazine to read, or your application to review, but leave any extraneous material in the waiting room when you go in for your interview. In any event, relax and compose yourself.

The matter of dress is important. The board is forming impressions about you – from your experience, your manners, your attitude, and your appearance. Give your personal appearance careful attention. Dress your best, but not your flashiest. Choose conservative, appropriate clothing, and be sure it is immaculate. This is a business interview, and your appearance should indicate that you regard it as such. Besides, being well groomed and properly dressed will help boost your confidence.

Sooner or later, someone will call your name and escort you into the interview room. *This is it.* From here on you are on your own. It is too late for any more preparation. But remember, you asked for this opportunity to prove your fitness, and you are here because your request was granted.

What happens when you go in?

The usual sequence of events will be as follows: The clerk (who is often the board stenographer) will introduce you to the chairman of the oral board, who will introduce you to the other members of the board. Acknowledge the introductions before you sit down. Do not be surprised if you find a microphone facing you or a stenotypist sitting by. Oral interviews are usually recorded in the event of an appeal or other review.

Usually the chairman of the board will open the interview by reviewing the highlights of your education and work experience from your application – primarily for the benefit of the other members of the board, as well as to get the material into the record. Do not interrupt or comment unless there is an error or significant misinterpretation; if that is the case, do not hesitate. But do not quibble about insignificant matters. Also, he will usually ask you some question about your education, experience or your present job – partly to get you to start talking and to establish the interviewing "rapport." He may start the actual questioning, or turn it over to one of the other members. Frequently, each member undertakes the questioning on a particular area, one in which he is perhaps most competent, so you can expect each member to participate in the examination. Because time is limited, you may also expect some rather abrupt switches in the direction the questioning takes, so do not be upset by it. Normally, a board member will not pursue a single line of questioning unless he discovers a particular strength or weakness.

After each member has participated, the chairman will usually ask whether any member has any further questions, then will ask you if you have anything you wish to add. Unless you are expecting this question, it may floor you. Worse, it may start you off on an extended, extemporaneous speech. The board is not usually seeking more information. The question is principally to offer you a last opportunity to present further qualifications or to indicate that you have nothing to add. So, if you feel that a significant qualification or characteristic has been overlooked, it is proper to point it out in a sentence or so. Do not compliment the board on the thoroughness of their examination – they have been sketchy, and you know it. If you wish, merely say, "No thank you, I have nothing further to add." This is a point where you can "talk yourself out" of a good impression or fail to present an important bit of information. Remember, *you close the interview yourself*.

The chairman will then say, "That is all, Mr. _____, thank you." Do not be startled; the interview is over, and quicker than you think. Thank him, gather your belongings and take your leave. Save your sigh of relief for the other side of the door.

How to put your best foot forward

Throughout this entire process, you may feel that the board individually and collectively is trying to pierce your defenses, seek out your hidden weaknesses and embarrass and confuse you. Actually, this is not true. They are obliged to make an appraisal of your qualifications for the job you are seeking, and they want to see you in your best light. Remember, they must interview all candidates and a non-cooperative candidate may become a failure in spite of their best efforts to bring out his qualifications. Here are 15 suggestions that will help you:

1) Be natural – Keep your attitude confident, not cocky

If you are not confident that you can do the job, do not expect the board to be. Do not apologize for your weaknesses, try to bring out your strong points. The board is interested in a positive, not negative, presentation. Cockiness will antagonize any board member and make him wonder if you are covering up a weakness by a false show of strength.

2) Get comfortable, but don't lounge or sprawl

Sit erectly but not stiffly. A careless posture may lead the board to conclude that you are careless in other things, or at least that you are not impressed by the importance of the occasion. Either conclusion is natural, even if incorrect. Do not fuss with your clothing, a pencil or an ashtray. Your hands may occasionally be useful to emphasize a point; do not let them become a point of distraction.

3) Do not wisecrack or make small talk

This is a serious situation, and your attitude should show that you consider it as such. Further, the time of the board is limited – they do not want to waste it, and neither should you.

4) Do not exaggerate your experience or abilities

In the first place, from information in the application or other interviews and sources, the board may know more about you than you think. Secondly, you probably will not get away with it. An experienced board is rather adept at spotting such a situation, so do not take the chance.

5) If you know a board member, do not make a point of it, yet do not hide it

Certainly you are not fooling him, and probably not the other members of the board. Do not try to take advantage of your acquaintanceship – it will probably do you little good.

6) Do not dominate the interview

Let the board do that. They will give you the clues – do not assume that you have to do all the talking. Realize that the board has a number of questions to ask you, and do not try to take up all the interview time by showing off your extensive knowledge of the answer to the first one.

7) Be attentive

You only have 20 minutes or so, and you should keep your attention at its sharpest throughout. When a member is addressing a problem or question to you, give him your undivided attention. Address your reply principally to him, but do not exclude the other board members.

8) Do not interrupt

A board member may be stating a problem for you to analyze. He will ask you a question when the time comes. Let him state the problem, and wait for the question.

9) Make sure you understand the question

Do not try to answer until you are sure what the question is. If it is not clear, restate it in your own words or ask the board member to clarify it for you. However, do not haggle about minor elements.

10) Reply promptly but not hastily

A common entry on oral board rating sheets is "candidate responded readily," or "candidate hesitated in replies." Respond as promptly and quickly as you can, but do not jump to a hasty, ill-considered answer.

11) Do not be peremptory in your answers

A brief answer is proper – but do not fire your answer back. That is a losing game from your point of view. The board member can probably ask questions much faster than you can answer them.

12) Do not try to create the answer you think the board member wants

He is interested in what kind of mind you have and how it works – not in playing games. Furthermore, he can usually spot this practice and will actually grade you down on it.

13) Do not switch sides in your reply merely to agree with a board member

Frequently, a member will take a contrary position merely to draw you out and to see if you are willing and able to defend your point of view. Do not start a debate, yet do not surrender a good position. If a position is worth taking, it is worth defending.

14) Do not be afraid to admit an error in judgment if you are shown to be wrong

The board knows that you are forced to reply without any opportunity for careful consideration. Your answer may be demonstrably wrong. If so, admit it and get on with the interview.

15) Do not dwell at length on your present job

The opening question may relate to your present assignment. Answer the question but do not go into an extended discussion. You are being examined for a *new* job, not your present one. As a matter of fact, try to phrase ALL your answers in terms of the job for which you are being examined.

Basis of Rating

Probably you will forget most of these "do's" and "don'ts" when you walk into the oral interview room. Even remembering them all will not ensure you a passing grade. Perhaps you did not have the qualifications in the first place. But remembering them will help you to put your best foot forward, without treading on the toes of the board members.

Rumor and popular opinion to the contrary notwithstanding, an oral board wants you to make the best appearance possible. They know you are under pressure – but they also want to see how you respond to it as a guide to what your reaction would be under the pressures of the job you seek. They will be influenced by the degree of poise you display, the personal traits you show and the manner in which you respond.

ABOUT THIS BOOK

This book contains tests divided into Examination Sections. Go through each test, answering every question in the margin. We have also attached a sample answer sheet at the back of the book that can be removed and used. At the end of each test look at the answer key and check your answers. On the ones you got wrong, look at the right answer choice and learn. Do not fill in the answers first. Do not memorize the questions and answers, but understand the answer and principles involved. On your test, the questions will likely be different from the samples. Questions are changed and new ones added. If you understand these past questions you should have success with any changes that arise. Tests may consist of several types of questions. We have additional books on each subject should more study be advisable or necessary for you. Finally, the more you study, the better prepared you will be. This book is intended to be the last thing you study before you walk into the examination room. Prior study of relevant texts is also recommended. NLC publishes some of these in our Fundamental Series. Knowledge and good sense are important factors in passing your exam. Good luck also helps. So now study this Passbook, absorb the material contained within and take that knowledge into the examination. Then do your best to pass that exam.

EXAMINATION SECTION

EXAMINATION SECTION
TEST 1

DIRECTIONS: Each question or incomplete statement is followed by several suggested answers or completions. Select the one that BEST answers the question or completes the statement. *PRINT THE LETTER OF THE CORRECT ANSWER IN THE SPACE AT THE RIGHT.*

Questions 1-5.

DIRECTIONS: Each of Questions 1 through 5 consists of a passage which contains one word that is incorrectly used because it is not in keeping with the meaning that the quotation is evidently intended to convey. Determine which word is incorrectly used. Select from the choices lettered A, B, C, and D the word which, when substituted for the incorrectly used word, would BEST to convey the meaning of the quotation.

1. Whatever the method, the necessity to keep up with the dynamics of an organization is the point on which many classification plans go awry. The budgetary approach to "positions," for example, often leads to using for recruitment and pay purposes a position authorized many years earlier for quite a different purpose than currently contemplated—making perhaps the title, the class, and the qualifications required inappropriate to the current need. This happens because executives overlook the stability that takes place in job duties and fail to reread an initial description of the job before saying, as they scan a list of titles, "We should fill this position right away." Once a classification plan is adopted, it is pointless to do anything less than provide for continuous, painstaking maintenance on a current basis, else once different positions that have actually become similar to each other remain in different classes, and some former cognates that have become quite different continue in the same class. Such a program often seems expensive. But to stint too much on this out-of-pocket cost may create still higher hidden costs growing out of lowered morale, poor production, delayed operating programs, excessive pay for simple work, and low pay for responsible work (resulting in poorly qualified executives and professional men)—all normal concomitants of inadequate, hasty, or out-of-date classification. 1.____

    A. evolution   B. personnel   C. disapproved   D. forward

2. At first sight, it may seem that there is little or no difference between the usableness of a manual and the degree of its use. But there is a difference. A manual may have all the qualities which make up the usable manual and still not be used. Take this instance as an example: Suppose you have a satisfactory manual but issue instructions from day to day through the avenue of bulletins, memorandums, and other informational releases. Which will the employee use, the manual or the bulletin which passes over his desk? He will, 2.____

of course, use the latter, for some obsolete material will not be contained in this manual. Here we have a theoretically usable manual which is unused because of the other avenues by which procedural information may be issued.
   A. countermand   B. discard   C. intentional   D. worthwhile

3. By reconcentrating control over its operations in a central headquarters, a firm is able to extend the influence of automation to many, if not all, of its functions—from inventory and payroll to production, sales, and personnel. In so doing, businesses freeze all the elements of the corporate function in their relationship to one another and to the overall objectives of the firm. From this total systems concept, companies learn that computers can accomplish much more than clerical and accounting jobs. Their capabilities can be tapped to perform the traditional applications (payroll processing, inventory control, accounts payable, and accounts receivable) as well as newer applications such as spotting deviations from planned programs (exception reporting), adjusting planning schedules, forecasting business trends, simulating market conditions, and solving production problems. Since the officer manage is a manager of information and each of these applications revolve around the processing of data, he must take an active role in studying and improving the system under his care.
   A. maintaining   B. inclusion   C. limited   D. visualize

3.____

4. In addition to the formal and acceptance theories of the source of authority, although perhaps more closely related to the latter, is the belief that authority is generated by personal qualifes of technical competence. Under this heading is the individual who has made, in effect, subordinates of others through sheer force of personality, and the engineer or economist who exerts influence by furnishing answers or sound advice. These may have no actual organizational authority, yet their advice may be so eagerly sought and so unerringly followed that it appears to carry the weight of an order. But, above all, one cannot discount the importance of formal authority with its institutional foundations. Buttressed by the qualities of leadership implicit in the acceptance theory, formal authority is basic to the managerial job. Once abrogated, it may be delegated or withheld, used or misused, and be effective in capable hands or be ineffective in inept hands.
   A. selected   B. delegation   C. limited   D. possessed

4.____

5. Since managerial operations in organization, staffing, directing, and controlling are designed to support the accomplishment of enterprise objectives, planning logically precedes the execution of all other managerial functions. Although all the functions intermesh in practice, planning is unique in that it establishes the objectives necessary for all group effort. Besides, plans must be made to accomplish these objectives before the manager knows what kind of organization relationships and personal qualifications are needed, along which course subordinates are to be directed, and what kind of control is to be applied. And, of course, each of the other managerial functions must be planned if they are to be effective.

5.____

Planning and control are inseparable—the Siamese twins of management. Unplanned action cannot be controlled, for control involves keeping activities on course by correcting deviations from plans. Any attempt to control without plans would be meaningless, since there are no way anyone can tell whether he is going where he wants to go—the task of control—unless first he knows where he wants to go—the task of planning. Plans thus preclude the standards of control.
   A. coordinating   B. individual   C. furnish   D. follow

Questions 6-7.

DIRECTIONS: Questions 6 and 7 are to be answered SOLELY on the basis of information given in the following paragraph.

    In-basket tests are often used to assess managerial potential. The exercise consists of a set of papers that would be likely to be found in the in-basket of an administrator or manager at any given time, and requires the individuals participating in the examination to indicate how they would dispose of each item found in the in-basket. In order to handle the in-basket effectively, they must successfully manage their time, refer and assign some work to subordinates, juggle potentially conflicting appointments and meetings, and arrange for follow-up of problems generated by the items in the in-basket. In other words, the in-basket test is attempting to evaluate the participants' abilities to organize their work, set priorities, delegate control, and make decisions.

6.   According to the above paragraph, to succeed in an in-basket test, an administrator must
    A. be able to read very quickly
    B. have a great deal of technical knowledge
    C. know when to delegate work
    D. arrange a lot of appointments and meetings

6.____

7.   According to the above paragraph, all of the following abilities are indications of managerial potential EXCEPT the ability to
    A. organize and control   B. manage time
    C. write effective reports   D. make appropriate decisions

7.____

Questions 8-9.

DIRECTIONS: Questions 8 and 9 are to be answered SOLELY on the basis of information given in the following paragraph.

    One of the biggest mistakes of government executives with substantial supervisory responsibility is failing to make careful appraisals of performance during employee probationary periods. Many a later headache could have been avoided by prompt and full appraisal during the early months of an employee's assignment. There is not much more to say about this except to emphasize the common prevalence of this oversight, and to underscore that for its consequences, which are many and sad, the offending managers have no one to blame but themselves.

8. According to the above paragraph, probationary periods are
   A. a mistake, and should not be used by supervisors with large responsibilities
   B. not used properly by government executives
   C. used only for those with supervisory responsibility
   D. the consequences of management mistakes

8.____

9. The one of the following conclusions that can MOST appropriately be drawn from the above paragraph is that
   A. management's failure to appraise employees during their probationary period is a common occurrence
   B. there is not much to say about probationary periods, because they are unimportant
   C. managers should blame employees for failing to use their probationary periods properly
   D. probationary periods are a headache to most managers

9.____

Questions 10-12.

DIRECTIONS: Questions 11 and 12 are to be answered SOLELY on the basis of the information given in the following paragraph.

The common sense character of the merit system seems so natural to most Americans that many people wonder why it should ever have been inoperative. After all, the American economic system, the most phenomenal the world has ever known, is also founded on a rugged selective process which emphasizes the personal qualities of capacity, industriousness, and productivity. The criteria may not have always been appropriate and competition has not always been fair, but competition there was, and the responsibilities and the rewards—with exceptions, of course—have gone to those who could measure up in terms of intelligence, knowledge, or perseverance. This has been true not only in the economic area, in the money-making process, but also in achievement in the professions and other walks of life.

10. According to the above paragraph, economic awards in the United States have
    A. always been based on appropriate, fair criteria
    B. only recently been based on a competitive system
    C. not gone to people who compete too ruggedly
    D. usually gone to those people with intelligence, knowledge, and perseverance

10.____

11. According to the above paragraph, a merit system is
    A. an unfair criterion on which to base rewards
    B. unnatural to anyone who is not American
    C. based only on common sense
    D. based on the same principles as the American economic system

11.____

12. According to the above paragraph, it is MOST accurate to say that 12.____
    A. the United States has always had a civil service merit system
    B. civil service employees are very rugged
    C. the American economic system has always been based on a merit objective
    D. competition is unique to the American way of life

Questions 13-15.

DIRECTIONS: The management study of employee absence due to sickness is an effective tool in planning. Questions 13 through 15 are to be answered SOLELY on the data given below.

Number of Days Absent Per Worker (Sickness)	1	2	3	4	5	6	7	8 or Over
Number of Workers	76	23	6	3	1	0	1	0
Total Number of Workers	400							
Period Covered	January 1 – December 31							

13. The total number of man-days lost due to illness was 13.____
    A. 110   B. 137   C. 144   D. 164

14. What percent of the workers had 4 or more days absence due to sickness? 14.____
    A. .25%   B. 2.5%   C. 1.25%   D. 12.5%

15. Of the 400 workers studied, the number who lost no days due to sickness was 15.____
    A. 190   B. 236   C. 290   D. 346

Questions 16-18.

DIRECTIONS: In the graph below, the lines labeled "A" and "B" represent the cumulative progress in the work of two file clerks, each of whom was given 500 consecutively numbered applications to file in the proper cabinets over a five-day work week. Questions 16 through 18 are to be answered SOLELY upon the data provided in the graph.

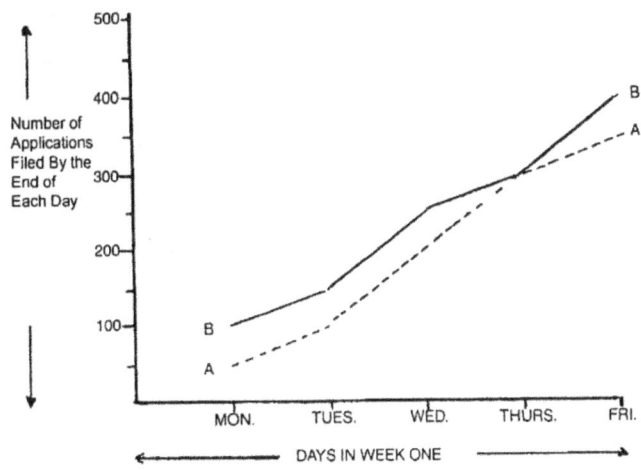

16. The day during which the LARGEST number of applications was filed by both clerks was
    A. Monday   B. Tuesday   C. Wednesday   D. Friday

17. At the end of the second day, the percentage of applications STILL to be filed was
    A. 25%   B. 50%   C. 66%   D. 75%

18. Assuming that the production pattern is the same the following week as the week shown in the chart, the day on which the file clerks will FINISH this assignment will be
    A. Monday   B. Tuesday   C. Wednesday   D. Friday

Questions 19-21.

DIRECTIONS: The following chart shows the differences between the rates of production of employees in Department D in 2009 and 2019. Questions 19 through 21 are to be answered SOLELY on the basis of the information given in the chart.

Number of Employees Producing Work-Units Within Range in 2009	Number of Work-Units Produced	Number of Employees Producing Work-Units Within Range in 2019
7	500 – 1000	4
14	1001 – 1500	11
26	1501 – 2000	28
22	2001 – 2500	36
17	2501 – 3000	39
10	3001 – 3500	23
4	3501 - 4000	9

19. Assuming that within each range of work-units produced the average production was at the mid-point at that range (e.g., category 500 – 1000 = 750), then the AVERAGE number of work-units produced per employee in 2009 fell into the range
    A. 1001 – 1500   B. 1501 – 2000   C. 2001 – 2500   D. 2501 – 3000

20. The ratio of the number of employees producing more than 2000 work-units in 2009 to the number of employees producing more than 2000 work-units in 2019 is MOST NEARLY
    A. 1:2   B. 2:3   C. 3:4   D. 4:5

21. In Department D, which of the following were GREATER in 2019 than in 2009?
    I. Total number of employees
    II. Total number of work-units produced
    III. Number of employees producing 2000 or fewer work-units
    The CORRECT answer is
    A. I, II, III   B. I, II   C. I, III   D. II, III

22. Unit S's production fluctuated substantially from one year to another. In 2018, Unit S's production was 100% greater than in 2017. In 2019, production decreased by 25% from 2018. In 2020, Unit S's production was 10% greater than in 2019.
On the basis of this information, it is CORRECT to conclude that Unit S's production in 2020 exceeded Unit S's production in 2017 by
   A. 65%   B. 85%   C. 95%   D. 135%

22.____

23. Agency "X" is moving into a new building. It has 1500 employees presently on its staff and does not contemplate much variance from this level. The new building contains 100 available offices, each with a maximum capacity of 30 employees. It has been decided that only 2/3 of the maximum capacity of each office will be utilized.
The TOTAL number of offices that will be occupied by Agency "X" is
   A. 30   B. 66   C. 75   D. 90

23.____

24. One typist completes a form letter every 5 minutes and another typist completes one every 6 minutes.
If the two typists start together, they will again start typing new letters simultaneously _____ minutes later and will have completed _____ letters by that time.
   A. 11; 30   B. 12; 24   C. 24; 12   D. 30; 11

24.____

25. During one week, a machine operator produces 10 fewer pages per hour of work than he usually does.
If it ordinarily takes him six hours to produce a 300-page report, it will take him _____ hours longer to produce that same 300-page report during the week when he produces more slowly.
   A. 1½   B. 1⅔   C. 2   D. 2¾

25.____

KEY (CORRECT ANSWERS)

		Incorrect Words
1.	A	stability
2.	D	obsolete
3.	D	freeze
4.	D	abrogated
5.	C	preclude

6.	C	16.	C
7.	C	17.	D
8.	B	18.	B
9.	A	19.	C
10.	D	20.	A

11.	D	21.	B
12.	C	22.	A
13.	D	23.	C
14.	C	24.	D
15.	C	25.	A

EXAMINATION SECTION
TEST 1

DIRECTIONS: Each question or incomplete statement is followed by several suggested answers or completions. Select the one that BEST answers the question or completes the statement. *PRINT THE LETTER OF THE CORRECT ANSWER IN THE SPACE AT THE RIGHT.*

1. An executive assigns A, the head of a staff unit, to devise plans for reducing the delay in submittal of reports by a local agency headed by C. The reports are under the supervision of C's subordinate line official B with whom A is to deal directly. In his investigation, A finds: (1) the reasons for the delay; and (2) poor practices which have either been overlooked or condoned by line official B.
   Of the following courses of action A could take, the BEST one would be to
   A. develop recommendations with line official B with regard to reducing the delay and correcting the poor practice and then report fully to his own executive
   B. discuss the findings with C in an attempt to correct the situation before making any formal report on the poor practices
   C. report both findings to his executive, attaching the explanation offered by C
   D. report to his executive on the first finding and discuss the second in a friendly way with line official B
   E. report the first finding to his executive, ignoring the second until his opinion is requested

1.____

2. Drafts of a proposed policy, prepared by a staff committee, are circulated to ten member of the field staff of the organization by route slips with a request for comments within two weeks. Two members of the field staff make extensive comments, four offer editorial suggestions, and the remainder make minor favorable comments. Shortly after, it found that the statement needs considerable revision by the field staff.
   Of the following possible reasons for the original failure of the field staff to identify difficulties, the MOST likely is that the
   A. field staff did not take sufficient time to review the manual
   B. field staff had not been advised of the type of contribution expected
   C. low morale of the field staff prevented their showing interest
   D. policy statement was too advanced for the staff
   E. staff committee was not sufficiently representative

2.____

3. Operator participation in management improvement work is LEAST likely to
   A. assure the use of best available management technique
   B. overcome the stigma of the outside expert
   C. place responsibility for improvement in the person who knows the job best
   D. simplify installation
   E. take advantage of the desire of most operators to seek self-improvement

3.____

4. In general, the morale of workers in an agency is MOST frequently and MOST significantly affected by the
   A. agency policies of organizational structure and operational procedures
   B. distance of the employee's job from his home community
   C. fringe benefits
   D. number of opportunities for advancement
   E. relationship with supervisors

5. Of the following, the PRIMARY function of a work distribution chart is to
   A. analyze the soundness of existing divisions of labor
   B. eliminate the unnecessary clerical detail
   C. establish better supervisory techniques
   D. simplify work methods
   E. weed out core functions

6. In analyzing a process chart, which one of the following should be asked FIRST?
   A. How   B. When   C. Where   D. Who   E. Why

7. Which one of the following is NOT an advantage of the interview method of collecting data? It
   A. enables interviewer to judge the person interviewed on such matters as general attitude, knowledge, etc.
   B. helps build up personal relations for later installation of changes
   C. is a flexible method that can be adjusted to changing circumstances
   D. permits the obtaining of *off the record* information
   E. produces more accurate information than other methods

8. Which one of the following may be defined as a *regularly recurring appraisal of the manner in which all elements of agency management are being carried out*?
   A. Functional survey   B. Operations audit
   C. Organization survey   D. Over-all survey
   E. Reconnaissance survey

9. An analysis of the flow of work in a department should begin with the _____ work.
   A. major routine   B. minor routine   C. supervisory
   D. technical   E. unusual

10. Which method would MOST likely be used to get first-hand information on complaints from the public?
    A. Study of correspondence
    B. Study of work volume
    C. Tracing specific transactions through a series of steps
    D. Tracing use of forms
    E. Worker desk audit

11. People will generally produce the MOST if
    A. management exercises close supervision over the work
    B. there is strict discipline in the group
    C. they are happy in their work
    D. they feel involved in their work
    E. they follow *the one best way*

12. The normal analysis of which chart listed below is MOST closely related to organizational analysis? _____ chart.
    A. Layout   B. Operation   C. Process
    D. Work count   E. Work distribution

13. The work count would be LEAST helpful in accomplishing which one of the following?
    A. Demonstrating personnel needs   B. Improving the sequence of steps
    C. Measuring the value of a step   D. Spotting bottlenecks
    E. Stimulating interest in work

14. Which one of the following seems LEAST useful as a guide in interviewing an employee in a procedure and methods survey?
    A. Explaining who you are and the purpose of your visit
    B. Having a general plan of what you intend to get from the interview
    C. Listening carefully and not interrupting
    D. Trying out his reactions to your ideas for improvements
    E. Trying to analyze his reasons for saying what he says

15. Which one of the following is an advantage of the questionnaire method of gathering facts as compared with the interview method?
    A. Different people may interpret the questions differently
    B. Less *off the record* information is given
    C. More time may be taken in order to give exact answers
    D. Personal relationships with the people involved are not established
    E. There is less need for follow-up

16. Which one of the following is generally NOT an advantage of the personal observation method of gathering facts? It
    A. enables staff to use *off the record* information if personally observed
    B. helps in developing valid recommendations
    C. helps the person making the observation acquire *know how* valuable for later installation and follow-up
    D. is economical in time and money
    E. may turn up other problems in need of solution

17. Which of the following would MOST often be the best way to minimize resistance to change?
    A. Break the news about the change gently to the people affected
    B. Increase the salary of the people affected by the change
    C. Let the people concerned participate at the decision to change

D. Notify all people concerned with the change, both orally and in writing
E. Stress the advantages of the new system

18. The functional organization chart   18.____
    A. does not require periodic revision
    B. includes a description of the duties of each organization segment
    C. includes positions and titles for each organization segment
    D. is the simplest type of organization chart
    E. is used primarily by newly established agencies

19. The principle of span of control has frequently been said to be in conflict with the   19.____
    A. principle of unity of command
    B. principle that authority should be commensurate with responsibility
    C. principle that like functions should be grouped into one unit
    D. principle that the number of levels between the top of an organization and the bottom should be small
    E. scalar principle

20. If an executive delegates to his subordinates authority to handle problems of a routine nature for which standard solutions have been established, he may expect that   20.____
    A. fewer complaint will be received
    B. he has made it more difficult for his subordinates to solve these problems
    C. he has opened the way for confusion in his organization
    D. there will be a lack of consistency in the methods applied to the solution of these problems
    E. these routine problems will be handled efficiently and he will have more time for other non-routine work

21. Which of the following would MOST likely be achieved by a change in the basic organization structure from the *process* or *functional* type to the *purpose* or *product* type?   21.____
    A. Easier recruitment of personnel in a tight labor market
    B. Fixing responsibility at a lower level in the organization
    C. Greater centralization
    D. Greater economy
    E. Greater professional development

22. Usually the MOST difficult problem in connection with a major reorganization is   22.____
    A. adopting a pay plan to fit the new structure
    B. bringing the organization manual up-to-date
    C. determining the new organization structure
    D. gaining acceptance of the new plan by the higher level employees
    E. gaining acceptance of the new plan by the lower level employees

23. Which of the following statements MOST accurately describes the work of the chiefs of MOST staff divisions in departments?
Chiefs
    A. focus more on getting the job done than on how it is done
    B. are mostly interested in short-range results
    C. nearly always advise but rarely advise
    D. usually command or control but rarely advise
    E. provide service to the rest of the organization and/or assist the chief executive in planning and controlling operations

23.____

24. In determining the type of organization structure of an enterprise, the one factor that might be given relatively greater weight in a small organization than in a larger organization of the same nature is the
    A. geographical location of the enterprise
    B. individual capabilities of incumbents
    C. method of financing to be employed
    D. size of the area served
    E. type of activity engaged in

24.____

25. Functional foremanship differs MOST markedly from generally accepted principle of administration in that it advocates
    A. an unlimited span of control
    B. less delegation of responsibility
    C. more than one supervisor for an employee
    D. nonfunctional organization
    E. substitution of execution for planning

25.____

KEY (CORRECT ANSWERS)

1.	A	11.	D
2.	B	12.	E
3.	A	13.	B
4.	E	14.	D
5.	A	15.	C
6.	E	16.	D
7.	E	17.	C
8.	B	18.	B
9.	A	19.	D
10.	A	20.	E

21.	B
22.	D
23.	E
24.	B
25.	C

TEST 2

DIRECTIONS: Each question or incomplete statement is followed by several suggested answers or completions. Select the one that BEST answers the question or completes the statement. *PRINT THE LETTER OF THE CORRECT ANSWER IN THE SPACE AT THE RIGHT.*

1. Decentralization of the authority to make decisions is a necessary result of increased complexity in an organization, but for the sake of efficiency and coordination of operations, such decentralization must be planned carefully. A good general rule is that
    A. any decision should be made at the lowest possible point in the organization where all the information and competence necessary for a sound decision are available
    B. any decision should be made at the highest possible point in the organization, thus guaranteeing the best decision
    C. any decision should be made at the lowest possible point in the organization, but always approved by management
    D. any decision should be made by management and referred to the proper subordinate for comment
    E. no decision should be made by any individual in the organization without approval by a superior

    1.____

2. One drawback of converting a conventional consecutive filing system to a terminal digit filing system for a large installation is that
    A. conversion would be expensive in time and manpower
    B. conversion would prevent the proper use of recognized numeric classification systems, such as the Dewey decimal, in classifying files material
    C. responsibility for proper filing cannot be pinpointed in the terminal digit system
    D. the terminal digit system requires considerably more space than a normal filing system

    2.____

3. The basic filing system that would ordinarily be employed in a large administrative headquarters unit is the _____ file system.
    A alphabetic   B. chronological
    C. mnemonic   D. retention
    E. subject classification

    3.____

4. A records center is of benefit in a records management program PRIMARILY because
    A. all the records of the organization are kept in one place
    B. inactive records can be stored economically in less expense storage areas
    C. it provides a place where useless records can be housed at little or no cost to the organization

    4.____

D. obsolete filing and storage equipment can be utilized out of view of the public
E. records analysts can examine an organization's files without affecting the unit's operation or upsetting the supervisors

5. In examining a number of different forms to see whether any could be combined or eliminated, which of the following would one be MOST likely to use?
   A. Forms analysis sheet of recurring data
   B. Forms control log
   C. Forms design and approval request
   D. Forms design and guide sheet
   E. Numerical file

5.____

6. The MOST important reason for control of *bootleg* forms is that
   A. they are more expensive than authorized forms
   B. they are usually poorly designed
   C. they can lead to unnecessary procedures
   D. they cannot be reordered as easily as authorized terms
   E. violation of rules and regulations should not be allowed

6.____

7. With a box design of a form, the caption title or question to be answered should be located in the _____ of the box.
   A. center at the bottom
   B. center at the top
   C. lower left corner
   D. lower right corner
   E. upper left corner

7.____

8. A two-part snapout form would be MOST properly justified if
   A. it is a cleaner operation
   B. it is prepared ten times a week
   C. it saves time in preparation
   D. it is to be filled out by hand rather than by typewriter
   E. proper registration is critical

8.____

9. When deciding whether or not to approve a request for a new form, which reference is normally MOST pertinent?
   A. Alphabetical Forms File
   B. Functional Forms File
   C. Numerical Forms File
   D. Project Completion Report
   E. Records Retention Data

9.____

10. Which of the following statements BEST explains the significance of the famed Hawthorne Plant experiments?
    They showed that
    A. a large span of control leads to more production than a small span of control
    B. morale has no relationship to production
    C. personnel counseling is of relatively little importance in a going organization

10.____

D. the special attention received by a group in an experimental situation has a greater impact on production than changes in working conditions
E. there is a direct relationship between the amount of illumination and production

11. Which of the following would most often NOT result from a highly efficient management control system?
    A. Facilitation of delegation
    B. Highlighting of problem areas
    C. Increase in willingness of people to experiment or to take calculated risks
    D. Provision of an objective test of new ideas or new methods and procedures
    E. Provision of information useful for revising objectives, programs, and operations

11.____

12. The PERT system is a
    A. method for laying out office space on a modular basis utilizing prefabricated partitions
    B. method of motivating personnel to be continuously alert and to improve their appearance
    C. method of program planning and control using a network or flow plan
    D. plan for expanding reporting techniques
    E. simplified method of cost accounting

12.____

13. The term *management control* is MOST frequently used to mean
    A. an objective and unemotional approach by management
    B. coordinating the efforts of all parts of the organization
    C. evaluation of results in relation to plan
    D. giving clear, precise orders to subordinates
    E. keeping unions from making managerial decisions

13.____

14. Which one of the following factors has the MOST bearing on the frequency with which a control report should be made?
    A. Degree of specialization of the work
    B. Degree of variability in activities
    C. Expense of the report
    D. Number of levels of supervision
    E. Number of personnel involved

14.____

15. The value of statistical records is MAINLY dependent upon the
    A. method of presenting the material
    B. number of items used
    C. range of cases sampled
    D. reliability of the information used
    E. time devoted to compiling the material

15.____

16. When a supervisor delegates an assignment, he should 16.____
    A. delegate his responsibility for the assignment
    B. make certain that the assignment is properly performed
    C. participate in the beginning and final stages of the assignment
    D. retail all authority needed to complete the assignment
    E. oversee all stages of the assignment

17. Assume that the department in which you are employed has never given 17.____
    official sanction to a mid-afternoon coffee break. Some bureaus have it and
    others do not. In the latter case, some individuals merely absent themselves
    for about 15 minutes at 3 P.M. while others remain on the job despite the
    fatigue which seems to be common among all employees in this department at
    that time.
    The course of action which you should recommend, if possible, is to
    A. arrange a schedule of mid-afternoon coffee breaks for all employees
    B. forbid all employees to take a mid-afternoon coffee break
    C. permit each bureau to decide for itself whether or not it will have a coffee break
    D. require all employees who wish a coffee break to take a shorter lunch period
    E. arrange a poll to discover the consensus of the department

18. The one of the following which is LEAST important in the management of a 18.____
    suggestion program is
    A. giving awards which are of sufficient value to encourage competition
    B. securing full support from the department's officers and executives
    C. publicizing the program and the awards given
    D. holding special conferences to analyze and evaluate some of the suggestions needed
    E. providing suggestion boxes in numerous locations

19. The one of the following which is MOST likely to decrease morale is 19.____
    A. insistence on strict adherence to safety rules
    B. making each employee responsible for the tidiness of his work area
    C. overlooking evidence of hostility between groups of employees
    D. strong, aggressive leadership
    E. allocating work on the basis of personal knowledge of the abilities and interests of the member of the department

20. Assume that a certain office procedure has been standard practice for many 20.____
    years.
    When a new employee asks why this particular procedure is followed, the
    supervisor should FIRST
    A. explain that everyone does it that way
    B. explain the reason for the procedure
    C. inform him that it has always been done that way in that particular office
    D. tell him to try it for a while before asking questions
    E. tell him he has never thought about it that way

5 (#2)

21. Several employees complain informally to their supervisor regarding some new procedures which have been instituted.
The supervisor should IMMEDIATELY
   A. explain that management is responsible
   B. state frankly that he had nothing to do with it
   C. refer the matter to the methods analyst
   D. tell the employees to submit their complaint as a formal grievance
   E. investigate the complaint

21.____

22. A new employee asks his supervisor how he is doing. Actually, he is not doing well in some phases of the job, but it is felt that he will learn in time.
The BEST response for the supervisor to make is:
   A. Some things you are doing well, and in others I am sure you will improve.
   B. Wait until the end of your probation period when we will discuss this matter.
   C. You are not doing too well.
   D. You are doing very well.
   E. I'll be able to tell you when I go over your record.

22.____

23. The PRINCIPAL aim of a supervisor is to
   A. act as liaison between employee and management
   B. get the work done
   C. keep up morale
   D. train his subordinates
   E. become chief of the department

23.____

24. When the work of two bureaus must be coordinated, direct contact between the subordinates in each bureau who are working on the problem is
   A. *bad*, because it violates the chain of command
   B. *bad*, because they do not have authority to make decisions
   C. *good*, because it enable quicker results
   D. *good*, because it relieves their superiors of any responsibilities
   E. *bad*, because they may work at cross purposes

24.____

25. Of the following, the organization defect which can be ascertained MOST readily merely by analyzing an accurate and well-drawn organization chart is
   A. ineffectiveness of an activity
   B. improper span of control
   C. inappropriate assignment of functions
   D. poor supervision
   E. unlawful delegation of authority

25.____

KEY (CORRECT ANSWERS)

1. A
2. A
3. E
4. B
5. A

6. C
7. E
8. E
9. B
10. D

11. C
12. C
13. C
14. B
15. D

16. B
17. A
18. E
19. C
20. B

21. E
22. A
23. B
24. C
25. B

EXAMINATION SECTION
TEST 1

DIRECTIONS: Each question or incomplete statement is followed by several suggested answers or completions. Select the one that BEST answers the question or completes the statement. *PRINT THE LETTER OF THE CORRECT ANSWER IN THE SPACE AT THE RIGHT.*

1. Professional staff members in large organizations are sometimes frustrated by a lack of vital work-related information because of the failure of some middle-management supervisors to pass along unrestricted information from top management.
   All of the following are considered to be reasons for such failure to pass along information EXCEPT the supervisors'
   A. belief that information affecting procedures will be ignored unless they are present to supervise their subordinates
   B. fear that specific information will require explanation or justification
   C. inclination to regard the possession of information as a symbol of higher status
   D. tendency to treat information a private property

   1.____

2. Increasingly in government, employees' records are being handled by automated data processing systems. However, employees frequently doubt a computer's ability to handle their records properly.
   Which of the following is the BEST way for management to overcome such doubts?
   A. Conduct a public relations campaign to explain the savings certain to result from the use of computers
   B. Use automated data processing equipment made by the firm which has the best repair facilities in the industry
   C. Maintain a clerical force to spot check on the accuracy of the computer's recordkeeping
   D. Establish automated data processing systems that are objective, impartial, and take into account individual factors as far as possible

   2.____

3. Some management experts question the usefulness of offering cash to individual employees for their suggestions.
   Which of the following reasons for opposing cash awards is MOST valid?
   A. Emphasis on individual gain deters cooperative effort.
   B. Money spent on evaluating suggestions may outweigh the value of the suggestions.
   C. Awards encourage employees to think about unusual methods of doing work.
   D. Suggestions too technical for ordinary evaluation are usually presented.

   3.____

4. The use of outside consultants, rather than regular staff, in studying and recommending improvements in the operations of public agencies has been criticized.
   Of the following, the BEST argument in favor of using regular staff is that such staff can better perform the work because they
   A. are more knowledgeable about operations and problems
   B. can more easily be organized into teams consisting of technical specialists
   C. may wish to gain additional professional experience
   D. will provide reports which will be more interesting to the public since they are more experienced

5. One approach to organizational problem-solving is to have all problem-solving authority centralized at the top of the organization.
   However, from the viewpoint of providing maximum service to the public, this practice is UNWISE chiefly because it
   A. reduces the responsibility of the decision-makers
   B. produces delays
   C. reduces internal communications
   D. requires specialists

6. Research has shown that problem-solving efficiency is optimal when the motivation of the problem-solver is at a moderate rather than an extreme level.
   Of the following, probably the CHIEF reason for this is that the problem-solver
   A. will cause confusion among his subordinates when his motivation is too high
   B. must avoid alternate solutions that tend to lead him up blind alleys
   C. can devote his attention to both the immediate problem as well as to other relevant problems in the general area
   D. must feel the need to solve the problem but not so urgently as to direct all his attention to the need and none to the means of solution

7. Don't be afraid to make mistakes. Many organizations are paralyzed from the fear of making mistakes. As a result, they don't do the things they should; they don't try new and different ideas.
   For the effective supervisor, the MOST valid implication of this statement is that
   A. mistakes should not be encouraged, but there are some unavoidable risks in decision-making
   B. mistakes which stem from trying new and different ideas are usually not serious
   C. the possibility of doing things wrong is limited by one's organizational position
   D. the fear of making mistakes will prevent future errors

8. The duties of an employee under your supervision may be either routine, problem-solving, innovative, or creative.
   Which of the following BEST describes duties which are both innovative and creative?

A. Checking to make sure that work is done properly
B. Applying principles in a practical matter
C. Developing new and better methods of meeting goals
D. Working at two or more jobs at the same time

9. According to modern management theory, a supervisor who uses as little authority as possible and as much as is necessary would be considered to be using a mode that is
    A. autocratic
    B. inappropriate
    C. participative
    D. directive

9._____

10. Delegation involves establishing and maintaining effective working arrangements between a supervisor and the persons who report to him.
    Delegation is MOST likely to have taken place when the
    A. entire staff openly discusses common problems in order to reach solutions satisfactory to the supervisor
    B. performance of specified work is entrusted to a capable person, and the expected results are mutually understood
    C. persons assigned to properly accomplish work are carefully evaluated and given a chance to explain shortcomings
    D. supervisor provides specific written instructions in order to prevent anxiety on the part of inexperienced persons

10._____

11. Supervisors often not aware of the effect that their behavior has on their subordinates.
    The one of the following training methods which would be BEST for changing such supervisory behavior is _____ training.
    A. essential skills
    B. off-the-job
    C. sensitivity
    D. developmental

11._____

12. A supervisor, in his role as a trainer, may have to decide on the length and frequency of training sessions.
    When the material to be taught is new, difficult, and lengthy, the trainer should be guided by the principle that for BEST results in such circumstances, sessions should be
    A. longer, relatively fewer in number, and held on successive days
    B. shorter, relatively greater in number, and spaced at intervals of several days
    C. of average length, relatively fewer in number, and held at intermittent intervals
    D. of random length and frequency, but spaced at fixed intervals

12._____

13. Employee training which is based on realistic simulation, sometimes known as *game play* or *role play*, is sometimes preferable to learning from actual experience on the job.
    Which of the following is NOT a correct statement concerning the value of simulation to trainees?

13._____

A. Simulation allows for practice in decision-making without any need for subsequent discussion.
B. Simulation is intrinsically motivating because it offers a variety of challenges.
C. Compared to other, more traditional training techniques, simulation is dynamic.
D. The simulation environment is nonpunitive as compared to real life.

14. Programmed instruction as a method of training has all of the following advantages EXCEPT:
    A. Learning is accomplished in an optimum sequence of distinct steps.
    B. Trainees have wide latitude in deciding what is to be learned within each program.
    C. The trainee takes an active part in the learning process.
    D. The trainee receives immediate knowledge of the results of his response.

15. In a work-study program, trainees were required to submit weekly written performance reports in order to insure that work assignments fulfilled the program objectives.
    Such reports would also assist the administrator of the work-study program PRIMARILY to
    A. eliminate personal counseling for the trainees
    B. identify problems requiring prompt resolution
    C. reduce the amount of clerical work for all concerned
    D. estimate the rate at which budgeted funds are being expended

16. Which of the following would be MOST useful in order to avoid misunderstanding when preparing correspondence or reports?
    A. Use vocabulary which is at an elementary level
    B. Present each sentence as an individual paragraph
    C. Have someone other than the writer read the material for clarity
    D. Use general words which are open to interpretation

17. Which of the following supervisory methods would be MOST likely to train subordinates to give a prompt response to memoranda in an organizational setting where most transactions are informal?
    A. Issue a written directive setting forth a schedule of strict deadlines
    B. Let it be known, informally, that those who respond promptly will be rewarded
    C. Follow up each memorandum by a personal inquiry regarding the receiver's reaction to it
    D. Direct subordinates to furnish a precise explanation for ignoring memos

18. Conferences may fail for a number of reasons. Still, a conference that is an apparent failure may have some benefit.
    Which of the following would LEAST likely be such a benefit?
    It may
    A. increase for most participants their possessiveness about information they have

B. produce a climate of good will and trust among many of the participants
C. provide most participants with an opportunity to learn things about the others
D. serve as a unifying force to keep most of the individuals functioning as a group

19. Assume that you have been assigned to study and suggest improvements in an operating unit of a delegate agency whose staff has become overwhelmed with problems, has had inadequate resources, and has become accustomed to things getting worse. The staff is indifferent to cooperating with you because they see no hope of improvement.
Which of the following steps would be LEAST useful in carrying out your assignment?
    A. Encourage the entire staff to make suggestions to you for change
    B. Inform the staff that management is somewhat dissatisfied with their performance
    C. Let staff know that you are fully aware of their problems and stresses
    D. Look for those problem area where changes can be made quickly

19.____

20. Which of the following statements about employer-employee relations is NOT considered to be correct by leading managerial experts?
    A. An important factor in good employer-employee relations is treating workers respectfully.
    B. Employer-employee relations are profoundly influenced by the fundamentals of human nature.
    C. Good employer-employee relations must stem from top management and reach downward.
    D. Employee unions are usually a major obstacle to establishing good employer-employee relations.

20.____

21. In connection with labor relations, the term *management rights* GENERALLY refers to
    A. a managerial review system in a grievance system
    B. statutory prohibitions that bar monetary negotiations
    C. the impact of collective bargaining on government
    D. those subjects which management considers to be non-negotiable

21.____

22. Barriers may exist to the utilization of women in higher level positions. Some of these barriers are attitudinal in nature.
Which of the following is MOST clearly attitudinal in nature?
    A. Advancement opportunities which are vertical in nature and thus require seniority
    B. Experience which is inadequate or irrelevant to the needs of a dynamic and progressive organization
    C. Inadequate means of early identification of employees with talent and potential for advancement
    D. Lack of self-confidence on the part of some women concerning their ability to handle a higher position

22.____

23. Because a reader reacts to the meaning he associates with a word, we can neve be sure what emotional impact a word may carry or how it may affect our readers.
The MOST logical implication of this statement for employees who correspond with members of the public is that
   A. a writer should try to select a neutral word that will not bias his writing by its hidden emotional meaning
   B. simple language should be used in writing letters denying requests so that readers are not upset by the denial
   C. every writer should adopt a writing style which he finds natural and easy
   D. whenever there is doubt as to how a word is defined, the dictionary should be consulted

23.____

24. A public information program should be based on clear information about the nature of actual public knowledge and opinion. One way of learning about the views of the public is through the use of questionnaires.
Which of the following is of LEAST importance in designing a questionnaire?
   A. A respondent should be asked for his name and address.
   B. A respondent should be asked to choose from among several statements the one which expresses his views.
   C. Questions should ask for responses in a form suitable for processing.
   D. Questions should be stated in familiar language.

24.____

25. Assume that you have accepted an invitation to speak before an interested group about a problem. You have brought with you for distribution a number of booklets and other informational material.
Of the following, which would be the BEST way to use this material?
   A. Distribute it before you begin talking so that the audience may read it at their leisure.
   B. Distribute it during your talk to increase the likelihood that it will be read.
   C. Hold it until the end of your talk, then announce that those who wish may take or examine the material.
   D. Before starting the talk, leave it on a table in the back of the room so that people may pick it up as they enter.

25.____

KEY (CORRECT ANSWERS)

1. A
2. D
3. A
4. A
5. B

6. D
7. A
8. C
9. C
10. B

11. C
12. B
13. A
14. B
15. B

16. C
17. C
18. A
19. B
20. D

21. D
22. D
23. A
24. A
25. C

TEST 2

DIRECTIONS: Each question or incomplete statement is followed by several suggested answers or completions. Select the one that BEST answers the question or completes the statement. *PRINT THE LETTER OF THE CORRECT ANSWER IN THE SPACE AT THE RIGHT.*

1. Of the following, the FIRST step in planning an operation is to
   A. obtain relevant information
   B. identify the goal to be achieved
   C. consider possible alternatives
   D. make necessary assignments

   1.____

2. A supervisor who is extremely busy performing routine tasks is MOST likely making INCORRECT use of what basic principle of supervision?
   A. Homogeneous Assignment
   B. Span of Control
   C. Work Distribution
   D. Delegation of Authority

   2.____

3. Controls help supervisors to obtain information from which they can determine whether their staffs are achieving planned goals.
   Which one of the following would be LEAST useful as a control device?
   A. Employee diaries
   B. Organization charts
   C. Periodic inspections
   D. Progress charts

   3.____

4. A certain employee has difficulty in effectively performing a particular portion of his routine assignments, but his overall productivity is average.
   As the direct supervisor of his individual, your BEST course of action would be to
   A. attempt to develop the man's capacity to execute the problematic facets of his assignments
   B. diversify the employee's work assignments in order to build up his confidence
   C. reassign the man to less difficult tasks
   D. request in a private conversation that the employee improve his work output

   4.____

5. A supervisor who uses persuasion as a means of supervising a unit would GENERALLY also use which of the following practices to supervise his unit?
   A. Supervise and control the staff with an authoritative attitude to indicate that he is a *take-charge* individual
   B. Make significant changes in the organizational operations so as to improve job efficiency
   C. Remove major communication barriers between himself, subordinates, and management
   D. Supervise everyday operations while being mindful of the problems of his subordinates

   5.____

6. Whenever a supervisor in charge of a unit delegate a routine task to a capable subordinate, he tells him exactly how to do it.

   6.____

This practice is GENERALLY
- A. *desirable*, chiefly because good supervisors should be aware of the traits of their subordinates and delegate responsibilities to them accordingly
- B. *undesirable*, chiefly because only non-routine tasks should be delegated
- C. *desirable*, chiefly because a supervisor should frequently test the willingness of his subordinates to perform ordinary tasks
- D. *undesirable*, chiefly because a capable subordinate should usually be allowed to exercise his own discretion in doing a routine job

7. The one of the following activities through which a supervisor BEST demonstrates leadership ability is by
   - A. arranging periodic staff meetings in order to keep his subordinates informed about professional developments in the field
   - B. frequently issuing definite orders and directives which will lessen the need for subordinates to make decisions in handling any tasks assigned to them
   - C. devoting the major part of his time to supervising subordinates so as to simulate continuous improvement
   - D. setting aside time for self-development and research so as to improve the skills, techniques, and procedures of his unit

8. The following three statements relate to the supervision of employees:
   I. The assignment of difficult tasks that offer a challenge is more conducive to good morale than the assignment of easy tasks.
   II. The same general principles of supervision that apply to men are equally applicable to women.
   III. The best retraining program should cover all phases of an employee's work in a general manner.
   Which of the following choices list ALL of the above statements that are generally correct?
   A. II, III   B. I   C. I, II   D. I, II, III

9. Which of the following examples BEST illustrates the application of the *exception principle* as a supervisory technique?
   - A. A complex job is divided among several employees who work simultaneously to complete the whole job in a shorter time.
   - B. An employee is required to complete any task delegated to him to such an extent that nothing is left for the superior who delegated the task except to approve it.
   - C. A superior delegates responsibility to a subordinate but retains authority to make the final decisions.
   - D. A superior delegates all work possible to his subordinates and retains that which requires his personal attention or performance

10. Assume that you are a supervisor. Your immediate superior frequently gives orders to your subordinates without your knowledge.
    Of the following, the MOST direct and effective way for you to handle this problem is to

A. tell our subordinates to take orders only from you
B. submit a report to higher authority in which you cite specific instances
C. discuss it with your immediate superior
D. find out to what extent your authority and prestige as a supervisor have been affected

11. In an agency which has as its primary purpose the protection of the public against fraudulent business practices, which of the following would GENERALLY be considered an *auxiliary* or *staff* rather than a *line* function?
    A. Interviewing victims of frauds and advising them about their legal remedies
    B. Daily activities directed toward prevention of fraudulent business practices
    C. Keeping records and statistics about business violations reported and corrected
    D. Follow-up inspections by investigators after corrective action has been taken

11.____

12. A supervisor can MOST effectively reduce the spread of false rumors through the *grapevine* by
    A. identifying and disciplining any subordinate responsible for initiating such rumors
    B. keeping his subordinates informed as much as possible about matters affecting them
    C. denying false rumors which might tend to lower staff morale and productivity
    D. making sure confidential matters are kept secure from access by unauthorized employees

12.____

13. A supervisor has tried to learn about the background, education, and family relationships of his subordinates through observation, personal contact, and inspection of their personnel records.
    These supervisor actions are GENERALLY
    A. *inadvisable*, chiefly because they may lead to charges of favoritism
    B. *advisable*, chiefly because they may make him more popular with his subordinates
    C. *inadvisable*, chiefly because his efforts may be regarded as an invasion of privacy
    D. *advisable*, chiefly because the information may enable him to develop better understanding of each of his subordinates

13.____

14. In an emergency situation, when action must be taken immediately, it is BEST for the supervisor to give orders in the form of
    A. direct commands which are brief and precise
    B. requests, so that his subordinates will not become alarmed
    C. suggestions which offer alternative courses of action
    D. implied directives, so that his subordinates may use their judgment in carrying them out

14.____

15. When demonstrating a new and complex procedure to a group of subordinates, it is ESSENTIAL that a supervisor
    A. go slowly and repeat the steps involved at least once
    B. show the employees common errors and the consequences of such errors
    C. go through the process at the usual speed so that the employees can see the rate at which they should work
    D. distribute summaries of the procedure during the demonstration and instruct his subordinates to refer to them afterwards

15.____

16. After a procedures manual has been written and distributed,
    A. continuous maintenance work is necessary to keep the manual current
    B. it is best to issue new manuals rather than make changes in the original manual
    C. no changes should be necessary
    D. only major changes should be considered

16.____

17. Of the following, the MOST important criterion of effective report writing is
    A. eloquence of writing style
    B. the use of technical language
    C. to be brief and to the point
    D. to cover all details

17.____

18. The use of electronic data processing
    A. has proven unsuccessful in most organizations
    B. has unquestionable advantages for all organizations
    C. is unnecessary in most organizations
    D. should be decided upon only after careful feasibility studies by individual organizations

18.____

19. The PRIMARY purpose of work measurement is to
    A. design and install a wage incentive program
    B. determine who should be promoted
    C. establish a yardstick to determine extent of progress
    D. set up a spirit of competition among employee

19.____

20. The action which is MOST effective in gaining acceptance of a study by the agency which is being studied is
    A. a directive from the agency head to install a study based on recommendations included in a report
    B. a lecture-type presentation following approval of the procedure
    C. a written procedure in narrative form covering the proposed system with visual presentations and discussions
    D. procedural charts showing the *before* situation, forms, steps, etc., to the employees affected

20.____

21. Which organization principle is MOST closely related to procedural analysis and improvement?
    A. Duplication, overlapping, and conflict should be eliminated.
    B. Managerial authority should be clearly defined.
    C. The objectives of the organization should be clearly defined.
    D. Top management should be freed of burdensome detail.

22. Which one of the following is the MAJOR objective of operational audits?
    A. Detecting fraud
    B. Determining organization problems
    C. Determining the number of personnel needed
    D. Recommending opportunities for improving operating and management practices

23. Of the following, the formalization of organization structure is BEST achieved by
    A. a narrative description of the plan of organization
    B. functional charts
    C. job descriptions together with organization charts
    D. multi-flow charts

24. Budget planning is MOST useful when it achieves
    A. cost control
    B. forecast of receipts
    C. performance review
    D. personnel reduction

25. GENERALLY, in applying the principle of delegation in dealing with subordinates, a supervisor
    A. allows his subordinates to set up work goals and to fix the limits within which they can work
    B. allows his subordinates to set up work goals and then gives detailed orders as to how they are to be achieved
    C. makes relatively few decisions by himself and frames his orders in broad, general terms
    D. provides externalized motivation for his subordinate

KEY (CORRECT ANSWERS)

1.	B	11.	C
2.	D	12.	B
3.	B	13.	D
4.	A	14.	A
5.	D	15.	A
6.	D	16.	A
7.	C	17.	C
8.	C	18.	D
9.	D	19.	C
10.	C	20.	C

21. A
22. D
23. C
24. A
25. C

INTERPRETING STATISTICAL DATA GRAPHS, CHARTS AND TABLES

EXAMINATION SECTION

TEST 1

DIRECTIONS: Each question or incomplete statement is followed by several suggested answers or completions. Select the one that BEST answers the question or completes the statement. *PRINT THE LETTER OF THE CORRECT ANSWER IN THE SPACE AT THE RIGHT.*

Questions 1-5.

DIRECTIONS: Questions 1 through 5 are to be answered on the basis of the following chart.

DEPT	MIN BAL	AUTO ALLOC	JAN	FEB	MARCH	APRIL	MAY	JUNE	BEG BAL	JAN	FEB	MARCH	APRIL	MAY	JUNE
A	300	600	300	350	200	150	400	250	800	500	750	550	400	600	350
B	500	900	400	350	600	500	450	300	1100						V
C	200	300	150	100	200	200	100	200	400						W
D	800	1200	600	700	500	450	350	700	1600						X
E	600	900	600	700	650	400	550	700	1400						Y
F	400	700	400	350	200	450	300	250	500						Z

The above table gives hypothetical information regarding monthly allocations, by department, for a certain agency. Each department has begun the year with money left over from 2018. The second column gives the minimum balance allowable for each department. As soon as expenses for a given month would bring the account below this minimum, the amount entered in the third column would automatically be put into that department's account. Columns 4-9 give each department's expenses for the first half of 2019. Column 10 gives the beginning balance for the year (the amount left over from 2018); the remaining columns show how much money is left in each department's account at the end of each month

By doing the operations necessary to fill in this table, you will be able to answer Questions 1 through 5.

1. Find the value of V.   1.____
    A. $1,200   B. $1,000   C. $1,100   D. $1,300

2. Find the value of W.   2.____
    A. $450   B. $300   C. $350   D. $250

3. Find the value of X.   3.____
    A. $800   B. $950   C. $1,600   D. $1,500

4. Find the value of Y.   4.____
    A. $1,300   B. $1,400   C. $750   D. $1,150

5. Find the value of Z.   5.____
    A. $550   B. $1,000   C. $700   D. $650

Questions 6-15.

DIRECTIONS: Questions 6 through 15 are to be answered on the basis of the following information and charts. The paragraphs below give hypothetical information regarding the number, by age groups, of individuals using five state-run lake facilities for the months of July and August 2019. Assume that no one participated in more than one activity. Also, if an activity is not mentioned, assume that it is not offered at that particular lake.

JULY

Seventy-five hundred people under the age of 13 swam in Lake Catharine while 50 people in that age group rowed. Of those 13-19, 5,400 swam in Lake Catharine, 170 canoed there, and 120 rowed. Sailing was more popular with people 20 and over, with 150 people over 60 and 350 people in the 20 to 60 age group using the lake for sailing. In the grouping of people over 60, 2,300 people swam, 50 people rowed, and 200 people canoed. Of those 20 to 60, 40 people rowed, 350 canoed, and 13,500 swam.

Lake Herman is a much smaller and more remote lake and the figures bear this out. No one under 13 was reported using the lake, and the activities are more limited. Of those over 60, most (400) fished from the pier. The remainder used small crafts: 350 canoed and 200 sailed. In the 20-60 age group, there were also more people (1,100) fishing from the pier than were occupied in other activities. Of the remaining people in this age group, 650 canoed and 400 sailed. Those in the 13 to 19 age group did not use the lake in great number, but those that did were more likely to canoe (75) than to sail (60) or to fish from the pier (10).

Lake Manichee is the largest and most developed lake of the five. The least represented group were those over 60. Thirty-five hundred swam in the lake, while 600 canoed, 600 more fished from the pier, 350 sailed, and 300 rowed. The numbers were also not as great for the 13-19 age group. Seventy-eight hundred young people swam on the lake but few people used small crafts. Only 200 canoed and 400 rowed. A very small number (30) fished from the pier. A great number of people in the other two age categories used the lake. Nine thousand children under 13 swam in the lake, 1,100 fished from the pier, and 40 rowed. Of those people 20 to 60, 15,400 swam, 1,000 canoed, 600 fished from the pier, 500 rowed, and 400 sailed.

Swimming, canoeing, and rowing are possible at Dragon Lake. Forty-five hundred children under 13 swam in the lake, while 100 rowed. Of those 13-19, 3,700 swam, 400 rowed, and 350 canoed. In the 20-60 age group, 7,300 swam, 900 canoed, and 750 rowed. Of those over 60, 2,300 swam, 450 canoed, and 250 rowed.

One thousand children under 13 swam in Dream Lake. Six hundred people aged 13 to 19 swam in the lake, while 25 people fished from the pier. Nine hundred people over 60 swam in the lake, 400 canoed there, and 300 fished from the pier. In the 20-60 age group, 2,500 swam, 950 canoed, and 640 fished from the pier.

AUGUST

In August, significantly more people used the facilities at the five lakes. The only exception to this was Lake Herman. Fishing in the lake was prohibited as of August first and that may have had something to do with the minimal increase in use of that facility. Of those who canoed, 80 were 13-19, 400 were over 60, and 750 were in the 20-60 age group. Of those using sailboats, 250 were over 60 years of age, 60 were 13-19, and 450 were 20-60.

Lake Manichee continued to be more popular than any other lake in the group. Record numbers of adults between the ages of 20 and 60 used the lake. Nearly nineteen thousand (18,850) swam in the lake, while 1,200 canoed, 600 rowed, 750 fished, and 450 sailed. The next highest group were the children under 13. More than 10,000 (10,500) swam in the lake, 50 rowed there, and 1,300 fished from the pier. Ninety-four hundred young people between the ages of 13 and 19 swam in the lake, 480 rowed, and 250 canoed, but only 45 fished from the pier. Forty-two hundred people over 60 swam in the lake. Those over 60 seemed to be the most well-rounded in terms of the other activities available. Seven hundred and twenty canoed, 650 fished, 400 rowed, and 370 sailed.

As in July, Lake Catharine was second in popularity to Lake Manichee. As usual, the largest numbers were found in the 20-60 age group. Sixteen thousand people in that age group swam in the lake, 870 canoed, 500 sailed, and 50 rowed. The lake was also very popular with children. Sixty children under 13 rowed on the lake, while 9,150 swam in it. Next, came the 13-19 age group. Two hundred young adults canoed on the lake, 140 rowed on it, and 6,450 swam in it. No one in this age group sailed on the lake. Finally, of those over 60, 2,700 swam, 220 canoed, 180 sailed, and 50 rowed.

Dream Lake also attracted significantly more people (about 19% more) in August than it had in July. Again, only those over 19 canoed on the lake (20-60: 1,000; over 60: 450). Twelve hundred children under 13 swam in the lake, while 750 of those between the ages of 13 and 19 swam. In addition, 40 people in the 13-19 age group rowed on the lake. Of those 20 to 60, 2,900 swam in the lake, and 750 fished from the pier. Eleven hundred people over 60 swam in the lake and 350 fished from the pier.

Finally, 5,200 children under 13 swam in Dragon Lake and 150 rowed there. Of those in the 13-19 age group, 4,100 swam, 500 rowed, and 400 canoed. Of those adults 20 to 60, 7,800 swam, 1,100 canoed, and 850 rowed. In the over 60 age group, 2,500 swam, 550 canoed, and 300 rowed.

By filling in the tables that follow, you will be able to answer Questions 6 through 15.

4 (#1)

	0-12	13-19	20-60	Over 60	TOTAL
Swim					A
Row					B
Canoe					C
Sail					D
Fish					E
TOTAL	F	G	H	I	J

6. Find the value of A.　　　　　　　　　　　　　　　　　　　6.____
   A. 190,000　　B. 143,000　　C. 173,000　　D. 145,000

7. Find the value of C.　　　　　　　　　　　　　　　　　　　7.____
   A. 14,855　　B. 13,945　　C. 15,855　　D. 14,845

8. Find the value of D.　　　　　　　　　　　　　　　　　　　8.____
   A. 4,220　　B. 5,620　　C. 5,200　　D. 4,170

9. Find the value of G.　　　　　　　　　　　　　　　　　　　9.____
   A. 50,850　　B. 42,255　　C. 38,385　　43,280

10. Find the value of I.　　　　　　　　　　　　　　　　　　　10.____
   A. 28,990　　B. 38,230　　C. 27,370　　D. 35,290

Listed below are per person fees for swimming and fishing privileges at the five lakes. Use this information and the information from the preceding chart to fill in the table below. Again, assume that no one participated in more than one activity, and that those activities which are not mentioned are not offered.

LAKE CATHERINE	0-12	13-19	20-60	Over 60
Swimming	.25	.50	1.00	.50

LAKE HERMAN	0-12	13-19	20-60	Over 60
Fishing	Free	.50	1.50	.50

LAKE MANICHEE	0-12	13-19	20-60	Over 60
Swimming	.50	1.00	1.00	Free
Fishing	Free	1.00	1.00	Free

DREAM LAKE	0-12	13-19	20-60	Over 60
Swimming	Free	.50	1.00	Free
Fishing	Free	Free	1.00	Free

DRAGON LAKE	0-12	13-19	20-60	Over 60
Swimming	.50	1.00	2.00	1.00

TOTAL REVENUES IN THE FIVE-LAKE REGION: SUMMER 2019					
	0-12	13-19	20-60	Over 60	TOTAL
Swimming					A
Fishing					B
Boat Rental					
Sailboat	N/A	$200	$12,750	$8,800	C
Canoe	N/A	$2,095	$20,000	$7,800	D
Rowboat	$350	$2,050	$3,750	$900	E
TOTAL	F	G	H	I	J

11. Find the value of A.
    A. $163,662.50
    B. $186,625.50
    C. $160,862.50
    D. $140,060.50

11._____

12. Find the value of B.
    A. $4,670   B. $46,700   C. $5,220   D. $4,570

12._____

13. Find the value of G.
    A. $27,925   B. $36,025   C. $33,845   D. $16,035

13._____

14. Find the value of H.
    A. $132,940   B. $140,240   C. $133,870   D. $143,990

14._____

15. Find the value of J.
    A. $195,397,50
    B. $199,297.50
    C. $190,227.50
    D. $224,227.50

15._____

Questions 16-20.

DIRECTIONS: Questions 16 through 20 are to be answered on the basis of the following information. The hypothetical information below concerns the 2019 operating budgets for three units in a particular department. Consolidate this information in the table on the next page and use your findings to answer Questions 16 through 20.

UNIT A

1st Quarter
Postal Fees: 250; Utilities, Elec.: 150; Utilities, Phone: 300; Expense Accounts: 1,500; Maintenance: 400; Non-Paper Supplies: 450; Paper Supplies: 500

2nd Quarter
Postal Fees: 200; Utilities, Elec.: 150; Utilities, Phone: 200; Expense Accounts: 1,700; Maintenance: 450; Paper Supplies: 200; Non-Paper Supplies: 150

3rd Quarter
Postal Fees: 150; Utilities, Elec.: 225; Utilities, Phone: 150; Expense Accounts: 1,000; Maintenance: 400; Paper Supplies: 150; Non-Paper Supplies: 100

4th Quarter
Postal Fees: 300; Utilities, Elec.: 200; Utilities, Phone: 350; Expense Accounts: 2,100; Maintenance: 350; Paper Supplies: 250; Non-Paper Supplies: 200

UNIT B

	1st	2nd	3rd	4th
Supplies:				
Paper	500	300	250	600
Non-Paper	450	300	250	300
Maintenance	450	400	350	400
Utilities:				
Electricity	200	150	250	250
Telephone	350	300	200	300
Expense Accounts	2,000	3,000	1,500	3,500
Postal	350	250	200	450

UNIT C

	Exp. Acct.	Main	P. Fees	Phone	Elec.	Paper	Non-Paper
1st Q.	4,100	800	300	800	600	300	400
2nd Q.	3,200	650	600	650	400	400	200
3rd Q.	3,000	850	300	450	450	250	350
4th Q.	3,600	750	550	700	500	350	350

	1st Q.	2nd Q.	3rd Q.	4th Q.	TOTAL
EXPENSE ACCTS.					
MAINTENANCE					
POSTAL FEES					

SUPPLIES:
  PAPER
  NON-PAPER					

UTILITIES
  ELECTRICITY
  TELEPHONE					

TOTAL					

16. The only expense that decreased between the 3rd and 4th quarter was
    A. maintenance
    B. electricity
    C. telephone
    D. non-paper supplies

    16._____

17. Between the 1st and 2nd quarter, the LARGEST percent decrease occurred in which category?
    A. Telephone
    B. Expense accounts
    C. Non-paper supplies
    D. Paper supplies

    17._____

18. If the rate of increase for expense accounts were to be the same from the 4th quarter of 2019 to the 1st quarter of 2020, what amount would be spent for expense accounts in the 1st quarter of 2019?
    A. $1,538   B. $6,164   C. $15,389   D. $6,189

    18._____

19. The category which had the MOST stable expenses throughout 2019 is
    A. electricity
    B. expense accounts
    C. postal fees
    D. maintenance

    19._____

20. On the whole, all the units are LEAST expensive to maintain during which quarter?
    A. 1st   B. 2nd   C. 3rd   D. 4th

    20._____

Questions 21-24.

DIRECTIONS: Questions 21 through 24 are to be answered on the basis of the following charts.

TYPES OF PUBLIC WAREHOUSES – 2019
(Hypothetical Data)

Category of Operation	Number	Total Revenue ($000)	Proportion of Total Revenue in 2019
Local trucking and storage (including household goods)	4687	823,959	?
General Merchandise Warehousing	?	610,566	28.74
Refrigerated Goods (including food lockers)	1534	?	16.55
Farm Products	744	155,085	7.30
Special Warehousing	?	136,861	6.44
Household Goods	423	46,698	?
TOTAL	10026	2,124,765	100.00

GENERAL MERCHANDISE WAREHOUSING
(Hypothetical Data)

Year	Number of Establishments	Public Floor Space (000 sq.ft.)	Number of Paid Employees	Revenue ($000)
1994	1,197	108,315	22,283	$171,542
1999	1,512	119,325	22,496	200,934
2004	1,483	129,170	22,880	248,282
2009	1,677	163,168	28,295	379,910
2019	2,170	296,067	32,495	620,566

21. Approximately how many square feet of public floor space were held by the average general merchandise warehousing establishment in 2019?
    A. 136   B. 973   C. 97,298   D. 136,440

22. If one-third as many new general merchandise warehouses opened between December of 2014 and December of 2016 as opened between January 2017 and December of 2019, approximately how many general merchandise warehousing establishments existed at the end of 2016? (Assume that the totals in the table are year-end figures and that no warehouse closed in that time.)
    A. 105   B. 1,302   C. 1,407   D. 1,276

23. What was the average amount of public space used for general merchandise warehousing from 2014 through 2019? _____ square feet.
    A. 103,995,000   B. 22,149,340   C. 129,995   D. 129,994,500

24. In which category of operation was the average revenue per establishment GREATEST?
    A. Local trucking and storage
    B. General merchandise warehousing
    C. Refrigerated goods
    D. Cannot be determined from information given

24.____

Questions 25-28.

DIRECTIONS: Questions 25 through 28 are to be answered on the basis of the following charts.

CUMMINGS EMPLOYMENT TRAINING
COMPARATIVE BUDGET DATA: 2017-2019
(Hypothetical Data)

Income	2017	2018	2019
Federal Funds:	57,900	64,070	?
Commodities Support Project	20,000	26,900	29,800
CSBG Grants	14,000	10,000	0
Training Contracts	?	27,170	54,840
County Funds	12,400	17,500	23,070
Grants:	0	?	16,000
Smith Foundation	0	8,000	12,000
Wealth-Rite Corp.	0	5,000	?
TOTAL	70,200	?	?

Expenses			
Personnel:	51,750	71,300	90,950
Salaries	45,000	?	?
Benefits	6,750	?	11,850
Office	10,120	13,540	17,505
Training Materials	6,800	8,500	9,540
Transportation	1,530	2,230	3,230
TOTAL	70,200	95,570	?

25. For each dollar spent on training materials in 2019, how many dollars were spent on salaries?
    A. 8.28   B. .12   C. 7.9   D. .79

25.____

26. By what percent did the program's spending increase from 2017 to 2018?
    A. 73%   B. 36%   C. 136%   D. 74%

26.____

27. It is MOST likely that which of the following amounts was spent in 2018?
    A. $45,000   B. $93,000   C. $62,000   D. $69,000

27.____

28. In 2019, 3,025 people were trained through the Cummings Program. Two women were trained for every five men.
    How much did it cost to train men in the 2019 Cummings Program?
    A. $48,400   B. $72,600   C. $34,560   D. $86,429

Questions 29-32.

DIRECTIONS: Questions 29 through 32 are to be answered on the basis of the following chart.

State	Total Below Poverty: All Ages		High Risk Age Groups Below Poverty							
			Pregnant Women		Children 0-4		Children 5-17		Age 60+	
	Number	%*	Number	%**	Number	%**	Number	%**	Number	%**
Conn.	242,650	8.0	2,325	8.0	27,346	15	65,260	10	38,446	8
Maine	140,996	13.0	1,606	13.0	13,847	18	36,015	15	27,002	15
Mass.	532,458	9.6	5,227	9.6	52,535	16	140,277	12	83,599	9
N.H.	75,364	8.5	875	8.5	6,851	11	17,130	9	14,635	11
R.I.	93,959	10.3	940	10.3	9,321	12	23,195	13	18,756	11
Vt.	59,059	12.1	706	12.1	5,961	17	13,940	13	9,476	13
Total	1,144,486	9.3	11,679	9.6	115,861	15.5	295,817	11.9	192,314	9.6

  * Percent of Total Population Within State
  ** Percent of Total Population Within Each High Risk Group

29. What proportion of the people in Massachusetts living below the poverty level are over 60 years of age?
    A. 9.6%   B. 16%   C. 8%   D. 53%

30. Approximately what percent of the total New England population is shown to be in high risk age groups?
    A. 54%   B. 46.6%   C. 9%   D. 5%

31. If among those individuals living below the poverty level the male to female ratio is 1:4, how many females were living below the poverty level in New England in 2019?
    A. 915,589   B. 286,122   C. 228,897   D. 968,542

32. In Massachusetts, 3,473 pregnant women living below the poverty level received federally-funded prenatal care.
    If the participation rate is consistent for Connecticut and Rhode Island, how many pregnant women living below the poverty level received federally-funded prenatal health care in Connecticut?
    A. 1,545
    B. 3,499
    C. 2,949
    D. Cannot be determined from information given

Questions 33-36.

DIRECTIONS: Questions 33 through 36 are to be answered on the basis of the following chart.

HYPERTENSION SCREENING PROGRAM, 2015-2019
(Hypothetical Data)

	2015	2016	2017	2018	2019
Persons Screened: (thousands)	3,040	3,810	2,950	2,600	2,540
% Over 65	10%	12%	11%	13%	9%
% Under 35	12%	14%	15%	17%	17%
Expenditures: From local, state, and federal funding sources (millions)	15.55	23.05	24.00	24.50	25.65
% Local	7%	8%	6%	4%	7%
% State	20%	14%	19%	22.5%	25%

33. In which three years were the amounts from federal sources APPROXIMATELY the same:
    A. 2015, 2016, 2017
    B. 2016, 2017, 2018
    C. 2017, 2018, 2019
    D. 2015, 2017, 2018

34. Between 2015 and 2016, the amount spent to screen individuals in the 35-65 age bracket increased by
    A. $.93   B. $4,915   C. 40.5%   D. 45%

35. For every $10 provided by the federal government in 2018, how many dollars were spent by the state governments?
    A. $3.06   B. $1.25   C. $.33   D. $4.30

36. From this table, one could conclude that
    A. there are more people under 35 who have hypertension than there are people over 65 with hypertension
    B. the number of people under 35 screened for hypertension steadily increased between 2016 and 2019
    C. the amount of local funds used for hypertension screening has remained approximately the same from 2017 to 2019
    D. the amount of federal funds used for hypertension screening increased from 2015 to 2017

Questions 37-40.

DIRECTIONS: Questions 37 through 40 are to be answered on the basis of the following graph and information.

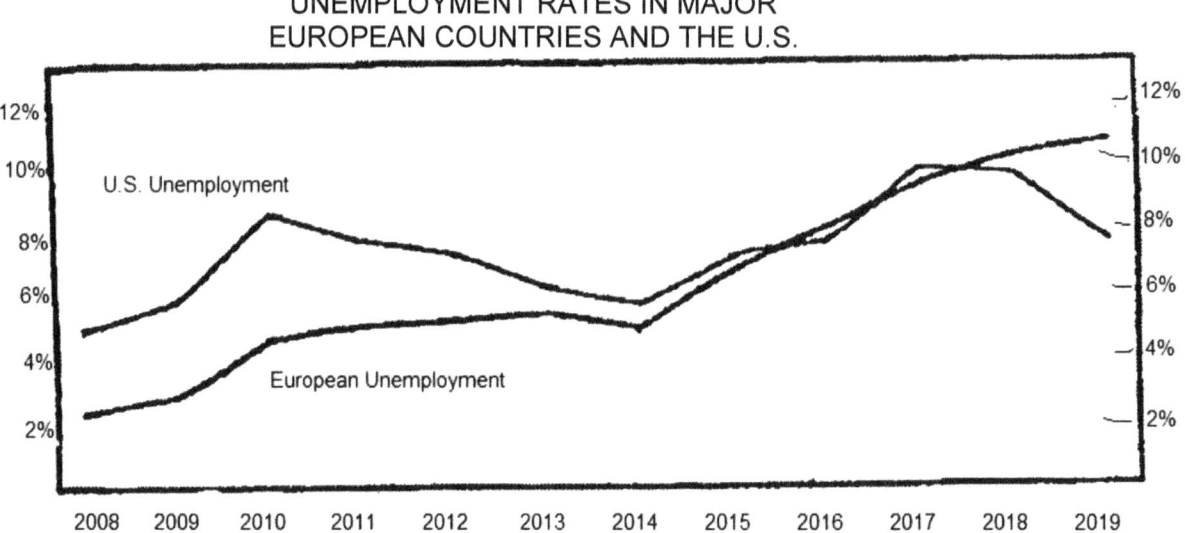

UNEMPLOYMENT RATES IN MAJOR EUROPEAN COUNTRIES AND THE U.S.

WHAT THE NUMBERS SAY: The economy is slowing down. GNP grew only by 1.3% in the first quarter.

MONTHLY DATA	3/2020	2/2020	1/2019	3/2019	2002
Employment (seasonally adjusted)					
Number of unemployed (millions)	8.396	8.399	8.484	8.793	2.975
Overall employment rate	7.3%	7.3%	7.4%	7.8%	3.8%
Black unemployment rate	15.2%	16.3%	14.%	16.6%	7.4%
Wages					
Average weekly earnings: current dollars	$297.70	$295.64	$295.80	$288.40	$101.84
Average weekly earnings: 2012 dollars	N/A	$170.99	$171.78	$172.59	$184.83
Prices					
All items Consumer Price Index	318.8	317.4	316.1	307.3	100.00
Increase from one year earlier	3.7%	3.5%	3.6%	4.7%	2.9%
Food increase from one year earlier	4.0%	2.4%	2.6%	4.0%	0.9%
Interest Rates					
Mortgage (effective, on new homes)	11.91%	12.21%	12.27%	12.02%	6.50%
Prime Interest Rate	10.5%	10.5%	10.61%	11.5%	5.61%

13 (#1)

QUARTERLY DATA (billions of dollars at annual rates, seasonally adjusted)	2020 1st	2019 4th	2019 1st	2002
Gross National Product	3819.9	3758.7	3553.3	796.3
Balance of Trade (exports minus imports)	N/A	-91.5	-103.1	+3.8
Wages, Salaries, and Benefits	1447.8	1427.4	1354.0	471.9
Corporate Profits	N/A	291.6	277.4	79.3
Gross National Product in 2007 dollars	1668.0	1662.4	1610.9	1007.7

NOTES: N/A means not available. Wages are the average for private-sector nonfarm workers; no taxes have been subtracted.
SOURCES: Employment, wages, and prices are from the Department of Labor, Bureau of Labor Statistics. Mortgage interest rate is from the Federal Home Loan Bank Board. GNP and its components are from the Department of Commerce, Bureau of Economic Analysis.

37. Compare the average weekly earnings, in current dollars, for February of 2007 with the average weekly earnings, in current dollars, for March of 2019.
    A. $7.24 more B. $1.60 less C. $7.40 more D. $9.30 more

    37.____

38. The average weekly earnings in 2012 dollars, from March of 2019 to February of 2020
    A. increased .009%
    B. decreased .009%
    C. increased .25%
    D. decreased .9%

    38.____

39. From 2002 to the last quarter of 2019, the Balance of Trade declined
    A. 4% B. 25.1% C. 23.1% D. 25.8%

    39.____

40. From this table, one could conclude that
    A. black unemployment will continue to decline throughout 2020
    B. buying power has increased since 2019
    C. the increase in buying power has not kept pace with the increase in wages since 2002
    D. from 2002 to the last quarter of 2019, corporate profits decreased more than 250%

    40.____

Questions 41-44.

DIRECTIONS: Questions 41 through 44 are to be answered on the basis of the following chart.

14 (#1)

NEW YORK STOCK EXCHANGE
(Hypothetical Data)

	CLOSING			CHANGE		
	4/28/2019	10/27/2019	10/28/2019	Change	Percent	Pct. 6 mos.
PlanResearch	18	$22^3/_8$	31	?	?	+72.2%
Unitrode	14	13	$11^3/_4$	$-1^1/_4$	-9.6%	-16.07%
Wurlitzer	$3^1/_4$	$2^3/_4$	$2^1/_2$	$-^1/_4$	-9.1%	-23.08%
Dow Indus.	1825.37	1841.79	?	$-3^2/_3$	-.2%	+.7%
IBM	159.25	119.44	$120^3/_4$	+1.31	+1.1%	-24.2%
PogoProd.	4.33	?	?	?	?	-13.5%
Cullinet	$9^1/_8$	$8^7/_8$	$8^3/_8$	$-^1/_2$	-5.6%	-8.2%
CM	81	70 1/3	70	+1/3	+.5%	+13.6%
NYSE Composite	138.44	137.62	137.89	$.27	+.2%	-.4%

41. PanResearch, from 10/27 to 10/18,
    A. increased 28.6%   B. decreased 8.6%
    C. increased 38.6%   D. increased 34.6%

41.____

42. On 10/28, the value of Dow Industrials, compared to the NYSE Composite, was
    A. $1,704.17   B. $1,703.90   C. $13^1/_3$ times   D. 130 times

42.____

43. If, on October 29, PogoProd increased 20% from the October 28 figure, its closing price on that day would have been
    A. 4%
    B. $4.49
    C. $5.90
    D. cannot be determined from information given

43.____

44. If Cullinet closed on 4/28/2019 at 35% less than it closed six months before, the closing price for Cullinet on 10/28/2018 would have been
    A. 10.125   B. 12.32   C. 14.04   D. 15.21

44.____

KEY (CORRECT ANSWERS)

1. A	11. C	21. D	31. A	41. C
2. C	12. A	22. D	32. A	42. C
3. C	13. B	23. D	33. B	43. B
4. B	14. B	24. B	34. C	44. C
5. D	15. D	25. A	35. A	
6. A	16. A	26. B	36. D	
7. A	17. C	27. C	37. A	
8. D	18. C	28. D	38. D	
9. B	19. D	29. B	39. D	
10. A	20. C	30. D	40. C	

LOGICAL REASONING
EVALUATING CONCLUSIONS IN LIGHT OF KNOWN FACTS
EXAMINATION SECTION
TEST 1

COMMENTARY

This section is designed to provide practice questions in evaluating conclusions when you are given specific data to work with.

We suggest you do the questions three at a time, consulting the answer key and then the solution section for any questions you may have missed. It's a good idea to try the questions again a week before the exam.

In the validity of conclusion type of question, you are first given a reading passage which describes a particular situation. The passage may be on any topic, as it is not your knowledge of the topic that is being tested, but your reasoning abilities. The passage is likely to detail several proposed courses of action and factors affecting these proposals. The reading passage is followed by a conclusion based on the facts in the passage, or a description of a decision taken regarding the situation. The conclusion is followed by a number of statements which have a possible connection to the conclusion. For each statement, you are to determine whether:

A. The statement proves the conclusion.
B. The statement supports the conclusion but does not prove it.
C. The statement disproves the conclusion.
D. The statement weakens the conclusion but does not disprove it.
E. The statement has no relevance to the conclusion.

Remember that the conclusion after the passage is to be accepted as the outcome of what actually happened, and that you are being asked to evaluate the impact each statement would have had on the conclusion.

Questions 1-8.

DIRECTIONS: Questions 1 through 8 are based on the following paragraph.

In May of 2018, Mr. Bryan inherited a clothing store on Main Street in a small New England town. The store has specialized in selling quality men's and women's clothing since 1920. Business has been stable throughout the years, neither increasing nor decreasing. He has an opportunity to buy two adjacent stores which would enable him to add a wider range and style of clothing. In order to do this, he would have to borrow a substantial amount of money. He also risks losing the goodwill of his present clientele.

CONCLUSION: On November 7, 2018, Mr. Bryan tells the owner of the two adjacent stores that he has decided not to purchase them. He feels that it would be best to simply maintain his present marketing position, as there would not be enough new business to support an expansion.

A. The statement proves the conclusion.
B. The statement supports the conclusion but does not prove it.
C. The statement disproves the conclusion.
D. The statement weakens the conclusion.
E. The statement is irrelevant to the conclusion.

1. A large new branch of the county's community college holds its first classes in September.   1.____

2. The town's largest factory shuts down with no indication that it will reopen.   2.____

3. The United States Census showed that the number of children per household dropped from 2.4 to 2.1 since the last census.   3.____

4. Mr. Bryan's brother tells him of a new clothing boutique specializing in casual women's clothing which is opening soon.   4.____

5. Mr. Bryan's sister buys her baby several items for Christmas at Mr. Bryan's store.   5.____

6. Mrs. McIntyre, the President of the Town Council, brings Mr. Bryan a home-baked pumpkin pie in honor of his store's 100th anniversary. They discuss the changes that have taken place in the town, and she comments on how his store has maintained the same look and feel over the years.   6.____

7. In October, Mr. Bryan's aunt lends him $50,000.   7.____

8. The Town Council has just announced that the town is eligible for funding from a federal project designed to encourage the location of new businesses in the central districts of cities and towns.   8.____

Questions 9-18.

DIRECTIONS: Questions 9 through 18 are based on the following paragraph.

A proposal was put before the legislative body of a country to require air bags in all automobiles manufactured for domestic use in that country after 2019. The air bag, made of nylon or plastic, is designed to inflate automatically within a car at the impact of a collision, thus protecting front-seat occupants from being thrown forward. There has been much support of the measure from consumer groups, the insurance industry, key legislators, and the general public. The country's automobile manufacturers, who contend the new crash equipment would add up to $1,000 to car prices and provide no more protection than existing seat belts, are against the proposed legislation

CONCLUSION: On April 21, 2014, the legislation requiring air bags in all automobiles manufactured for domestic use in that country after 2019.

A. The statement proves the conclusion.
B. The statement supports the conclusion but does not prove it.
C. The statement disproves the conclusion.
D. The statement weakens the conclusion.
E. The statement is irrelevant to the conclusion.

9. A study has shown that 59% of car occupants do not use seat belts. 9.____

10. The country's Department of Transportation has estimated that the crash protection equipment would save up to 5,900 lives each year. 10.____

11. On April 27, 2013, Augusta Raneoni was named head of an advisory committee to gather and analyze data on the costs, benefits, and feasibility of the proposed legislation on air bags in automobiles. 11.____

12. Consumer groups and the insurance industry accuse the legislature of rejecting passage of the regulation for political reasons. 12.____

13. A study by the Committee on Imports and Exports projected that the sales of imported cars would rise dramatically in 2019 because imported cars do not have to include air bags, and can be sold more cheaply. 13.____

14. Research has shown that air bags, if produced on a large scale, would cost about $200 apiece, and would provide more reliable protection than any other type of seat belt. 14.____

15. Auto sales in 2011 increased 3% over the previous year. 15.____

16. A Department of Transportation report in July of 2020 credits a drop in automobile deaths of 4,100 to the use of air bags. 16.____

17. In June of 2014, the lobbyist of the largest insurance company receives a bonus for her work on the passage of the air bag legislation. 17.____

18. In 2020, the stock in crash protection equipment has risen three-fold over the previous year. 18.____

Questions 19-25.

DIRECTIONS: Questions 19 through 25 are based on the following paragraph.

On a national television talk show, Joan Rivera, a famous comedienne, has recently insulted the physical appearances of a famous actress and the dead wife of an ex-President. There has been a flurry of controversy over her comments, and much discussion of the incident has appeared in the press. Most of the comments have been negative. It appears that this tie she might have gone too far. There have been cancellations of two of her five scheduled performances in the two weeks since the show was televised, and Joan's been receiving a lot of negative mail. Because of the controversy, she has an interview with a national news magazine at the end of the week, and her press agent is strongly urging her to apologize publicly. She feels strongly that her comments were no worse than any other she has ever made, and that the whole incident will *blow over* soon. She respects her press agent's judgment, however, as his assessment of public sentiment tends to be very accurate.

CONCLUSION: Joan does not apologize publicly, and during the interview she challenges the actress to a weight-losing contest. For every pound the actress loses, Joan says she will donate $1 to the Cellulite Prevention League.

A. The statement proves the conclusion.
B. The statement supports the conclusion but does not prove it.
C. The statement disproves the conclusion.
D. The statement weakens the conclusion.
E. The statement is irrelevant to the conclusion.

19. Joan's mother, who she is very fond of, is very upset with Joan's comments. 19.____

20. Six months after the interview, Joan's income has doubled. 20.____

21. Joan's agent is pleased with the way Joan handles the interview. 21.____

22. Joan's sister has been appointed Treasurer of the Cellulite Prevention League In her report, she states that Joan's $12 contribution is the only amount that has been donated to the League in its first six months. 22.____

23. The magazine receives many letters commending Joan for the courage it took for her to apologize publicly in the interview. 23.____

24. Immediately after the interview appears, another one of Joan's performances is cancelled. 24.____

25. Due to a printers' strike, the article was not published until the following week. 25.____

Questions 26-30.

DIRECTIONS: Questions 25 through 30 are based on the following paragraph.

The law-making body of Country X must decide what to do about the issue of recording television shows for home use. There is currently no law against recording shows directly from the TV as long as the DVDs are not used for commercial purposes. The increasing popularity of pay TV and satellite systems, combined with the increasing number of homes that own recording equipment, has caused a great deal of concern in some segments of the entertainment industry. Companies that own the rights to films, popular television shows, and sporting events feel that their copyright privileges are being violated, and they are seeking compensation or the banning of TV recording. Legislation has been introduced to make it illegal to record television programs for home use. Separate proposed legislation is also pending that would continue to allow recording of TV shows for home use, but would place a tax of 10% on each DVD that is purchased for home use. The income from that tax would then be proportionately distributed as royalties to those owning the rights to programs being aired. A weighted point system coupled with the averaging of several national viewing rating systems would be used to determine the royalties. There is a great deal of lobbying being done for both bills, as the manufacturers of DVDs and recording equipment are against the passage of the bills.

CONCLUSION: The legislature of Country X rejects both bills by a wide margin.

A. The statement proves the conclusion.
   B. The statement supports the conclusion but does not prove it.
   C. The statement disproves the conclusion.
   D. The statement weakens the conclusion.
   E. The statement is irrelevant to the conclusion.

26. Country X's Department of Taxation hires 500 new employees to handle the increased paperwork created by the new tax on DVDs.

27. A study conducted by the country's most prestigious accounting firm shows that the cost of implementing the proposed new DVD tax would be greater than the income expected from it.

28. It is estimated that 80% of all those working in the entertainment industry, excluding performers, own DVD recorders.

29. The head of Country X's law enforcement agency states that legislation banning the home recording of TV shows would be unenforceable.

30. Financial experts predict that unless a tax is placed on DVDs, several large companies in the entertainment industry will have to file for bankruptcy.

Questions 31-38.

DIRECTIONS: Questions 31 through 38 are variations on the type of question you just had. It is important that you read the question very carefully to determine exactly what is required.

31. In this question, select the choice that is MOST relevant to the conclusion.
    I. The Buffalo Bills football team is in second place in its division.
    II. The New England Patriots are in first place in the same division.
    III. There are two games left to play in the season, and the Bills will not play the Patriots again.
    IV. The New England Patriots won ten games and lost four games, and the Buffalo Bills have won eight games and lost six games.
    CONCLUSION: The Buffalo Bills win their division.
    A. The conclusion is proved by sentences I-IV.
    B. The conclusion is disproved by sentences I-IV.
    C. The facts are not sufficient to prove or disprove the conclusion.

32. In this question, select the choice that is MOST relevant to the conclusion.
    I. On the planet of Zeinon there are only two different eye colors and only two different hair colors.
    II. Half of those beings with purple hair have golden eyes.
    III. There are more inhabitants with purple hair than there are inhabitants with silver hair.
    IV. One-third of those with silver hair have green eyes.
    CONCLUSION: There are more golden-eyed beings on Zeinon than green-eyed ones.
    A. The conclusion is proved by sentences I-IV.
    B. The conclusion is disproved by sentences I-IV.
    C. The facts are not sufficient to prove or disprove the conclusion.

33. In this question, select the choice that is MOST relevant to the conclusion.
    John and Kevin are leaving Amaranth to go to school in Bethany. They've decided to rent a small truck to move their possessions. Joe's Truck Rental charges $100 plus 30¢ a mile. National Movers charges $50 more but gives free mileage for the first 100 miles. After the first 100 miles, they charge 25¢ a mile.
    CONCLUSION: John and Kevin rent their truck from National Movers because it is cheaper.
    A. The conclusion is proved by the facts in the above paragraph.
    B. The conclusion is disproved by the facts in the above paragraph.
    C. The facts are not sufficient to prove or disprove the conclusion.

34. For this question, select the choice that supports the information given in the passage.
    Municipalities in Country X are divided into villages, towns, and cities. A village has a population of 5,000 or less. The population of a town ranges from 5,001 to 15,000. In order to be incorporated as a city, the municipality must have a population over 15,000. If, after a village becomes a town, or a town becomes a city, the population drops below the minimum required (for example, the population of a city goes below 15,000), and stays below the minimum for more than ten years, it loses its current status, and drops to the next category. As soon as a municipality rises in population to the next category (village to town, for example), however, it is immediately reclassified to the next category.
    In the 2000 census, Plainfield had a population of 12,000. Between 2000 and 2010, Plainfield grew 10%, and between 2010 and 2020 Plainfield grew another 20%. The population of Springdale doubled from 2000 to 2010, and increased 25% from 2010 to 2020. The city of Smallville's population, 20,283, has not changed significantly in recent years. Granton had a population of 25,000 people in 1990, and has decreased 25% in each ten year period since then. Ellenville had a population of 4,283 in 1990, and grew 5% in each ten year period since 1990.

In 2020,
- A. Plainfield, Smallville, and Granton are cities.
- B. Smallville is a city, Granton is a town, and Ellenville is a village.
- C. Springdale, Granton, and Ellenville are towns.
- D. Plainfield and Smallville are cities, and Ellenville is a town.

35. For this question, select the choice that is MOST relevant to the conclusion.
    A study was done for a major food-distributing firm to determine if there is any difference in the kind of caffeine containing products used by people of different ages. A sample of one thousand people between the ages of twenty and fifty were drawn from selected areas in the country. They were divided equally into three groups.
    Those individuals who were 20-29 were designated Group A, those 30-39 were Group B, and those 40-50 were placed in Group C.
    It was found that on the average, Group A drank 1.8 cups of coffee, Group B 3.1, and Group C 2.5 cups of coffee daily. Group A drank 2.1 cups of tea, Group B drank 1.2, and Group C drank 2.6 cups of tea daily. Group A drank 3 1.8 ounces glasses of cola, Group B drank 1.9, and Group C drank 1.5 glasses of cola daily.
    CONCLUSION: According to the study, the average person in the 20-29 age group drinks less tea daily than the average person in the 40-50 age group, but drinks more coffee daily than the average person in the 30-39 age group drinks cola.
    - A. The conclusion is proved by the facts in the above paragraph.
    - B. The conclusion is disproved by the facts in the above paragraph.
    - C. The facts are not sufficient to prove or disprove the conclusion.

36. For this question, select the choice that is MOST relevant to the conclusion
    I. Mary is taller than Jane but shorter than Dale.
    II. Fred is taller than Mary but shorter than Steven.
    III. Dale is shorter than Steven but taller than Elizabeth.
    IV. Elizabeth is taller than Mary but not as tall as Fred.
    CONCLUSION: Dale is taller than Fred.
    - A. The conclusion is proved by sentences I-IV.
    - B. The conclusion is disproved by sentences I-IV.
    - C. The facts are not sufficient to prove or disprove the conclusion.

37. For this question, select the choice that is MOST relevant to the conclusion.
    I. Main Street is between Spring Street and Glenn Blvd.
    II. Hawley Avenue is one block south of Spring Street and three blocks north of Main Street.
    III. Glenn Street is five blocks south of Elm and four blocks south of Main.
    IV. All the streets mentioned are parallel to one another.
    CONCLUSION: Elm Street is between Hawley Avenue and Glenn Blvd.
    - A. The conclusion is proved by the facts in sentences I-IV.
    - B. The conclusion is disproved by the facts in sentences I-IV.
    - C. The facts are not sufficient to prove or disprove the conclusion.

38. For this question, select the choice that is MOST relevant to the conclusion. 38._____
   I. Train A leaves the town of Hampshire every day at 5:50 A.M. and arrives in New London at 6:42 A.M.
   II. Train A leaves New London at 7:00 A.M. and arrives in Kellogsville at 8:42 A.M.
   III. Train B leaves Kellogsville at 8:00 A.M. and arrives in Hampshire at 10:45 A.M.
   IV. Due to the need for repairs, there is just one railroad track between New London and Hampshire.
   CONCLUSION: It is impossible for Train A and Train B to follow these schedules without colliding.
   A. The conclusion is proved by the facts in sentences I-IV.
   B. The conclusion is disproved by the facts in sentences I-IV.
   C. The facts are not sufficient to prove or disprove the conclusion.

KEY (CORRECT ANSWERS)

1.	D	11.	C	21.	D	31.	C
2.	B	12.	C	22.	A	32.	A
3.	E	13.	D	23.	C	33.	C
4.	B	14.	B	24.	B	34.	B
5.	C	15.	E	25.	E	35.	B
6.	A	16.	B	26.	C	36.	C
7.	D	17.	A	27.	B	37.	A
8.	B	18.	B	28.	E	38.	B
9.	B	19.	D	29.	B		
10.	B	20.	E	30.	D		

SOLUTIONS TO QUESTIONS

1. The answer is D. This statement weakens the conclusion, but does not disprove it. If a new branch of the community college opened in September, it could possibly bring in new business for Mr. Bryant. Since it states in the conclusion that Mr. Bryant felt there would not be enough new business to support the additional stores, this would tend to disprove the conclusion. Choice C would not be correct because it's possible that he felt that the students would not have enough additional money to support his new venture, or would not be interested in his clothing styles. It's also possible that the majority of the students already live in the area, so that they wouldn't really be a new customer population. This type of question is tricky, and can initially be very confusing, so don't feel badly if you missed it. Most people need to practice with a few of these types of questions before they feel comfortable recognizing exactly what they're being asked to do.

2. The answer is B. It supports the conclusion because the closing of the factory would probably take money and customers out of the town, causing Mr. Bryant to lose some of his present business. It doesn't prove the conclusion, however, because we don't know how large the factory was. It's possible that only a small percentage of the population was employed there, or that they found other jobs.

3. The answer is E. The fact that the number of children per household dropped slightly nationwide in the decade is irrelevant. Statistics showing a drop nationwide doesn't mean that there was a drop in the number of children per household in Mr. Bryant's hometown. This is a tricky question, as choice B, supporting the conclusion but not proving it, may seem reasonable. If the number of children per household declined nationwide, then it may not seem unreasonable to feel that this would support Mr. Bryant's decision not to expand his business. However, we're preparing you for promotional exams, not "real life." One of the difficult things about taking exams is that sometimes you're forced to make a choice between two statements that both seem like they could be the possible answer. What you need to do in that case is choose the best choice. Becoming annoyed or frustrated with the question won't really help much. If there's a review of the exam, you can certainly appeal the question. There have been many cases where, after an appeal, two possible choices have been allowed as correct answers. We've included this question, however, to help you see what to do should you get a question like this. It's most important not to get rattled, and to select the BEST choice. In this case, the connection between the statistical information and Mr. Bryant's decision is pretty remote. If the question had said that the number of children in Mr. Bryant's town had decreased, then choice B would have been a more reasonable choice. It could also help in this situation to visualize the situation. Picture Mr. Bryant in his armchair reading that, nationwide, the average number of children per household has declined slightly. How likely would this be to influence his decision, especially since he sells men's and women's clothing? It would take a while for this decline in population to show up, and we're not even sure if it applies to Mr. Bryant's hometown. Don't feel badly if you missed this; it was tricky. The more of these you do, the more comfortable you'll feel.

4. The answer is B. If a new clothing boutique specializing in casual women's clothing were to open soon, this would lend support to Mr. Bryant's decision not to expand, but would not prove that he had actually made the decision to expand. A new women's clothing boutique would most likely be in competition with his existing business, thus making any possible expansion a riskier venture. We can't be sure from this, however, that he didn't go ahead and expand his business despite the increased competition. Choice A, proves the conclusion, would only be the answer if we could be absolutely sure from the statement that Mr. Bryant had actually not expanded his business.

5. The answer is C. This statement disproves the conclusion. In order for his sister to buy several items for her baby at Mr. Bryant's store, he would have to have changed his business to include children's clothing.

6. The answer is A. It definitely proves the conclusion. The passage states that Mr. Bryan's store had been in business since 1920. A pie baked in honor of his store's 100th anniversary would have to be presented sometime in 2020. The conclusion states that he made his decision not to expand on November 7, 2018. If, more than a year later Mrs. MacIntyre comments that his store has maintained the same look and feel over the years, it could not have been expanded, or otherwise significantly changed.

7. The answer is D. If Mr. Bryant's aunt lent him $50,000 in October, this would tend to weaken the conclusion, which took place in November. Because it was stated that Mr. Bryant would need to borrow money in order to expand his business, it would be logical to assume that if he borrowed money he had decided to expand his business, weakening the conclusion. The reason C, disproves the conclusion, is not the correct answer is because we can't be sure Mr. Bryant didn't borrow the money for another reason.

8. The answer is B. If Mr. Bryant's town is eligible for federal funds to encourage the location of new businesses in the central district, this would tend to support his decision not to expand his business. Funds to encourage new business would increase the likelihood of there being additional competition for Mr. Bryant's store to contend with. Since we can't say for sure that there would be direct competition from a new business, however, choice A would be incorrect. Note that this is also a tricky question. You might have thought that the new funds weakened the conclusion because it would mean that Mr. Bryant could easily get the money he needed. Mr. Bryant is expanding his present business, not creating a new business. Therefore, he is not eligible for the funding.

9. The answer is B. This is a very tricky question. It's stated that 59% of car occupants don't use seat belts. The legislature is considering the use of air bags because of safety issues. The advantage of air bags over seat belts is that they inflate upon impact, and don't require car occupants to do anything with them ahead of time. Since the population has strongly resisted using seat belts, the air bags could become even more important in saving lives. Since saving lives is the purpose of the proposed legislation, the information that a small percentage of people use seat belts could be helpful to the passage of the legislation. We can't be sure that this is reason enough for the legislature to vote for the legislation, however, so choice A in incorrect.

10. The answer is B, as the information that 5,900 lives could be saved would tend to support the conclusion. Saving that many lives through the use of air bags could be a very persuasive reason to vote for the legislation. Since we don't know for sure that it's enough of a compelling reason for the legislature to vote for the legislation, however, choice A could not be the answer.

11. The answer is C, disproves the conclusion. If the legislation had been passed as stated in the conclusion, there would be no reason to appoint someone head of an advisory committee six days later to analyze the "feasibility of the proposed legislation." The key word here is "proposed." If it has been proposed, it means it hasn't been passed. This contradicts the conclusion and, therefore, disproves it.

12. The answer is C, disproves the conclusion. If the legislation had passed, there would be no reason for supporters of the legislation to accuse the legislature of rejecting the legislation for political reasons. This question may have seemed so obvious that you might have thought there was a trick to it. Exams usually have a few obvious questions, which will trip you up if you begin reading too much into them.

13. The answer is D, as this would tend to disprove the conclusion. A projected dramatic rise in imported cars could be very harmful to the country's economy and could be a very good reason for some legislators to vote against the proposed legislation. It would be assuming too much to choose C, however, because we don't know if they actually did vote against it.

14. The answer is B. This information would tend to support the passage of the legislation. The estimate of the cost of the air bags is $800 less than the cost estimated by opponents, and it's stated that the protection would be more reliable than any other type of seat belt. Both of these would be good arguments in favor of passing the legislation. Since we don't know for sure, however, how persuasive they actually were, choice A would not be the correct choice.

15. The answer is E, as this is irrelevant information. It really doesn't matter whether auto sales in 2001 have increased slightly over the previous year. If the air bag legislation were to go into effect in 2004, that might make the information somehow more relevant. But the air bag legislation would not take effect until 2009, so the information is irrelevant, since it tells us nothing about the state of the auto industry then.

16. The answer is B, supports the conclusion. This is a tricky question. While at first it might seem to prove the conclusion, we can't be sure that the air bag legislation is responsible for the drop in automobile deaths. It's possible air bags came into popular use without the legislation, or with different legislation. There's no way we can be sure that it was the proposed legislation mandating the use of air bags that was responsible.

17. The answer is A. If, in June of 2009, the lobbyist received a bonus "for her work on the air bag legislation," we can be sure that the legislation passed. This proves the conclusion.

18. The answer is B. This is another tricky question. A three-fold stock increase would strongly suggest that the legislation had been passed, but it's possible that factors other than the air bag legislation caused the increase. Note that the stock is in "crash protection

equipment." Nowhere in the statement does it say air bags. Seat belts, motorcycle helmets, and collapsible bumpers are all crash protection equipment and could have contributed to the increase. This is just another reminder to read carefully because the questions are often designed to mislead you.

19. The answer is D. This would tend to weaken the conclusion because Joan is very fond of her mother and she would not want to upset her unnecessarily. It does not prove it, however, because if Joan strongly feels she is right, she probably wouldn't let her mother's opinion sway her. Choice E would also not be correct, because we cannot assume that Joan's mother's opinion is of so little importance to her as to be considered irrelevant.

20. The answer is E. The statement is irrelevant. We are told that Joan's income has doubled but we are not old why. The phrase "six months after the interview" can be misleading in that it leads us to assume that the increase and the interview are related. Her income could have doubled because she regained her popularity but it could also have come from stocks or some other business venture. Because we are not given any reason for her income doubling, it would be impossible to say whether or not this statement proves or disproves the conclusion. Choice E is the best choice of the five possible choices. One of the problems with promotional exams is that sometimes you need to select a choice you're not crazy about. In this case, "not having enough information to made a determination" would be the best choice. However, that's not an option, so you're forced to work with what you've got. On these exams it's sometimes like voting for President; you have to pick the "lesser of the two evils" or the least awful choice. In this case, the information is more irrelevant to the conclusion than it is anything else.

21. The answer is D, weakens the conclusion. We've been told that Joan's agent feels that she should apologize. If he is pleased with her interview, then it would tend to weaken the conclusion but not disprove it. We can't be sure that he hasn't had a change of heart, or that there weren't other parts of the interview he liked so much that they outweighed her unwillingness to apologize.

22. The answer is A. The conclusion states that Joan will donate $1 to the Cellulite Prevention League for every pound the actress loses. Joan's sister's financial report on the League's activities directly supports and proves the conclusion.

23. The answer is C, disproves the conclusion. If the magazine receives many letters commending Joan for her courage in apologizing, this directly contradicts the conclusion, which states that Joan didn't apologize.

24. The answer is B. It was stated in the passage that two of Joan's performances were cancelled after the controversy first occurred. The cancellation of another performance immediately after her interview was published would tend to support the conclusion that she refused to apologize. Because we can't be sure, however, that her performance wasn't cancelled for another reason, choice A would be incorrect.

25. The answer is E, as this information is irrelevant. Postponing the article an extra week does not affect Joan's decision or the public's reaction to it.

13 (#1)

26. The answer is C. If 500 new employees are hired to handle the "increased paperwork created by the new tax on DVDs," this would directly contradict the conclusion, which states that the legislature defeated both bills. (They should all be this easy.)

27. The answer is B. The results of the study would support the conclusion. If implementing the legislation was going to be so costly, it is likely that the legislature would vote against it. Choice A is not the answer, however, because we can't be sure that the legislature didn't pass it anyway.

28. The answer is E. It's irrelevant to the conclusion that 80% of all those working in the entertainment industry own DVD recorders. Sometimes if you're not sure about these, it can help a lot to try and visualize the situation. Why would someone voting on this legislation care about this fact? It doesn't seem to be the kind of information that would make any difference or impact upon the conclusion.

29. The answer is B. The head of the law enforcement agency's statement that the legislation would be unenforceable would support the conclusion. It's possible that many legislators would question why they should bother to pass legislation that would be impossible to enforce. Choice A would be incorrect, however, because we can't be sure that the legislation wasn't passed in spite of his statement.

30. The answer is D. This would tend to weaken the conclusion because the prospect of several large companies going bankrupt would seem to be a good argument in favor of the legislation. The possible loss of jobs and businesses would be a good reason for some people to vote for the legislation. We can't be sure, however, that this would be a competing enough reason to ensure passage of the legislation so choice C is incorrect.

This concludes our section on the "Validity of Conclusion" type of questions. We hope these weren't too horrible for you. It's important to keep in mind exactly what you've been given and exactly what they want you to do with it. It's also necessary to remember that you may have to choose between two possible answers. In that case, you must choose the one that seems the best. Sometimes you may think there is no good answer. You will probably be right, but you can't let that upset you. Just choose the one you dislike the least.

We want to repeat that it is unlikely that this exact format will appear on the exam. The skills required to answer these questions, however, are the same as those you'll need for the exam so we suggest that you review this section before taking the actual exam.

31. The answer is C. This next set of questions requires you to "switch gears" slightly, and get used to different formats. In this type of question, you have to decide whether the conclusion is proved by the facts give, disproved by the facts given, or neither because note enough information has been provided. Fortunately, unlike the previous questions, you don't have to decide whether particular facts support or don't support the conclusion. This type of question is more straight forward, but the reasoning behind it is the same. We are told that the Bills have won two games less than the Patriots, and that the Patriots are in first place and the Bills are in second place. We are also told that there are two games left to play, and that they won't play each other again. The conclusion states that the Bills won the division. Is there anything in the four statements that would prove this? We have

no idea what the outcome of the last two games of the season was. The Bills and Patriots could have ended up tied at the end of the season, or the Bills could have lost both or one of their last games while the Patriots did the same. There might even be another team tied for first or second place with the Bills or Patriots. Since we don't know for sure, Choice A is incorrect. Choice B is trickier. It might seem at first glance that the best the Bills could do would be to tie the Patriots if the Patriots lost their last two games and the Bills won their last two games. But it would be too much to assume that there is no procedure for a tiebreaker that wouldn't give the Bills the division championship. Since we don't know what the rules are in the event of a tie (for example, what if a tie was decided on the results of what happened when the two teams had played each other, or on the best record in the division, or on most points scored?), we can't say for sure that it would be impossible for the Bills to win their division. For this reason, choice C is the answer, as we don't have enough information to prove or disprove the conclusion. This question looked more difficult than it actually was. It's important to disregard any factors outside of the actual question, and to focus only on what you've been given. In this case, as on all of these types of questions, what you know or don't know about a subject is actually irrelevant. It's best to concentrate only on the actual facts given.

32. The answer is A. The conclusion is proved by the facts given.

In this type of problem, it is usually best to pull as many facts as possible from the sentences and then put them into a simpler form. The phrasing and the order of exam questions are designed to be confusing so you need to restate things as clearly as possible by eliminating the extras.

Sentence I tells us that there are only two possible colors for eyes and two for hair. Looking at the other sentences we learn that eyes are either green or gold and that hair is either silver or purple. If half the beings with purple hair have golden eyes, then the other half must have green eyes since it is the only other eye color. Likewise, if one-third of those with silver hair have green eyes, the other two-thirds must have golden eyes.

This information makes it clear that there are more golden-eyed beings on Zeinon than green-eyed ones. It doesn't matter that we don't know exactly how many are actually living on the planet. The number of those with gold eyes (1/2 plus 2/3) will always be greater than the number of those with green eyes (1/2 plus 1/3), no matter what the actual figures might be. Sentence III is totally irrelevant because even if there were more silver-haired inhabitants it would not affect the conclusion.

33. The answer is C. The conclusion is neither proved nor disproved by the facts because we don't know how many miles Bethany is from Amoranth.

With this type of question, if you're not sure how to approach it, you can always substitute in a range of "real numbers" to see what the result would be. If they were 200 miles apart, Joe's Truck Rental would be cheaper because they would charge a total of $160 while National Movers would charge $175.

    Joe's - $100 plus .30 x 200 (or $60) = $160
    National - $150 plus .25 x 100 (or $25) = $175

If the towns were 600 miles apart, however, National Movers would be cheaper. The cost of renting from National would be $275 compared to the $280 charged by Joe's Trucking.

    Joe's - $100 plus .30 x 600 (or $180) = $280
    National - $150 plus .25 x 500 (or $125) = $275

15 (#1)

34. The answer is B. We've varied the format once more, but the reasoning is similar. This is a tedious question that is more like a math question, but we wanted to give you some practice with this type, just in case. You won't be able to do this question if you've forgotten how to do percents. Many exams require this knowledge, so if you feel you need a review we suggest you read Booklets 1, 2 or 3 in this series.

The only way to attack this problem is to go through each choice until you find the one that is correct. Choice A states that Plainfield, Smallville, and Granton are cities. Let's begin with Plainfield. The passage states that in 1990 Plainfield had a population of 12,000, and that it grew 10% between 1990 and 2000, and another 20% between 2000 and 2010. Ten percent of 12,000 is 1200 (12,000 x .10 = 1200). Therefore, the population grew from 12,000 in 1990 to 12,000 + 1200 between 1990 and 2000. At the time of the 2000 Census, Plainfield's population was 13,200. It then grew another 20% between 2000 and 2010, so, 13,200 x .20 = 2640. 13,200 plus the additional increase of 2640 would make the population of Plainfield 15,840. This would qualify it as a city, since its population is over 15,000. Since a change upward in the population of a municipality is re-classified immediately, Plainfield would have become a city right away. So far, statement A is true. The passage states that Smallville's population has not changed significantly in the last twenty years. Since Smallville's population was 20,283, Smallville would still be a city. Granton had a population of 25,000 (what a coincidence that so any of these places have such nice, even numbers) in 1980. The population has decreased 25% in each ten year period since that time. So from 1980 to 1990, the population decreased 25%. 25,000 x .25 = 6,250. 25,000 minus 6,250 = 18,750. So the population of Granton in 1990 would have been 18,750. (Or, you could have saved a step and multiplied 25,000 by .75 to get 18,750.) The population from 1990 to 2000 decreased an additional 25%. So: 18,750 x .25 = 4,687.50. 18,750 minus 4,687.50 = 14,062.50. Or: 18,750 x .75 = 14,062.50. (Don't let the fact that a half of a person is involved confuse you; these are exam questions, not real life.) From 2000 to 2010 the population decreased an additional 25%. This would mean that Granton's population was below 15,000 for more than ten years, so it's status as a city would have changed to that of a town, which would make choice A incorrect.

Choice B states that Smallville is a city and Granton is a town, which we know to be true from the information above. Choice B is correct so far. We next need to determine if Ellenville is a village. Ellenville had a population of 4,283 in 1980, and increased 5% in each ten year period since 1980. 4,283 x .05 = 214.15. 4,283 plus 214.15 = 4,497.15, so Ellenville's population from 1980 to 1990 increased to 4,497.15. (Or: 4,283 x 1.05 – 4,497.15.) From 1990 to 2000 Ellenville's population increased another 5%: 4,497.15 x .05 = 224.86. 4,497.15 plus 224.86 = 4,772.01 (or: 4,497.15 x 1.05 = 4,722.01.) From 2000 to 2010, Ellenville's population increased another 5%: 4,722.01 x .05 = 236.10. 4,722.01 plus 236.10 = 4,958.11. (Or: 4,722.01 x 1.05 = 4,958.11.).

Ellenville's population is still under 5,000 in 2010, so it would continue to be classified as a village. Since all three statements in choice B are true, choice B must be the answer. However, we'll go through the other choices. Choice C states that Springdale is a town. The passage tells us that the population of Springdale doubled from 1990 to 2000, and increased 25% from 2000 to 2010. It doesn't give us any actual population figures, however, so it's impossible to know what the population of Springdale is, making choice C incorrect. Choice C also states that Granton is a town, which is true, and that Ellenville is a town, which is false (from choice B we know it's a village). Choice D states that Plainfield and Smallville are cities, which is information we already know is true, and that Ellenville is a town. Since Ellenville is a village, choice D is also incorrect.

This was a lot of work for just one question and we doubt you'll get one like this on this section of the exam, but we included it just in case. On an exam, you can always put a check mark next to a question like this and come back to it later, if you feel you're pressed for time and cold spend your time more productively on other, less time-consuming problems.

35. The answer is B. This question requires very careful reading. It's best to break the conclusion down into smaller parts in order to solve the problem. The first half of the conclusion states that the average person in the 20-29 age group (Group A) drinks less tea daily than the average person in the 40-50 age group (Group C). The average person in Group A drinks 2.1 cups of tea daily, while the average person in Group C drinks 2.6 cups of tea daily. Since 2.1 is less than 2.6, the conclusion is correct so far. The second half of the conclusion states that the average person in Group A drinks more coffee daily than the average person in the 30-39 age group (Group B) drinks cola. The average person in Group A drinks 1.8 cups of coffee daily, while the average person in Group B drinks 1.9 glasses of cola. This disproves the conclusion, which states that the average person in Group A drinks more coffee daily than the average person in Group B drinks cola.

36. The answer is C. The easiest way to approach a problem that deals with the relationship between a number of different people or things is to set up a diagram. This type of problem is usually too confusing to do in your head. For this particular problem, the "diagram" could be a line, one end of which would be labeled tall and the other end labeled short. Then, taking one sentence at a time, place the people on the line to see where they fall in relation to one another.

   The diagram of the first sentence would look like this:

   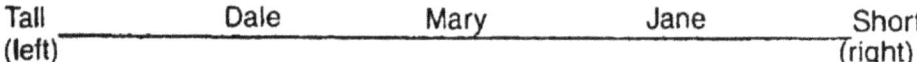

   Mary is taller than Jane but shorter than Dale, so she would fall somewhere between the two of them. We have placed tall on the left and labeled it left just to make the explanation easier. You could just as easily have reversed the position.

   The second sentence places Fred somewhere to the left of Mary because he is taller than she is. Steven would be to the left of Fred for the same reason. At this point we don't know whether Steven and Fred are taller or shorter than Dale. The new diagram would look like this:

   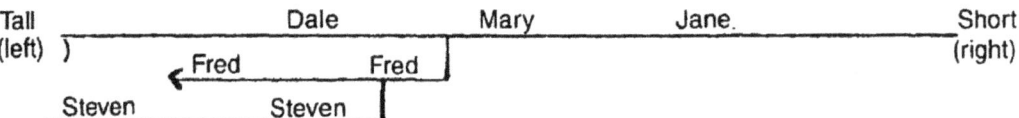

17 (#1)

The third sentence introduces Elizabeth, presenting a new problem. Elizabeth can be anywhere to the right of Dale. Don't make the mistake of assuming she falls between Dale and Mary. At this point we don't know where she fits in relation to Mary, Jane, or even Fred.

We do get information about Steven, however. He is taller than Dale so he would be to the left of Dale. Since he is also taller than Fred (see sentence II), we know that Steven is the tallest person thus far. The diagram would now look like this:

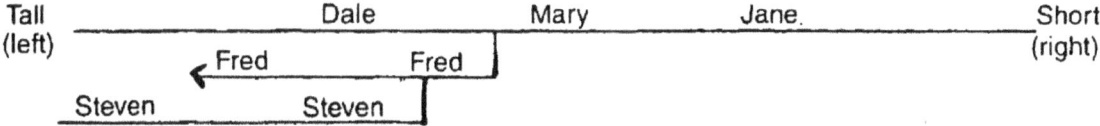

Fred's height is somewhere between Steven and Mary, Elizabeth's anywhere between Dale and the end of the line.

The fourth sentence tells us where Elizabeth stands, in relation to Fred and the others in the problem. The fact that she is taller than Mary means she is also taller than Jane. The final diagram would look like this:

| Tall (left) | Steven | Dale | Elizabeth | Mary | Jane | Short (right) |

with Fred bracketed between Steven and Elizabeth.

We still don't know whether Dale or Fred is taller, however. Therefore, the conclusion that Dale is taller than Fred can't be proved. It also can't be disproved because we don't know for sure that he isn't. The answer has to be choice C, as the conclusion can't be proved or disproved.

37. The answer is A. This is another problem that is easiest for most people if they make a diagram. Sentence I states that Main Street is between Spring Street and Glenn Blvd. At this point we don't know if they are next to each other or if they are separated by a number of streets. Therefore, you should leave space between streets as you plot your first diagram.

The order of the streets could go either:

    Spring St.   or   Glenn Blvd.
    Main St.   Main St.
    Glenn Blvd.   Spring St.

Sentence II states that Hawley Street is one block south of Spring Street and 3 blocks north of Main Street. Because most people think in terms of north as above and south as below and because it was stated that Hawley is one block south of Spring Street and three blocks north of Main Street, the next diagram could look like this:

18 (#1)

<u>Spring</u>
<u>Hawley</u>

———

———
<u>Main</u>
<u>Glenn</u>

The third sentence states that Glenn Street is five blocks south of Elm and four blocks south of Main. It could look like this:

<u>Spring</u>
<u>Hawley</u>

———

<u>Elm</u>
<u>Main</u>

———

———

<u>Glenn</u>

The conclusion states that Elm Street is between Hawley Avenue and Glenn Blvd. From the above diagram, we can see that this is the case.

38. The answer is B. For most people, the best way to do this problem is to draw a diagram, plotting the course of both trains. Sentence I states that Train A leaves Hampshire at 5:50 A.M. and reaches New London at 6:42. Your first diagram might look like this:

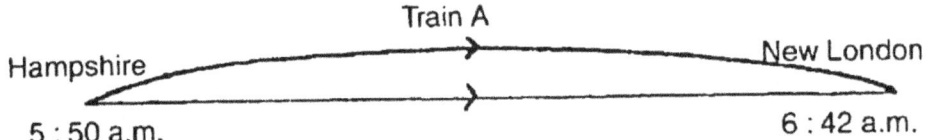

Sentence II states that the train leaves New London at 7:00 a.m. and arrives in Kellogsville at 8:42 a.m. The diagram might now look like this:

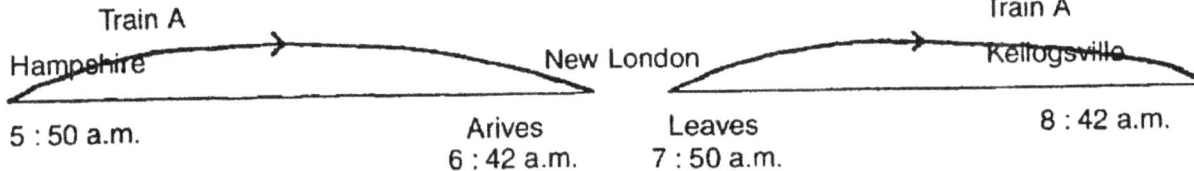

Sentence III gives us the rest of the information that must be included in the diagram. It introduces Train B, which moves in the opposite direction, leaving Kellogsville at 8:00 a.m. and arriving at Hampshire at 10:42 a.m. The final diagram might look like this:

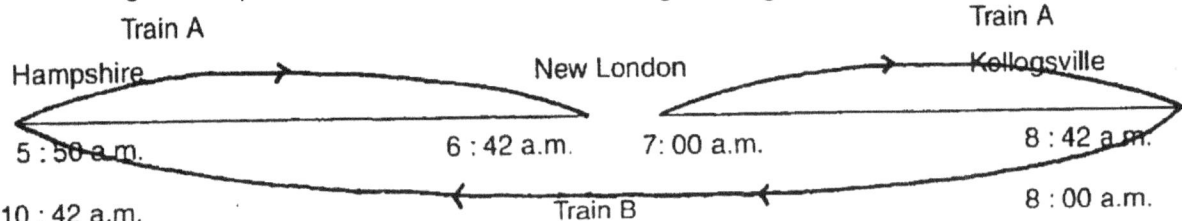

19 (#1)

As you can see from the diagram, the routes of the two trains will overlap somewhere between Kellogsville and New London. If you read sentence IV quickly and assumed that that was the section with only one track, you probably would have assumed that there would have had to be a collision. Sentence IV states, however, that there is only one railroad track between New London and Hampshire. That is the only section, then, where the two trains could collide. By the time Train B gets to that section, however, Train A will have passed it. The two trains will pass each other somewhere between New London and Kellogsville, not New London and Hampshire.

EXAMINATION SECTION
TEST 1

DIRECTIONS: Each question or incomplete statement is followed by several suggested answers or completions. Select the one that BEST answers the question or completes the statement. *PRINT THE LETTER OF THE CORRECT ANSWER IN THE SPACE AT THE RIGHT.*

QUESTIONS 1-4.

Questions 1-4 refer to the following information.

A recent study shows that of the 1000 graduates of Learnmore High School, 40% claimed that they smoked during their high school years, 30% said they started smoking before entering high school and continued smoking during high school years. Of the people who didn't smoke at all during their high school year, 70% claim that they have no medical problems. However, only 10% of those who did smoke during their high school years reported no medical problem.

1. What percent of all these graduates claim they have NO medical problem?

    A. 30
    B. 42
    C. 60
    D. 70
    E. None of the above

2. How many non-smokers have had at LEAST one medical problem?

    A. 70   B. 180   C. 280   D. 350   E. 450

3. What is the MAXIMUM number of people who began smoking before entering high school, and have had NO medical problems?

    A. 10   B. 30   C. 40   D. 100   E. over 100

4. Counting only individuals who have experienced at least one medical problem, what is the ratio of those who didn't smoke during high school years to those who did smoke during that time period?

    A. 3:2   B. 1:2   C. 1:3   D. 2:3   E. 3:1

5. If John enjoys the taste of pineapple, he'll like the taste of all fruit. The preceding statement is MOST similar to which of the following?

    A. If a dog has a liking for human food, he'll like all dog food
    B. If a person can understand algebra, he can understand all mathematics
    C. If a Chevrolet gets good gas mileage, then so will a Datsun
    D. If Sue's favorite color is red, then she won't buy a green dress
    E. If Bob can fix any electrical item, then he can fix a toaster

6. Only a few people who are heavy smokers will live past the age of 90. Since Eve is a 30-year-old non-smoker, she will probably live beyond the age of 90.
The argument is MOST similar to which of the following?

A. Only a few cities like Cleanville have a low crime rate. Thus, if a person lives in a low crime rate city, that city must be Cleanville.
B. Only birds have feathers. Thus, some birds have morefeathers than other birds.
C. All weight-lifters are light sleepers. Since Bob is a heavy sleeper, he doesn't lift weights.
D. Not many individuals who worry a lot can get a good night's rest. Since John does not worry at all, he can probably get a good night's rest.
E. Some mathematicians enjoy all sports. Since William is a mathematician, he may not enjoy any sports.

7. Since Jack is left-handed, he is an excellent tennis player. Assuming that the preceding statement is true, from which one(s) of the following can this quoted statement be logically deduced?
    I. All tennis players are left-handed.
    II. None of the excellent tennis players is right-handed.
    III. Either Jack is right-handed or he is an excellent tennis player.

    A. I only   B. II only   C. III only
    D. II and III   E. I, II, and III

8. Gamblers are boisterous individuals. Yesterday, I went to the racetrack and there was a lot of shouting after every race. The above argument assumes:
    I. Gamblers frequent racetracks.
    II. Noisy people are gamblers.
    III. Quiet people don't go to racetracks.

    A. I only   B. II only   C. III only
    D. I, III   E. I, II, III

QUESTIONS 9-14.

Questions 9-14 refer to the facts below. It is to be assumed that it is the month of July, the first day of which is a Monday.

The All-Weather appliance store sells televisions, radios, toasters, and refrigerators. Certain conditions govern this store:

   I. The store is open only Monday through Friday every month. Thus, all purchases and deliveries can only be made Monday through Friday.
   II. TV's and radios are only delivered on even numbered days.
   III. Refrigerators are delivered only on Tuesdays and Thursdays.
   IV. Toasters are delivered on any date of the month which can be divided evenly by 3 or 5.
   V. A customer may purchase a radio or a toaster on the day of delivery.
   VI. Since refrigerators and TV's are more expensive items, they are immediately inspected on the day of delivery. However, a customer may not purchase these items until 3 business days after delivery.

9. Which item(s) could be neither delivered nor purchased on Wednesdays?
    A. TV's and radios   B. TV's, radios, and refrigerators
    C. Refrigerators and toasters   D. Refrigerators *only*
    E. Toasters *only*

3 (#1)

10. On how many days during this month can toasters be purchased?   10._____

    A. At least 4 but fewer than 7   B. 9
    C. 11   D. More than 11
    E. None of the above

11. During the first week, on which dates may a TV either be purchased or delivered?   11._____

    A. 2nd, 3rd, 4th   B. 2nd, 4th, 5th   C. 3rd, 4th, 5th
    D. 2nd, 5th, 6th   E. 2nd, 3rd

12. On how many days during this month can TV's be delivered?   12._____

    A. Fewer than 6   B. 8   C. 9
    D. 10   E. 11

13. What is the *earliest* date on which both a TV and toaster can be purchased?   13._____

    A. 3rd   B. 5th   C. 7th   D. 9th   E. 11th

14. Which appliance(s) has(have) exactly 2 delivery dates on Fridays?   14._____

    A. Toasters, radios, TV's   B. Toasters, TV's
    C. TV's, radios   D. Toasters, radios
    E. Only toasters

15. If a person studies hard, he can pass any high school course.   15._____
    This statement can be logically deduced from which of the following?

    A. Some people study while others don't study.
    B. A person who has passed a particular high school course must have studied hard.
    C. A high school course can be passed if a person is willing to study hard.
    D. If a person doesn't study, he can't expect to pass a high school course.
    E. Some high school courses require more studying than do other courses.

QUESTIONS 16-17.

Questions 16 and 17 are to be answered on the basis of the following.

The most dangerous sport in the world is thoroughbred horseracing, since more participants per thousand are killed than in any other sport. Hang-gliding is the second most dangerous sport. By contrast, boxing ranks tenth on the list of most dangerous sports.

16. The author of the above paragraph is *most likely* trying to convey the message that: 16._____

    A. Most sports are dangerous
    B. Hang-gliding is popular despite its danger
    C. Only ten sports are considered dangerous
    D. The most number of injuries occur in horseracing
    E. Boxing is not the most dangerous sport

17. The author would *probably* be opposed to:

    A. Any dangerous sport
    B. A ban on boxing
    C. Amateur boxing
    D. Horseracing
    E. A ban on horseracing

QUESTIONS 18-22.

Questions 18-22 are to be answered on the basis of the following.
The Expanding Food Company has outlet stores on each of First Ave., Second Ave., Third Ave., Fourth Ave., and Fifth Ave. Also, it is known that:

   I.   There is at least one store on each avenue.
   II. The number of stores on Fifth Ave. equals the sum of the number of stores on First Ave. plus those on Second Ave.
   III. The number of stores on Second Ave. is double the number of stores on Third Ave.
   IV. The number of stores on Fourth Ave. is greater than the number of stores on Fifth Ave.
   V.   There are an even number of stores on First Ave.

18. What is the *fewest* number of stores that must exist on Fourth Ave.?

    A. 2   B. 3   C. 4   D. 5   E. 6

19. Which avenue has the MOST stores?

    A. Fifth Ave.   B. Fourth Ave.
    C. Third Ave.   D. All of the above
    E. None of the above

20. Suppose NO avenue has *more* than 7 stores. Find the total number of stores on all 5 avenues.

    A. 16 or 19   B. 20
    C. 21   D. 16, 19 or 20
    E. 16, 20 or 21

21. The number of stores on Fifth Ave

    A. must be even
    B. must be odd
    C. could equal the number of stores on First Ave.
    D. could equal the number of stores on Second Ave.
    E. none of the above

22. Suppose it is known that there are 4 stores on Third Ave. and that there are *more* than 4 stores on First Ave.
    Find the *minimum* number of stores on all 5 avenues.

    A. 45   B. 49   C. 46   D. 48   E. 47

QUESTIONS 23-25.

Questions 23 through 25 are to be answered on the basis of the following.

In a particular group of 21 people, each individual is one of three professions: doctor, engineer, or teacher. Half the number of people who smoke are engineers. One-third of the number of non-smokers are doctors. The number of engineers who smoke equals the number of non-smokers who are not doctors.

23. How many of the non-smokers are doctors? 23.____

    A. 2   B. 3   C. 5   D. 6   E. 9

24. If all the teachers are smokers, and there are only 2 doctors who smoke, then the teachers represent _____ Percent of the entire group. 24.____

    A. 19   B. 25   C. 29   D. 33   E. 40

25. Using the information from the preceding question, *how many* engineers are there in the entire group? 25.____

    A. 3   B. 6   C. 9   D. 12   E. 15

KEY (CORRECT ANSWERS)

1.	E	11.	B
2.	B	12.	E
3.	C	13.	B
4.	B	14.	A
5.	B	15.	C
6.	D	16.	E
7.	C	17.	B
8.	A	18.	D
9.	D	19.	B
10.	E	20.	E

21. A
22. E
23. B
24. A
25. D

SOLUTIONS

1. (.70)(.60) = .42 of all the graduates didn't smoke and didn't have any medical problems, whereas (.10)(.40) = .04 of all the graduates did smoke but yet didn't experience any medical problems. Thus, .42 + .04 = .46 or 46% of all graduates claimed they had no medical problems.

   (ANSWER E).

2. (.30)(.60) = .18 of the population were non-smokers and yet had at least one medical problem. Now (.18)(1000) = 180.

   (ANSWER B).

3. (.10)(.40) = .04 indicates the number of people who did smoke during their high school years and had no medical problem. Of the .04, it is not possible to determine what fraction actually started smoking before entering high school. So, (.04)(1000) = 40.

   (ANSWER C).

4. (.30)(.60) = .18 of the non-smokers had at least one medical problem, whereas (.90)(.40) = .36 of the smokers had at least one medical problem. Then .18/.36 = 1:2 ratio.

   (ANSWER B).

5. The original statement uses the truth of a specific item in order to imply the truth of a general item containing that specific item. Only choice B illustrates that kind of reasoning.

   (ANSWER B).

6. The original statement can be written: "If A, then B. If not A, then not B." This argument is not necessarily valid, but choice D resembles it most closely.

   (ANSWER D).

7. Statement I is false, since we can assume that there exist both left-handed and right-handed players. Statement II is also false, because there may be excellent right-handed players. Statement III is true, since Jack is not right-handed and thus would have to be an excellent tennis player.

   (ANSWER C).

8. The only valid implication is Statement I, since one can assume that gamblers do visit racetracks. (This statement could be false, since it is only an assumption). Statement II is not valid since many types of people are noisy. Statement III is also invalid since one can assume that both noisy and quiet people frequent racetracks.

   (ANSWER A).

QUESTIONS 9-14.

Questions 9-14 see calendars below showing days of receiving and purchasing of each of the 4 different appliances. Note that for question #10, the actual answer is 10.

7 (#1)

Radio Delivered / TV Delivered

Sun	Mon	Tu	Wed	Th	Fri	Sat
	1	(2)	3	(4)	5	6
7	(8)	9	(10)	11	(12)	13
14	15	(16)	17	(18)	19	20
21	(22)	23	(24)	25	(26)	27
28	29	(30)	31			

Toaster Delivered

Sun	Mon	Tu	Wed	Th	Fri	Sat
	1	2	(3)	4	(5)	6
7	8	(9)	(10)	11	(12)	13
14	(15)	16	17	(18)	19	20
21	22	23	(24)	(25)	26	27
28	29	(30)	31			

Refrigerator Delivered

Sun	Mon	Tu	Wed	Th	Fri	Sat
	1	(2)	3	(4)	5	6
7	8	(9)	10	(11)	12	13
14	15	(16)	17	(18)	19	20
21	22	(23)	24	(25)	26	27
28	29	(30)	31			

Radio Purchased

Sun	Mon	Tu	Wed	Th	Fri	Sat
	1	(2)	3	(4)	5	6
7	(8)	9	(10)	11	(12)	13
14	15	(16)	17	(18)	19	20
21	(22)	23	(24)	25	(26)	27
28	29	(30)	31			

8 (#1)

Radio Purchased

Sun	Mon	Tu	Wed	Th	Fri	Sat
	1	②	3	④	5	6
7	⑧	9	⑩	11	⑫	13
14	15	⑯	17	⑱	19	20
21	㉒	23	㉔	25	㉖	27
28	29	㉚	31			

Toaster Purchased

Sun	Mon	Tu	Wed	Th	Fri	Sat
	1	2	③	4	⑤	6
7	8	⑨	⑩	11	⑫	13
14	⑮	16	17	⑱	19	20
21	22	23	㉔	㉕	26	27
28	29	㉚	31			

TV Purchased

Sun	Mon	Tu	Wed	Th	Fri	Sat
	1	2	3	4	⑤	6
7	8	⑨	10	⑪	12	13
14	⑮	16	⑰	18		20
21	22	㉓	24	㉕	26	27
28	㉙	30	㉛			

Refrigerator Purchased

Sun	Mon	Tu	Wed	Th	Fri	Sat
	1	2	3	4	⑤	6
7	8	⑨	10	11	⑫	13
14	15	⑯	17	18	⑲	20
21	22	㉓	24	25	㉖	27
28	29	㉚	31			

9. (ANSWER D).

10. (ANSWER E).

11. (ANSWER B).

12. (ANSWER E).

13. (ANSWER B).

14. (ANSWER A).

15. The original statement follows logically from choice C, since it implies that studying hard is a prerequisite to passing any high school course.

    (ANSWER C).

16. Although the general public perceives boxing as the most dangerous sport(or at least one of the most dangerous), the author is relying on a certain type of statistic to illustrate that there are nine other sports which could be considered more dangerous than boxing.

    (ANSWER E).

17. The author, by his argument, appears to be defending any ban on the sport of boxing. He does not make any case for or against another sport.

    (ANSWER B).

18. Let x, $2y$, y, w, z be the number of stores respectively on First, Second, Third, Fourth, and Fifth Avenues. Also, $z = x + 2y$, $w > z$, and x must be an even number. Since the smallest values for x and y are 2 and 1 respectively, the minimum value of $z = 2 + (2)(1) = 4$. Now w = the number of stores on Fourth Ave., and since $w > z$, then $w > 4$. Thus, 5 is the minimum value of w.

    (ANSWER D).

19. Since $z = x + 2y$, $z > x$ and $z > y$. But $w > z$, so that w is the variable with the highest value. We know that w = the number of stores on Fourth Ave.

    (ANSWER B).

20. Assume $z = 7$. Then there are two e possible combinations of numbers associated with the number of stores on First, Second, Third, Fourth, and Fifth Avenues respectively. The 1st combination is 2, 4, 2, 7, 6; the 2nd combination is 4, 2, 1, 7, 6; the 3rd combination is 2, 2, 1, 7, 4. Thus, only 16, 20, or 21 are the possible totals.

    (ANSWER E).

21. Since $z = x + 2y$ and x must be even, then z must also be an even number. Note that $2y$ is already even. Thus, even number + even number = even number.

    (ANSWER A).

22. Since Third Ave. has 4 stores, Second Ave. has 8 stores. We also know that First Ave. has more than 4 stores; thus it must have a minimum of 6 stores (even number). Fifth Ave. has $6 + 8 = 14$ stores at minimum, and 15 = the minimum stores on Fourth Ave. Thus, the number of stores on all 5 avenues (minimum) = $6 + 8 + 4 + 14 + 15 = 47$.

    (ANSWER E).

23. Let x = # of smokers, so that $21 - x$ = # of non-smokers. Then $1/2x$ = # of smokers who are also engineers. This number must equal the number of non-smokers who are not doctors. We can infer that 2/3 of the non-smokers (i.e. $2/3 [21 - x]$) are not doctors. Thus, $1/2x = 2/3 (21 - x)$. So, $x = 12$ and $21 - x = 9$. This implies that there are a total of 9 non-smokers. Since 1/3 of this number are doctors, there are 3 non-smoking doctors.

(ANSWER B).

24. Since 1/2 of the smokers are engineers, this translates to (1/2)(12) = 6 people. Only 2 doctors smoke, so the number of teachers who smoke = 12 - 6 - 2 = 4. (All teachers are smokers). Now 4/21 = .1905 or approximately 19%.

(ANSWER A).

25. The non-smokers must consist of only doctors and engineers. Of the 9 non-smokers, 3 are doctors. Thus 6 non-smokers are engineers. We already know that there are 6 engineers who smoke, so that there are a total of 12 engineers.

(ANSWER D).

EXAMINATION SECTION
TEST 1

DIRECTIONS: Each question or incomplete statement is followed by several suggested answers or completions. Select the one that BEST answers the question or completes the statement. *PRINT THE LETTER OF THE CORRECT ANSWER IN THE SPACE AT THE RIGHT.*

1. When conducting a needs assessment for the purpose of education planning, an agency's FIRST step is to identify or provide
   A. a profile of population characteristics
   B. barriers to participation
   C. existing resources
   D. profiles of competing resources

   1.____

2. Research has demonstrated that of the following, the MOST effective medium for communicating with external publics is(are)
   A. video news releases   B. television
   C. radio   D. newspapers

   2.____

3. Basic ideas behind the effort to influence the attitudes and behaviors of a constituency include each of the following EXCEPT the idea that
   A. words, rather than actions or events, are most likely to motivate
   B. demands for action are a usual response
   C. self-interest usually figures heavily into public involvement
   D. the reliability of change programs is difficult to assess

   3.____

4. An agency representative is trying to craft a pithy message to constituents in order to encourage the use of agency program resources.
   Choosing an audience for such messages is easiest when the message
   A. is project- or behavior-based   B. is combined with other messages
   C. is abstract   D. has a broad appeal

   4.____

5. Of the following factors, the MOST important to the success of an agency's external education or communication programs is the
   A. amount of resources used to implement them
   B. public's prior experiences with the agency
   C. real value of the program to the public
   D. commitment of the internal audience

   5.____

6. A representative for a state agency is being interviewed by a reporter from a local news network. The representative is being asked to defend a program that is extremely unpopular in certain parts of the municipality.
   When a constituency is known to be opposed to a position, the MOST useful communication strategy is to present

   6.____

A. only the arguments that are consistent with constituents' views
B. only the agency's side of the issue
C. both sides of the argument as clearly as possible
D. both sides of the argument, omitting key information about the opposing position

7. The MOST significant barriers to effective agency community relations include
   I. widespread distrust of communication strategies
   II. the media's "watchdog" stance
   III. public apathy
   IV. statutory opposition

   The CORRECT answer is:
   A. I only   B. I and II   C. II and III   D. III and IV

7.____

8. In conducting an education program, many agencies use workshops and seminars in a classroom setting.
   Advantages of classroom-style teaching over other means of educating the public include each of the following, EXCEPT
   A. enabling an instructor to verify learning through testing and interaction with the target audience
   B. enabling hands-on practice and other participatory learning techniques
   C. ability to reach an unlimited number of participants in a given length of time
   D. ability to convey the latest, most up-to-date information

8.____

9. The _____ model of community relations is characterized by an attempt to persuade the public to adopt the agency's point of view.
   A. two-way symmetric   B. two-way asymmetric
   C. public information   D. press agency/publicity

9.____

10. Important elements of an internal situation analysis include the
    I. list of agency opponents   II. communication audit
    III. updated organizational almanac   IV. stakeholder analysis

    The CORRECT answer is:
    A. I and II   B. I, II, and III   C. II and III   D. I, II, III and IV

10.____

11. Government agency information efforts typically involve each of the following objectives, EXCEPT to
    A. implement changes in the policies of government agencies to align with public opinion
    B. communicate the work of agencies
    C. explain agency techniques in a way that invites input from citizens
    D. provide citizen feedback to government administrators

11.____

12. Factors that are likely to influence the effectiveness of an educational campaign include the
    I. level of homogeneity among intended participants
    II. number and types of media used
    III. receptivity of the intended participants
    IV. level of specificity in the message or behavior to be taught

    The CORRECT answer is:
    A. I and II   B. I, II, and III   C. II and III   D. I, II, III, and IV

13. An agency representative is writing instructional objectives that will later help to measure the effectiveness of an educational program.
    Which of the following verbs, included in an objective, would be MOST helpful for the purpose of measuring effectiveness?
    A. Know   B. Identify   C. Learn   D. Comprehend

14. A state education agency wants to encourage participation in a program that has just received a boost through new federal legislation. The program is intended to include participants from a wide variety of socioeconomic and other demographic characteristics. The agency wants to launch a broad-based program that will inform virtually every interested party in the state about the program's new circumstances.
    In attempting to deliver this message to such a wide-ranging constituency, the agency's BEST practice would be to
    A. broadcast the same message through as many different media channels as possible
    B. focus on one discrete segment of the public at a time
    C. craft a message whose appeal is as broad as the public itself
    D. let the program's achievements speak for themselves and rely on word-of-mouth

15. Advantages associated with using the World Wide Web as an educational tool include
    I. an appeal to younger generations of the public
    II. visually-oriented, interactive learning
    III. learning that is not confined by space, time, or institutional association
    IV. a variety of methods for verifying use and learning

    The CORRECT answer is:
    A. I only   B. I and II   C. I, II, and III   D. I, II, II, and IV

16. In agencies involved in health care, community relations is a critical function because it
    A. serves as an intermediary between the agency and consumers
    B. generates a clear mission statement for agency goals and priorities
    C. ensures patient privacy while satisfying the media's right to information
    D. helps marketing professionals determine the wants and needs of agency constituents

17. After an extensive campaign to promote its newest program to constituents, an agency learns that most of the audience did not understand the intended message.
MOST likely, the agency has
    A. chosen words that were intended to inform, rather than persuade
    B. not accurately interpreted what the audience really needed to know
    C. overestimated the ability of the audience to receive and process the message
    D. compensated for noise that may have interrupted the message

18. The necessary elements that lead to conviction and motivation in the minds of participants in an educational or information program include each of the following, EXCEPT the _____ of the message.
    A. acceptability   B. intensity
    C. single-channel appeal   D. pervasiveness

19. Printed materials are often at the core of educational programs provided by public agencies.
The PRIMARY disadvantage associated with print is that it
    A. does not enable comprehensive treatment of a topic
    B. is generally unreliable in term of assessing results
    C. is often the most expensive medium available
    D. is constrained by time

20. Traditional thinking on public opinion holds that there is about _____ percent of the public who are pivotal to shifting the balance and momentum of opinion—they are concerned about an issue, but not fanatical, and interested enough to pay attention to a reasoned discussion.
    A. 2   B. 10   C. 33   D. 51

21. One of the most useful guidelines for influencing attitude change among people is to
    A. invite the target audience to come to you, rather than approaching them
    B. use moral appeals as the primary approach
    C. use concrete images to enable people to see the results of behaviors or indifference
    D. offer tangible rewards to people for changes in behavior

22. An agency is attempting to evaluate the effectiveness of its educational program. For this purpose, it wants to observe several focus groups discussing the same program.
Which of the following would NOT be a guideline for the use of focus groups?
    A. Focus groups should only include those who have participated in the program.
    B. Be sure to accurately record the discussion.
    C. The same questions should be asked at each focus group meeting.
    D. It is often helpful to have a neutral, non-agency employee facilitate discussions.

23. Research consistently shows that _____ is the determinant most likely to make a newspaper editor run a news release.
    A. novelty   B. prominence   C. proximity   D. conflict

24. Which of the following is NOT one of the major variables to take into account when considering a population-needs assessment?
    A. State of program development   B. Resources available
    C. Demographics   D. Community attitudes

25. The FIRST step in any communications audit is to
    A. develop a research instrument
    B. determine how the organization currently communicates
    C. hire a contractor
    D. determine which audience to assess

KEY (CORRECT ANSWERS)

1.	A		11.	A
2.	D		12.	D
3.	A		13.	B
4.	A		14.	B
5.	D		15.	C
6.	C		16.	A
7.	D		17.	B
8.	C		18.	C
9.	B		19.	B
10.	C		20.	B

21. C
22. A
23. C
24. C
25. D

TEST 2

DIRECTIONS: Each question or incomplete statement is followed by several suggested answers or completions. Select the one that BEST answers the question or completes the statement. *PRINT THE LETTER OF THE CORRECT ANSWER IN THE SPACE AT THE RIGHT.*

1. A public relations practitioner at an agency has just composed a press release highlighting a program's recent accomplishments and success stories.
   In pitching such releases to print outlets, the practitioner should
   I. e-mail, mail, or send them by messenger
   II. address them to "editor" or "news director"
   III. have an assistant call all media contacts by telephone
   IV. ask reporters or editors how they prefer to receive them

   The CORRECT answer is:
   A. I and II   B. I and IV   C. II, III, and IV   D. III only

   1.____

2. The "output goals" of an educational program are MOST likely to include
   A. specified ratings of services by participants on a standardized scale
   B. observable effects on a given community or clientele
   C. the number of instructional hours provided
   D. the number of participants served

   2.____

3. An agency wants to evaluate satisfaction levels among program participants, and mails out questionnaires to everyone who has been enrolled in the last year.
   The PRIMARY problem associated with this method of evaluative research is that it
   A. poses a significant inconvenience for respondents
   B. is inordinately expensive
   C. does not allow for follow-up or clarification questions
   D. usually involves a low response rate

   3.____

4. A communications audit is an important tool for measuring
   A. the depth of penetration of a particular message or program
   B. the cost of the organization's information campaigns
   C. how key audiences perceive an organization
   D. the commitment of internal stakeholders

   4.____

5. The "ABCs" of written learning objectives include each of the following, EXCEPT
   A. Audience   B. Behavior   C. Conditions   D. Delineation

   5.____

6. When attempting to change the behaviors of constituents, it is important to keep in mind that
   I. most people are skeptical of communications that try to get them to change their behaviors
   II. in most cases, a person selects the media to which he exposes himself
   III. people tend to react defensively to messages or programs that rely on fear as a motivating factor
   IV. programs should aim for the broadest appeal possible in order to include as many participants as possible

   The CORRECT answer is:
   A. I and II   B. I, II and III   C. II and III   D. I, II, III, and IV

7. The "laws" of public opinion include the idea that it is
   A. useful for anticipating emergencies
   B. not sensitive to important events
   C. basically determined by self-interest
   D. sustainable through persistent appeals

8. Which of the following types of evaluations is used to measure public attitudes before and after an information/educational program?
   A. Retrieval study
   B. Copy test
   C. Quota sampling
   D. Benchmark study

9. The PRIMARY source for internal communications is(are) usually
   A. flow charts
   B. meetings
   C. voice mail
   D. printed publications

10. An agency representative is putting together informational materials—brochures and a newsletter—outlining changes in one of the state's biggest benefits programs.
    In assembling print materials as a medium for delivering information to the public, the representative should keep in mind each of the following trends:
    I. For various reasons, the reading capabilities of the public are in general decline
    II. Without tables and graphs to help illustrate the changes, it is unlikely that the message will be delivered effectively
    III. Professionals and career-oriented people are highly receptive to information written in the form of a journal article or empirical study
    IV. People tend to be put off by print materials that use itemized and bulleted (●) lists

    The CORRECT answer is:
    A. I and II   B. I, II and III   C. II and III   D. I, II, III, and IV

11. Which of the following steps in a problem-oriented information campaign would typically be implemented FIRST?
    A. Deciding on tactics
    B. Determining a communications strategy
    C. Evaluating the problem's impact
    D. Developing an organizational strategy

12. A common pitfall in conducting an educational program is to
    A. aim it at the wrong target audience
    B. overfund it
    C. leave it in the hands of people who are in the business of education, rather than those with expertise in the business of the organization
    D. ignore the possibility that some other organization is meeting the same educational need for the target audience

13. The key factors that affect the credibility of an agency's educational program include
    A. organization
    B. scope
    C. sophistication
    D. penetration

14. Research on public opinion consistently demonstrates that it is
    A. easy to move people toward a strong opinion on anything, as long as they are approached directly through their emotions
    B. easier to move people away from an opinion they currently hold than to have them form an opinion about something they have not previously cared about
    C. easy to move people toward a strong opinion on anything, as long as the message appeals to their reason and intellect
    D. difficult to move people toward a strong opinion on anything, no matter what the approach

15. In conducting an education program, many agencies use meetings and conferences to educate an audience about the organization and its programs. Advantages associated with this approach include
    I. a captive audience that is known to be interested in the topic
    II. ample opportunities for verifying learning
    III. cost-efficient meeting space
    IV. the ability to provide information on a wider variety of subjects

    The CORRECT answer is:
    A. I and II   B. I, III and IV   C. II and III   D. I, II, III and IV

16. An agency is attempting to evaluate the effectiveness of its educational programs. For this purpose, it wants to observe several focus groups discussing particular programs.
    For this purpose, a focus group should never number more than _____ participants.
    A. 5   B. 10   C. 15   D. 20

17. A _____ speech is written so that several agency members can deliver it to different audiences with only minor variations.
    A. basic   B. printed   C. quota   D. pattern

18. Which of the following statements about public opinion is generally considered to be FALSE?
    A. Opinion is primarily reactive rather than proactive.
    B. People have more opinions about goals than about the means by which to achieve them.
    C. Facts tend to shift opinion in the accepted direction when opinion is not solidly structured.
    D. Public opinion is based more on information than desire.

19. An agency is trying to promote its educational program.
    As a general rule, the agency should NOT assume that
    A. people will only participate if they perceive an individual benefit
    B. promotions need to be aimed at small, discrete groups
    C. if the program is good, the audience will find out about it
    D. a variety of methods, including advertising, special events, and direct mail, should be considered

20. In planning a successful educational program, probably the first and most important question for an agency to ask is:
    A. What will be the content of the program?
    B. Who will be served by the program?
    C. When is the best time to schedule the program?
    D. Why is the program necessary?

21. Media kits are LEAST likely to contain
    A. fact sheets   B. memoranda
    C. photographs with captions   D. news releases

22. The use of pamphlets and booklets as media for communication with the public often involves the disadvantage that
    A. the messages contained within them are frequently nonspecific
    B. it is difficult to measure their effectiveness in delivering the message
    C. there are few opportunities for people to refer to them
    D. color reproduction is poor

23. The MOST important prerequisite of a good educational program is an
    A. abundance of resources to implement it
    B. individual staff unit formed for the purpose of program delivery
    C. accurate needs assessment
    D. uneducated constituency

24. After an education program has been delivered, an agency conducts a program evaluation to determine whether its objectives have been met.
General rules about how to conduct such an education program valuation include each of the following, EXCEPT that it
   A. must be done immediately after the program has been implemented
   B. should be simple and easy to use
   C. should be designed so that tabulation of responses can take place quickly and inexpensively
   D. should solicit mostly subjective, open-ended responses if the audience was large

25. Using electronic media such as television as means of educating the public is typically recommended ONLY for agencies that
   I. have a fairly simple message to begin with
   II. want to reach the masses, rather than a targeted audience
   III. have substantial financial resources
   IV. accept that they will not be able to measure the results of the campaign with much precision

   The CORRECT answer is:
   A. I and II   B. I, II and III   C. II and IV   D. I, II, III and IV

KEY (CORRECT ANSWERS)

1. B	11. C
2. C	12. D
3. D	13. A
4. C	14. D
5. D	15. B
6. B	16. B
7. C	17. D
8. D	18. D
9. D	19. C
10. A	20. D

21. B
22. B
23. C
24. D
25. D

EXAMINATION SECTION
TEST 1

DIRECTIONS: Each question or incomplete statement is followed by several suggested answers or completions. Select the one that BEST answers the question or completes the statement. *PRINT THE LETTER OF THE CORRECT ANSWER IN THE SPACE AT THE RIGHT.*

1. In public agencies, communications should be based PRIMARILY on a
   A. two-way flow from the top down and from the bottom up, most of which should be given in writing to avoid ambiguity
   B. multi-direction flow among all levels and with outside persons
   C. rapid, internal one-way flow from the top down
   D. two-way flow of information, most of which should be given orally for purposes of clarity

   1._____

2. In some organizations, changes in policy or procedures are often communicated by word of mouth from supervisors to employees with no prior discussion or exchange of viewpoints with employees.
   This procedure often produces employee dissatisfaction CHIEFLY because
   A. information is mostly unusable since a considerable amount of time is required to transmit information
   B. lower-level supervisors tend to be excessively concerned with minor details
   C. management has failed to seek employees' advice before making changes
   D. valuable staff time is lost between decision-making and the implementation of decisions

   2._____

3. For good letter writing, you should try to visualize the person to whom you are writing, especially if you know him.
   Of the following rules, it is LEAST helpful in such visualization to think of
   A. the person's likes and dislikes, his concerns, and his needs
   B. what you would be likely to say if speaking in person
   C. what you would expect to be asked if speaking in person
   D. your official position in order to be certain that your words are proper

   3._____

4. One approach to good informal letter writing is to make letters and conversational.
   All of the following practices will usually help to do this EXCEPT:
   A. If possible, use a style which is similar to the style used when speaking
   B. Substitute phrases for single words (e.g., *at the present time* for *now*)
   C. Use contractions of words (e.g., *you're* for *you are*)
   D. Use ordinary vocabulary when possible

   4._____

91

5. All of the following rules will aid in producing clarity in report-writing EXCEPT:
   A. Give specific details or examples, if possible
   B. Keep related words close together in each sentence
   C. Present information in sequential order
   D. Put several thoughts or ideas in each paragraph

6. The one of the following statements about public relations which is MOST accurate is that
   A. in the long run, appearance gains better results than performance
   B. objectivity is decreased if outside public relations consultants are employed
   C. public relations is the responsibility of every employee
   D. public relations should be based on a formal publicity program

7. The form of communication which is usually considered to be MOST personally directed to the intended recipient is the
   A. brochure   B. film   C. letter   D. radio

8. In general, a document that presents an organization's views or opinions on a particular topic is MOST accurately known as a
   A. tear sheet   B. position paper
   C. flyer   D. journal

9. Assume that you have been asked to speak before an organization of persons who oppose a newly announced program in which you are involved. You feel tense about talking to this group.
   Which of the following rules generally would be MOST useful in gaining rapport when speaking before the audience?
   A. Impress them with your experience
   B. Stress all areas of disagreement
   C. Talk to the group as to one person
   D. Use formal grammar and language

10. An organization must have an effective public relations program since, at its best, public relations is a bridge to change.
    All of the following statements about communication and human behavior have validity EXCEPT:
    A. People are more likely to talk about controversial matters with like-minded people than with those holding other views
    B. The earlier an experience, the more powerful its effect since it influences how later experiences will be interpreted
    C. In periods of social tension, official sources gain increased believability
    D. Those who are already interested in a topic are the ones who are most open to receive new communications about it

11. An employee should be encouraged to talk easily and frankly when he is dealing with his supervisor.
    In order to encourage such free communication, it would be MOST appropriate for a supervisor to behave in a(n)
    A. sincere manner; assure the employee that you will deal with him honestly and openly
    B. official manner; you are a supervisor and must always act formally with subordinates
    C. investigative manner; you must probe and question to get to a basis of trust
    D. unemotional manner; the employee's emotions and background should play no part in your dealings with him

11.____

12. Research findings show that an increase in free communication within an agency GENERALLY results in which one of the following?
    A. Improved morale and productivity
    B. Increased promotional opportunities
    C. An increase in authority
    D. A spirit of honesty

12.____

13. Assume that you are a supervisor and your superiors have given you a new-type procedure to be followed.
    Before passing this information on to your subordinates, the one of the following actions that you should take FIRST is to
    A. ask your superiors to send out a memorandum to the entire staff
    B. clarify the procedure in your own mind
    C. set up a training course to provide instruction on the new procedure
    D. write a memorandum to your subordinates

13.____

14. Communication is necessary for an organization to be effective.
    The one of the following which is LEAST important for most communication systems is that
    A. messages are sent quickly and directly to the person who needs them to operate
    B. information should be conveyed understandably and accurately
    C. the method used to transmit information should be kept secret so that security can be maintained
    D. senders of messages must know how their messages are received and acted upon

14.____

15. Which one of the following is the CHIEF advantage of listening willingly to subordinates and encouraging them to talk freely and honestly?
    It
    A. reveals to supervisors the degree to which ideas that are passed down are accepted by subordinates
    B. reduces the participation of subordinates in the operation of the department
    C. encourages subordinates to try for promotion
    D. enables supervisors to learn more readily what the *grapevine* is saying

15.____

16. A supervisor may be informed through either oral or written reports. 16.____
Which one of the following is an ADVANTAGE of using oral reports?
    A. There is no need for a formal record of the report.
    B. An exact duplicate of the report is not easily transmitted to others.
    C. A good oral report requires little time for preparation.
    D. An oral report involves two-way communication between a subordinate and his supervisor.

17. Of the following, the MOST important reason why supervisors should 17.____
communicate effectively with the public is to
    A. improve the public's understanding of information that is important for them to know
    B. establish a friendly relationship
    C. obtain information about the kinds of people who come to the agency
    D. convince the public that services are adequate

18. Supervisors should generally NOT use phrases like *too hard*, *too easy*, and 18.____
a lot PRINCIPALLY because such phrases
    A. may be offensive to some minority groups
    B. are too informal
    C. mean different things to different people
    D. are difficult to remember

19. The ability to communicate clearly and concisely is an important element in 19.____
effective leadership.
Which of the following statements about oral and written communication is GENERALLY true?
    A. Oral communication is more time-consuming.
    B. Written communication is more likely to be misinterpreted.
    C. Oral communication is useful only in emergencies.
    D. Written communication is useful mainly when giving information to fewer than twenty people.

20. Rumors can often have harmful and disruptive effects on an organization. 20.____
Which one of the following is the BEST way to prevent rumors from becoming a problem?
    A. Refuse to act on rumors, thereby making them less believable.
    B. Increase the amount of information passed along by the *grapevine*.
    C. Distribute as much factual information as possible.
    D. Provide training in report writing.

21. Suppose that a subordinate asks you about a rumor he has heard. The rumor 21.____
deals with a subject which your superiors consider *confidential*.
Which of the following BEST describes how you should answer the subordinate? Tell

A. the subordinate that you don't make the rules and that he should speak to higher ranking officials
B. the subordinate that you will ask your superior for information
C. him only that you cannot comment on the matter
D. him the rumor is not true

22. Supervisors often find it difficult to *get their message across* when instructing newly appointed employees in their various duties.
The MAIN reason for this is generally that the
    A. duties of the employees have increased
    B. supervisor is often so expert in his area that he fails to see it from the learner's point of view
    C. supervisor adapts his instruction to the slowest learner in the group
    D. new employees are younger, less concerned with job security and more interested in fringe benefits

23. Assume that you are discussing a job problem with an employee under your supervision. During the discussion, you see that the man's eyes are turning away from you and that he is not paying attention.
In order to get the man's attention, you should FIRST
    A. ask him to look you in the eye
    B. talk to him about sports
    C. tell him he is being very rude
    D. change your tone of voice

24. As a supervisor, you may find it necessary to conduct meetings with your subordinates.
Of the following, which would be MOST helpful in assuring that a meeting accomplishes the purpose for which it was called?
    A. Give notice of the conclusions you would like to reach at the start of the meeting.
    B. Delay the start of the meeting until everyone is present.
    C. Write down points to be discussed in proper sequence.
    D. Make sure everyone is clear on whatever conclusions have been reached and on what must be done after the meeting.

25. Every supervisor will occasionally be called upon to deliver a reprimand to a subordinate. If done properly, this can greatly help an employee improve his performance.
Which one of the following is NOT a good practice to follow when giving a reprimand?
    A. Maintain your composure and temper
    B. Reprimand a subordinate in the presence of other employees so they can learn the same lesson
    C. Try to understand why the employee was not able to perform satisfactorily
    D. Let your knowledge of the man involved determine the exact nature of the reprimand

KEY (CORRECT ANSWERS)

1. C
2. B
3. D
4. B
5. D

6. C
7. C
8. B
9. C
10. C

11. A
12. A
13. B
14. C
15. A

16. D
17. A
18. C
19. B
20. C

21. B
22. B
23. D
24. D
25. B

TEST 2

DIRECTIONS: Each question or incomplete statement is followed by several suggested answers or completions. Select the one that BEST answers the question or completes the statement. *PRINT THE LETTER OF THE CORRECT ANSWER IN THE SPACE AT THE RIGHT.*

1. Usually one thinks of communication as a single step, essentially that of transmitting an idea.
   Actually, however, this is only part of a total process, the FIRST step of which should be
   A. the prompt dissemination of the idea to those who may be affected by it
   B. motivating those affected to take the required action
   C. clarifying the idea in one's own mind
   D. deciding to whom the idea is to be communicated

   1.____

2. Research studies on patterns of informal communication have concluded that most individuals in a group tend to be passive recipients of news, while a few make it their business to spread it around in an organization.
   With this conclusion in mind, it would be MOST correct for the supervisor to attempt to identify these few individuals and
   A. give them the complete facts on important matters in advance of others
   B. inform the other subordinates of the identity of these few individuals so that their influence may be minimized
   C. keep them straight on the facts on important matters
   D. warn them to cease passing along any information to others

   2.____

3. The one of the following which is the PRINCIPAL advantage of making an oral report is that it
   A. affords an immediate opportunity for two-way communication between the subordinate and superior
   B. is an easy method for the superior to use in transmitting information to others of equal rank
   C. saves the time of all concerned
   D. permits more precise pinpointing of praise or blame by means of follow-up questions by the superior

   3.____

4. An agency may sometimes undertake a public relations program of a defensive nature.
   With reference to the use of defensive public relations, it would be MOST correct to state that it
   A. is bound to be ineffective since defensive statements, even though supported by factual data, can never hope to even partly overcome the effects of prior unfavorable attacks
   B. proves that the agency has failed to establish good relationships with newspapers, radio stations, or other means of publicity

   4.____

97

C. shows that the upper echelons of the agency have failed to develop sound public relations procedures and techniques
D. is sometimes required to aid morale by protecting the agency from unjustified criticism and misunderstanding of policies or procedures

5. Of the following factors which contribute to possible undesirable public attitudes towards an agency, the one which is MOST susceptible to being changed by the efforts of the individual employee in an organization is that
    A. enforcement of unpopular regulations as offended many individuals
    B. the organization itself has an unsatisfactory reputation
    C. the public is not interested in agency matters
    D. there are many errors in judgment committed by individual subordinates

5.____

6. It is not enough for an agency's services to be of a high quality; attention must also be given to the acceptability of these services to the general public.
This statement is GENERALLY
    A. *false*; a superior quality of service automatically wins public support
    B. *true*; the agency cannot generally progress beyond the understanding and support of the public
    C. *false*; the acceptance by the public of agency services determines their quality
    D. *true*; the agency is generally unable to engage in any effective enforcement activity without public support

6.____

7. Sustained agency participation in a program sponsored by a community organization is MOST justified when
    A. the achievement of agency objectives in some area depends partly on the activity of this organization
    B. the community organization is attempting to widen the base of participation in all community affairs
    C. the agency is uncertain as to what the community wants
    D. the agency is uncertain as to what the community wants

7.____

8. Of the following, the LEAST likely way in which a records system may serve a supervisor is in
    A. developing a sympathetic and cooperative public attitude toward the agency
    B. improving the quality of supervision by permitting a check on the accomplishment of subordinates
    C. permit a precise prediction of the exact incidences in specific categories for the following year
    D. helping to take the guesswork out of the distribution of the agency

8.____

9. Assuming that the *grapevine* in any organization is virtually indestructible, the one of the following which it is MOST important for management to understand is:
   A. What is being spread by means of the *grapevine* and the reason for spreading it
   B. What is being spread by means of the *grapevine* and how it is being spread
   C. Who is involved in spreading the information that is on the *grapevine*
   D. Why those who are involved in spreading the information are doing so

9._____

10. When the supervisor writes a report concerning an investigation to which he has been assigned, it should be LEAST intended to provide
    A. a permanent official record of relevant information gathered
    B. a summary of case findings limited to facts which tend to indicate the guilt of a suspect
    C. a statement of the facts on which higher authorities may base a corrective or disciplinary action
    D. other investigators with information so that they may continue with other phases of the investigation

10._____

11. In survey work, questionnaires rather than interviews are sometimes used. The one of the following which is a DISADVANTAGE of the questionnaire method as compared with the interview is the
    A. difficulty of accurately interpreting the results
    B. problem of maintaining anonymity of the participant
    C. fact that it is relatively uneconomical
    D. requirement of special training for the distribution of questionnaires

11._____

12. in his contacts with the public, an employee should attempt to create a good climate of support for his agency.
    This statement is GENERALLY
    A. *false*; such attempts are clearly beyond the scope of his responsibility
    B. *true*; employees of an agency who come in contact with the public have the opportunity to affect public relations
    C. *false*; such activity should be restricted to supervisors trained in public relations techniques
    D. *true*; the future expansion of the agency depends to a great extent on continued public support of the agency

12._____

13. The repeated use by a supervisor of a call for volunteers to get a job done is objectionable MAINLY because it
    A. may create a feeling of animosity between the volunteers and the non-volunteers
    B. may indicate that the supervisor is avoiding responsibility for making assignments which will be most productive
    C. is an indication that the supervisor is not familiar with the individual capabilities of his men
    D. is unfair to men who, for valid reasons, do not, or cannot volunteer

13._____

14. Of the following statements concerning subordinates' expressions to a supervisor of their opinions and feelings concerning work situations, the one which is MOST correct is that
    A. by listening and responding to such expressions the supervisor encourages the development of complaints
    B. the lack of such expressions should indicate to the supervisor that there is a high level of job satisfaction
    C. the more the supervisor listens to and responds to such expressions, the more he demonstrates lack of supervisory ability
    D. by listening and responding to such expressions, the supervisor will enable many subordinates to understand and solve their own problems on the job

15. In attempting to motivate employees, rewards are considered preferable to punishment PRIMARILY because
    A. punishment seldom has any effect on human behavior
    B. punishment usually results in decreased production
    C. supervisors find it difficult to punish
    D. rewards are more likely to result in willing cooperation

16. In an attempt to combat the low morale in his organization, a high level supervisor publicized an *open-door policy* to allow employees who wished to do so to come to him with their complaints.
    Which of the following is LEAST likely to account for the fact that no employee came in with a complaint?
    A. Employees are generally reluctant to go over the heads of their immediate supervisor.
    B. The employees did not feel that management would help them.
    C. The low morale was not due to complaints associated with the job.
    D. The employees felt that they had more to lose than to gain.

17. It is MOST desirable to use written instructions rather than oral instructions for a particular job when
    A. a mistake on the job will not be serious
    B. the job can be completed in a short time
    C. there is no need to explain the job minutely
    D. the job involves many details

18. If you receive a telephone call regarding a matter which your office does not handle, you should FIRST
    A. give the caller the telephone number of the proper office so that he can dial again
    B. offer to transfer the caller to the proper office
    C. suggest that the caller re-dial since he probably dialed incorrectly
    D. tell the caller he has reached the wrong office and then hang up

19. When you answer the telephone, the MOST important reason for identifying yourself and your organization is to
    A. give the caller time to collect his or her thoughts
    B. impress the caller with your courtesy
    C. inform the caller that he or she has reached the right number
    D. set a business-like tone at the beginning of the conversation

19._____

20. As soon as you pick up the phone, a very angry caller begins immediately to complain about city agencies and *red tape*. He says that he has been shifted to two or three different offices. It turs out that he is seeking information which is not immediately available to you. You believe, you know, however, where it can be found.
    Which of the following actions is the BEST one for you to take?
    A. To eliminate all confusion, suggest that the caller write the agency stating explicitly what he wants.
    B. Apologize by telling the caller how busy city agencies now are, but also tell him directly that you do not have the information he needs.
    C. Ask for the caller's telephone number and assure him you will call back after you have checked further.
    D. Give the caller the name and telephone number of the person who might be able to help, but explain that you are not positive he will get results/

20._____

21. Which of the following approaches usually provides the BEST communication in the objectives and values of a new program which is to be introduced?
    A. A general written description of the program by the program manager for review by those who share responsibility
    B. An effective verbal presentation by the program manager to those affected
    C. Development of the plan and operational approach in carrying out the program by the program manager assisted by his key subordinates
    D. Development of the plan by the program manager's supervisor

21._____

22. What is the BEST approach for introducing change?
    A
    A. combination of written and also verbal communication to all personnel affected by the change
    B. general bulletin to all personnel
    C. meeting pointing out all the values of the new approach
    D. written directive to key personnel

22._____

23. Of the following, committees are BEST used for
    A. advising the head of the organization
    B. improving functional work
    C. making executive decisions
    D. making specific planning decisions

23._____

24. An effective discussion leader is one who
    A. announces the problem and his preconceived solution at the start of the discussion
    B. guides and directs the discussion according to pre-arranged outline
    C. interrupts or corrects confused participants to save time
    D. permits anyone to say anything at any time

25. The human relations movement in management theory is basically concerned with
    A. counteracting employee unrest
    B. eliminating the *time and motion* man
    C. interrelationships among individuals in organizations
    D. the psychology of the worker

KEY (CORRECT ANSWERS)

1.	C	11.	A
2.	C	12.	B
3.	A	13.	B
4.	D	14.	D
5.	D	15.	D
6.	B	16.	C
7.	A	17.	D
8.	C	18.	B
9.	A	19.	C
10.	B	20.	C

21.	C
22.	A
23.	A
24.	B
25.	C

COMMUNICATION

EXAMINATION SECTION
TEST 1

DIRECTIONS: Each question or incomplete statement is followed by several suggested answers or completions. Select the one that BEST answers the question or completes the statement. *PRINT THE LETTER OF THE CORRECT ANSWER IN THE SPACE AT THE RIGHT.*

1. In some agencies the counsel to the agency head is given the right to bypass the chain of command and issue orders directly to the staff concerning matters that involve certain specific processes and practices.
   This situation MOST nearly illustrates the principle of _____ authority.
   A. the acceptance theory of
   B. multiple-linear
   C. splintered
   D. functional

2. It is commonly understood that communication is an important part of the administrative process.
   Which of the following is NOT a valid principle of the communication process in administration?
   A. The channels of communication should be spontaneous.
   B. The lines of communication should be as direct and as short as possible.
   C. Communications should be authenticated.
   D. The persons serving in communications centers should be competent.

3. Of the following, the one factor which is generally considered LEAST essential to successful committee operations is
   A. stating a clear definition of the authority and scope of the committee
   B. selecting the committee chairman carefully
   C. limiting the size of the committee to four persons
   D. limiting the subject matter to that which can be handled in group discussion

4. Of the following, the failure by line managers to accept and appreciate the benefits and limitations of a new program or system VERY FREQUENTLY can be traced to the
   A. budgetary problems involved
   B. resultant need to reduce staff
   C. lack of controls it engenders
   D. failure of top management to support its implementation

5. If a manager were thinking about using a committee of subordinates to solve an operating problem, which of the following would generally NOT be an advantage of such use of the committee approach?
   A. Improved coordination
   B. Low cost
   C. Increased motivation
   D. Integrated judgment

103

6. Every supervisor has many occasions to lead a conference or participate in a conference of some sort.
Of the following statements that pertain to conferences and conference leadership, which is generally considered to be MOST valid?
   A. Since World War II, the trend has been toward fewer shared decisions and more conferences.
   B. The most important part of a conference leader's job is to direct discussion.
   C. In providing opportunities for group interaction, management should avoid consideration of its past management philosophy.
   D. A good administrator cannot lead a good conference if he is a poor public speaker.

6.____

7. Of the following, it is usually LEAST desirable for a conference leader to
   A. call the name of a person after asking a question
   B. summarize proceedings periodically
   C. make a practice of repeating questions
   D. ask a question without indicating who is to reply

7.____

8. Assume that, in a certain organization, a situation has developed in which there is little difference in status or authority between individuals.
Which of the following would be the MOST likely result with regard to communication in this organization?
   A. Both the accuracy and flow of communication will be improved.
   B. Both the accuracy and flow of communication will substantially decrease.
   C. Employees will seek more formal lines of communication.
   D. Neither the flow nor the accuracy of communication will be improved over the former hierarchical structure.

8.____

9. The main function of many agency administrative officers is "information management." Information that is received by an administrative officer may be classified as active or passive, depending upon whether or not it requires the recipient to take some action.
Of the following, the item received which is clearly the MOST active information is
   A. an appointment of a new staff member
   B. a payment voucher for a new desk
   C. a press release concerning a past event
   D. the minutes of a staff meeting

9.____

10. Of the following, the one LEAST considered to be a communication barrier is
    A. group feedback   B. charged words
    C. selective perception   D. symbolic meanings

10.____

11. Management studies support the hypothesis that, in spite of the tendency of employees to censor the information communicated to their supervisor, subordinates are more likely to communicate problem-oriented information UPWARD when they have a
    A. long period of service in the organization
    B. high degree of trust in the supervisor
    C. high educational level
    D. low status on the organizational ladder

    11._____

12. Electronic data processing equipment can produce more information faster than can be generated by any other means.
    In view of this, the MOST important problem faced by management at present is to
    A. keep computers fully occupied
    B. find enough computer personnel
    C. assimilate and properly evaluate the information
    D. obtain funds to establish appropriate information systems

    12._____

13. A well-designed management information system essentially provides each executive and manager the information he needs for
    A. determining computer time requirements
    B. planning and measuring results
    C. drawing a new organization chart
    D. developing a new office layout

    13._____

14. It is generally agreed that management policies should be periodically reappraised and restated in accordance with current conditions.
    Of the following, the approach which would be MOST effective in determining whether a policy should be revised is to
    A. conduct interviews with staff members at all levels in order to ascertain the relationship between the policy and actual practice
    B. make proposed revisions in the policy and apply it to current problems
    C. make up hypothetical situations using both the old policy and a revised version in order to make comparisons
    D. call a meeting of top level staff in order to discuss ways of revising the policy

    14._____

15. Your superior has asked you to notify division employees of an important change in one of the operating procedures described in the division manual. Every employee presently has a copy of this manual.
    Which of the following is normally the MOST practical way to get the employees to understand such a change?
    A. Notify each employee individually of the change and answer any questions he might have
    B. Send a written notice to key personnel, directing them to inform the people under them

    15._____

C. Call a general meeting, distribute a corrected page for the manual, and discuss the change
D. Send a memo to employees describing the change in general terms and asking them to make the necessary corrections in their copies of the manual

16. Assume that the work in your department involves the use of any technical terms.
    In such a situation, when you are answering inquiries from the general public, it would usually be BEST to
    A. use simple language and avoid the technical terms
    B. employ the technical terms whenever possible
    C. bandy technical terms freely, but explain each term in parentheses
    D. apologize if you are forced to use a technical term

17. Suppose that you receive a telephone call from someone identifying himself as an employee in another city department who asks to be given information which your own department regards as confidential.
    Which of the following is the BEST way of handling such a request?
    A. Give the information requested, since your caller as official standing
    B. Grant the request, provided the caller gives you a signed receipt
    C. Refuse the request, because you have no way of knowing whether the caller is really who he claims to be
    D. Explain that the information is confidential and inform the caller of the channels he must go through to have the information released to him

18. Studies show that office employees place high importance on the social and human aspects of the organization. What office employees like best about their jobs is the kind of people with whom they work. So strive hard to group people who are most likely to get along well together.
    Based on this information, it is MOST reasonable to assume that office workers are most pleased to work in a group which
    A. is congenial   B. has high productivity
    C. allows individual creativity   D. is unlike other groups

19. A certain supervisor does not compliment members of his staff when they come up with good ideas. He feels that coming up with good ideas is part of the job and does not merit special attention.
    This supervisor's practice is
    A. *poor*, because recognition for good ideas is a good motivator
    B. *poor*, because the staff will suspect that the supervisor has no good ideas of his own
    C. *good*, because it is reasonable to assume that employees will tell their supervisor of ways to improve office practice
    D. *good*, because the other members of the staff are not made to seem inferior by comparison

20. Some employees of a department have sent an anonymous letter containing many complaints to the department head.
Of the following, what is this MOST likely to show about the department?
    A. It is probably a good place to work.
    B. Communications are probably poor.
    C. The complaints are probably unjustified.
    D. These employees are probably untrustworthy.

21. Which of the following actions would usually be MOST appropriate for a supervisor to take after receiving an instruction sheet from his superior explaining a new procedure which is to be followed?
    A. Put the instruction sheet aside temporarily until he determines what is wrong with the old procedure.
    B. Call his superior and ask whether the procedure is one he must implement immediately.
    C. Write a memorandum to the superior asking for more details.
    D. Try the new procedure and advise the superior of any problems or possible improvements.

22. Of the following, which one is considered the PRIMARY advantage of using a committee to resolved a problem in an organization?
    A. No one person will be held accountable for the decision since a group of people was involved.
    B. People with different backgrounds give attention to the problem.
    C. The decision will take considerable time so there is unlikely to be a decision that will later be regretted.
    D. One person cannot dominate the decision-making process.

23. Employees in a certain office come to their supervisor with all their complaints about the office and the work. Almost every employee has had at least one minor complaint at some time.
The situation with respect to complaints in this office may BEST be described as probably
    A. *good*; employees who complain care about their jobs and work hard
    B. *good*; grievances brought out into the open can be corrected
    C. *bad*; only serious complaints should be discussed
    D. *bad*; it indicates the staff does not have confidence in the administration

24. The administrator who allows his staff to suggest ways to do their work will usually find that
    A. this practice contributes to high productivity
    B. the administrator's ideas produce greater output
    C. clerical employees suggest inefficient work methods
    D. subordinate employees resent performing a management function

25. The MAIN purpose for a supervisor's questioning the employees at a conference he is holding is to
    A. stress those areas of information covered but not understood by the participants
    B. encourage participants to think through the problem under discussion
    C. catch those subordinates who are not paying attention
    D. permit the more knowledgeable participants to display their grasp of the problems being discussed

25._____

KEY (CORRECT ANSWERS)

1.	D		11.	B
2.	A		12.	C
3.	C		13.	B
4.	D		14.	A
5.	B		15.	C
6.	B		16.	A
7.	C		17.	D
8.	D		18.	A
9.	A		19.	A
10.	A		20.	B

21. D
22. B
23. B
24. A
25. B

TEST 2

DIRECTIONS: Each question or incomplete statement is followed by several suggested answers or completions. Select the one that BEST answers the question or completes the statement. *PRINT THE LETTER OF THE CORRECT ANSWER IN THE SPACE AT THE RIGHT.*

1. For a superior to use *consultative supervision* with his subordinates effectively, it is ESSENTIAL that he
   A. accept the fact that his formal authority will be weakened by the procedure
   B. admit that he does not know more than all his men together and that his ideas are not always best
   C. utilize a committee system so that the procedure is orderly
   D. make sure that all subordinates are consulted so that no one feels left out

1.____

2. The *grapevine* is an informal means of communication in an organization. The attitude of a supervisor with respect to the grapevine should be to
   A. ignore it since it deals mainly with rumors and sensational information
   B. regard it as a serious danger which should be eliminated
   C. accept it as a real line of communication which should be listened to
   D. utilize it for most purposes instead of the official line of communication

2.____

3. The supervisor of an office that must deal with the public should realize that planning in this type of work situation
   A. is useless because he does not know how many people will request service or what service they will request
   B. must be done at a higher level but that he should be ready to implement the results of such planning
   C. is useful primarily for those activities that are not concerned with public contact
   D. is useful for all the activities of the office, including those that relate to public contact

3.____

4. Assume that it is your job to receive incoming telephone calls. Those calls which you cannot handle yourself have to be transferred to the appropriate office.
   If you receive an outside call for an extension line which is busy, the one of the following which you should do FIRST is to
   A. interrupt the person speaking on the extension and tell him a call is waiting
   B. tell the caller the line is busy and let him know every thirty seconds whether or not it is free
   C. leave the caller on "hold" until the extension is free
   D. tell the caller the line is busy and ask him if he wishes to wait

4.____

109

5. Your superior has subscribed to several publications directly related to your division's work, and he has asked you to see to it that the publications are circulated among the supervisory personnel in the division. There are eight supervisors involved.
The BEST method of insuring that all eight see these publications is to
   A. place the publication in the division's general reference library as soon as it arrives
   B. inform each supervisor whenever a publication arrives and remind all of them that they are responsible for reading it
   C. prepare a standard slip that can be stapled to each publication, listing the eight supervisors and saying, "Please read, initial your name, and pass along"
   D. send a memo to the eight supervisors saying that they may wish to purchase individual subscriptions in their own names if they are interested in seeing each issue

5._____

6. Your superior has telephoned a number of key officials in your agency to ask whether they can meet at a certain time next month. He has found that they can all make it, and he has asked you to confirm the meeting.
Which of the following is the BEST way to confirm such a meeting?
   A. Note the meeting on your superior's calendar.
   B. Post a notice of the meeting on the agency bulletin board.
   C. Call the officials on the day of the meeting to remind them of the meeting.
   D. Write a memo to each official involved, repeating the time and place of the meeting.

6._____

7. Assume that a new city regulation requires that certain kinds of private organizations file information forms with your department. You have been asked to write the short explanatory message that will be printed on the front cover of the pamphlet containing the forms and instructions.
Which of the following would be the MOST appropriate way of beginning this message?
   A. Get the readers' attention by emphasizing immediately that there are legal penalties for organizations that fail to file before a certain date.
   B. Briefly state the nature of the enclosed forms and the types of organizations that must file.
   C. Say that your department is very sorry to have to put organizations to such an inconvenience.
   D. Quote the entire regulation adopted by the city, even if it is quite long and is expressed din complicated legal language.

7._____

8. Suppose that you have been told to make up the vacation schedule for the 18 employees in a particular unit. In order for the unit to operate effectively, only a few employees can be on vacation at the same time.
Which of the following is the MOST advisable approach in making up the schedule?
   A. Draw up a schedule assigning vacations in alphabetical order
   B. Find out when the supervisors want to take their vacations, and randomly assign whatever periods are left to the non-supervisory personnel

8._____

C. Assign the most desirable times to employees of longest standing and the least desirable times to the newest employees
D. Have all employees state their own preference, and then work out any conflicts in consultation with the people involved

9. Assume that you have been asked to prepare job descriptions for various positions in your department.
Which of the following are the basic points that should be covered in a *job description*?
    A. General duties and responsibilities of the position, with examples of day-to-day tasks
    B. Comments on the performances of present employees
    C. Estimates of the number of openings that may be available in each category during the coming year
    D. Instructions for carrying out the specific tasks assigned to your department

9.____

10. Of the following, the biggest DISADVANTAGE in allowing a free flow of communications in an agency is that such a free flow
    A. decreases creativity
    B. increases the use of the *grapevine*
    C. lengthens the chain of command
    D. reduces the executive's power to direct the flow of information

10.____

11. A downward flow of authority in an organization is one example of _____ communication.
    A. horizontal   B. informal   C. circular   D. vertical

11.____

12. Of the following, the one that would MOST likely block effective communication is
    A. concentration only on the issues at hand
    B. lack of interest or commitment
    C. use of written reports
    D. use of charts and graphs

12.____

13. An ADVANTAGE of the *lecture* as a teaching tool is that it
    A. enables a person to present his ideas to a large number of people
    B. allows the audience to retain a maximum of the information given
    C. holds the attention of the audience for the longest time
    D. enables the audience member to easily recall the main points

13.____

14. An ADVANTAGE of the *small-group* discussion as a teaching tool is that
    A. it always focuses attention on one person as the leader
    B. it places collective responsibility on the group as a whole
    C. its members gain experience by summarizing the ideas of others
    D. each member of the group acts as a member of a team

14.____

15. The one of the following that is an ADVANTAGE of a *large-group* discussion, when compared to a small-group discussion, is that the large-group discussion
    A. moves along more quickly than a small-group discussion
    B. allows its participants to feel more at ease, and speak out more freely
    C. gives the whole group a chance to exchange ideas on a certain subject at the same occasion
    D. allows its members to feel a greater sense of personal responsibility

KEY (CORRECT ANSWERS)

1.	D	6.	D	11.	D
2.	C	7.	B	12.	B
3.	D	8.	D	13.	A
4.	D	9.	A	14.	D
5.	C	10.	D	15.	C

PREPARING WRITTEN MATERIAL

PARAGRAPH REARRANGEMENT
COMMENTARY

The sentences that follow are in scrambled order. You are to rearrange them in proper order and indicate the letter choice containing the correct answer at the space at the right.

Each group of sentences in this section is actually a paragraph presented in scrambled order. Each sentence in the group has a place in that paragraph; no sentence is to be left out. You are to read each group of sentences and decide upon the best order in which to put the sentences so as to form a well-organized paragraph.

The questions in this section measure the ability to solve a problem when all the facts relevant to its solution are not given.

More specifically, certain positions of responsibility and authority require the employee to discover connection between events sometimes, apparently, unrelated. In order to do this, the employee will find it necessary to correctly infer that unspecified events have probably occurred or are likely to occur. This ability becomes especially important when action must be taken on incomplete information.

Accordingly, these questions require competitors to choose among several suggested alternatives, each of which presents a different sequential arrangement of the events. Competitors must choose the MOST logical of the suggested sequences.

In order to do so, they may be required to draw on general knowledge to infer missing concepts or events that are essential to sequencing the given events. Competitors should be careful to infer only what is essential to the sequence. The plausibility of the wrong alternatives will always require the inclusion of unlikely events or of additional chains of events which are NOT essential to sequencing the given events.

It's very important to remember that you are looking for the best of the four possible choices, and that the best choice of all may not even be one of the answers you're given to choose from.

There is no one right way to solve these problems. Many people have found it helpful to first write out the order of the sentences, as they would have arranged them, on their scrap paper before looking at the possible answers. If their optimum answer is there, this can save them some time. If it isn't, this method can still give insight into solving the problem. Others find it most helpful to just go through each of the possible choices, contrasting each as they go along. You should use whatever method feels comfortable and works for you.

While most of these types of questions are not that difficult, we've added a higher percentage of the difficult type, just to give you more practice. Usually there are only one or two questions on this section that contain such subtle distinctions that you're unable to answer confidently. And you then may find yourself stuck deciding between two possible choices, neither of which you're sure about.

PREPARING WRITTEN MATERIAL
PARAGRAPH REARRANGEMENT
EXAMINATION SECTION
TEST 1

DIRECTIONS: The following groups of sentences need to be arranged in an order that makes sense. Select the letter preceding the sequence that represents the best sentence order. *PRINT THE LETTER OF THE CORRECT ANSWER IN THE SPACE AT THE RIGHT.*

1.
   I. The ostrich egg shell's legendary toughness makes it an excellent substitute for certain types of dishes or dinnerware, and in parts of Africa ostrich shells are cut and decorated for use as containers for water.
   II. Since prehistoric times, people have used the enormous egg of the ostrich as a part of their diet, a practice which has required much patience and hard work—to hard boil an ostrich egg takes about four hours.
   III. Opening the egg's shell, which is rock hard and nearly an inch thick, requires heavy tools, such as a saw or chisel; from inside, a baby ostrich must use a hornlike projection on its beak as a miniature pick-axe to escape from the egg.
   IV. The offspring of all higher-order animals originate from single egg cells that are carried by mothers, and most of these eggs are relatively small, often microscopic.
   V. The egg of the African ostrich, however, weighs a massive thirty pounds, making it the largest single cell on earth, and a common object of human curiosity and wonder.

   The BEST order is:
   A. V, IV, I, II, III   B. I, IV, V, III, II   C. IV, II, III, V, I   D. IV, V, II, III, I

   1.____

2.
   I. Typically only a few feet high on the open sea, individual tsunami have been known to circle the entire globe two or three times if their progress is not interrupted, but are not usually dangerous until they approach the shallow water that surrounds land masses.
   II. Some of the most terrifying and damaging hazards caused by earthquakes are tsunami, which were once called "tidal waves"—a poorly chosen name, since these waves have nothing to do with tides.
   III. Then a wave, slowed by the sudden drag on the lower part of its moving water column, will pile upon itself, sometimes reaching a height of over 100 feet.
   IV. Tsunami (Japanese for "great harbor wave") are seismic waves that are caused by earthquakes near oceanic trenches, and once triggered, can travel up to 600 miles an hour on the open ocean.
   V. A land-shoaling tsunami is capable of extraordinary destruction; some tsunami have deposited large boats miles inland, washed out two-foot-thick seawalls, and scattered locomotive trains over long distances.

   The BEST order is:
   A. IV, I, III, II, V   B. I, III, IV, II, V   C. V, I, III, II, IV   D. II, IV, I, III, V

   2.____

3.
I. Soon, by the 1940s, jazz was the most popular type of music among American intellectuals and college students.
II. In the early days of jazz, it was considered "lowdown" music, or music that was played only in rough, disreputable bars and taverns.
III. However, jazz didn't take too long to develop from early ragtime melodies into more complex, sophisticated forms, such as Charlie Parker's "bebop" style of jazz.
IV. After charismatic band leaders such as Duke Ellington and Count Basie brought jazz to a larger audience, and jazz continued to evolve into more complicated forms, white audiences began to accept and even to enjoy the new American art form.
V. Many white Americans, who then dictated the tastes of society, were wary of music that was played almost exclusively in black clubs in the poorer sections of cities and towns.

The BEST order is:
A. V, IV, III, II, I   B. II, V, III, IV, I   C. IV, V, III, I, II   D. I, II, IV, III, V

4.
I. Then, hanging in a windless place, the magnetized end of the needle would always point to the south.
II. The needle could then be balanced on the rim of a cup, or the edge of a fingernail, but this balancing act was hard to maintain, and the needle often fell off.
III. Other needles would point to the north, and it was important for any traveler finding his way with a compass to remember which kind of magnetized needle he was carrying.
IV. To make some of the earliest compasses in recorded history, ancient Chinese "magicians" would rub a needle with a piece of magnetized iron called a lodestone.
V. A more effective method of keeping the needle free to swing with its magnetic pull was to attach a strand of silk to the center of the needle with a tiny piece of wax.

The BEST order is:
A. IV, II, V, I, III   B. IV, III, V, II, I   C. IV, V, II, I, III   D. IV, I, III, V, II

5.
I. The now-famous first mate of the *H.M.S. Bounty*, Fletcher Christian, founded one of the world's most peculiar civilizations in 1790.
II. The men knew they had just committed a crime for which they could be hanged, so they set sail for Pitcairn, a remote, abandoned island in the far eastern region of the Polynesian archipelago, accompanied by twelve Polynesian women and six men.
III. In a mutiny that has become legendary, Christian and the others forced Captain Bligh into a lifeboat and set him adrift off the coast of Tonga in April of 1789.
IV. In early 1790, the *Bounty* landed at Pitcairn Island, where the men lived out the rest of their lives and founded an isolated community which to this day includes direct descendants of Christian and the other Crewmen.

V. The *Bounty*, commanded by Captain William Bligh, was in the middle of a global voyage, and Christian and his shipmates had come to the conclusion that Bligh was a reckless madman who would lead them to their deaths unless they took the ship from him.
The BEST order is:
   A. IV, V, III, II, I   B. I, III, V, II, IV   C. I, V, III, II, IV   D. III, I, V, IV, II

6.   I. But once the vines had been led to make orchids, the flowers had to be carefully hand-pollinated, because unpollinated orchids usually lasted less than a day, wilting and dropping off the vine before it had even become dark.
  II. The Totonac farmers discovered that looping a vine back around once it reached a five-foot height on its host tree would cause the vine to flower.
  III. Though they knew how to process the fruit pods and extract vanilla's flavoring agent, the Totonacs also knew that a wild vanilla vine did not produce abundant flowers or fruit.
  IV. Wild vines climbed along the trunks and canopies of trees, and this constant upward growth diverted most of the vine's energy to making leaves instead of the orchid flowers that once pollinated, would produce the flavorful pods.
  V. Hundreds of years before vanilla became a prized food flavoring in Europe and the Western World, the Totonac Indians of the Mexican Gulf Coast were skilled cultivators of the vanilla vine, whose fruit they literally worshipped as a goddess.
The BEST order is:
   A. II, III, IV, I, V   B. II, IV, III, I, V   C. V, III, IV, II, I   D. III, IV, I, II, V

6.____

7.   I. Once airborne, the spider is at the mercy of the air currents—usually the spider takes a brief journey, traveling close to the ground, but some have been found in air samples collected as high as 10,000 feet, or been reported landing on ships far out at sea.
  II. Once a young spider has hatched, it must leave the environment into which it was born as quickly as possible, in order to avoid competing with its hundreds of brothers and sisters for food.
  III. The silk rises into warm air currents, and as soon as the pull feels adequate the spider lets go and drifts up into the air, suspended from the silk strand in the same way that a person might parasail.
  IV. To help young spiders do this, many species have adapted a practice known as "aerial dispersal," or, in common speech, "ballooning."
  V. A spider that wants to leave its surroundings quickly will climb to the top of a grass system or twig, face into the wind, and aim its back end into the air, releasing a long stream of silk from the glands near the tip of its abdomen.
The BEST order is:
   A. V, IV, II, III, I   B. V, II, IV, I, III   C. II, V, IV, III, I   D. II, IV, V, III, I

7.____

8. I. For about a year, Tycho worked at a castle in Prague with a scientist named Johannes Kepler, but their association was cut short by another argument that drove Kepler out of the castle, to later develop, on his own, the theory of planetary orbits.
    II. Tycho found life without a nose embarrassing, so he made a new nose for himself out of silver, which reportedly remained glued to his face for the rest of his life.
    III. Tycho Brahe, the 17th-century Danish astronomer, is today more famous for his odd and arrogant personality than for any contribution he has made to our knowledge of the stars and planets.
    IV. Early in his career, as a student at Rostock University, Tycho got into an argument with another student about who was the better mathematician, and the two became so angry that the argument turned into a sword fight, during which Tycho's nose was sliced off.
    V. Later in his life, Tycho's arrogance may have kept him from playing a part in one of the greatest astronomical discoveries in history: the elliptical orbits of the solar system's planets.
    The BEST order is:
    A. I, IV, II, III, V   B. IV, II, III, V, I   C. IV, II, I, III, V   D. III, IV, II, V, I

9. I. The processionaries are so used to this routine that if a person picks up the end of a silk line and brings it back to the origin—creating a closed circle—the caterpillars may travel around and around for days, sometimes starving or freezing, without changing course.
    II. Rather than relying on sight or sound, the other caterpillars, who are lined up end-to-end behind the leader, travel to and from their nests by walking on this silk line, and each will reinforce it by laying down its own marking line as it passes over.
    III. In order to insure the safety of individuals, the processionary caterpillar nests in a tree with dozens of other caterpillars, and at night, when it is safest, they all leave together in search of food.
    IV. The processionary caterpillar of the European continent is a perfect illustration of how much some inspect species rely on instinct in their daily routines.
    V. As they leave their nests, the processionaries form a single-file line behind a leader who spins and lays out a silk line to mark the chosen path.
    The BEST order is:
    A. IV, III, V, II, I   B. III, V, IV, II, I   C. III, V, II, I, IV   D. IV, V, III, I, II

10. I. Often, the child is also given a handcrafted walker or push cart, to provide support for its first upright explorations.
    II. In traditional Indian families, a child's first steps are celebrated as a ceremonial event, rooted in ancient myth.
    III. These carts are often intricately designed to resemble the chariot of Krishna, an important figure in Indian mythology.
    IV. The sound of these anklet bells is intended to mimic the footsteps of the legendary child Rama, who is celebrated in devotional songs throughout India.

V. When the child's parents see that the child is ready to begin walking, they will fit it with specially designed ankle bracelets, adorned with gently ringing bells.

The BEST order is:
A. II, III, IV, I, V   B. II, V, III, I, IV   C. V, IV, I, III, II   D. V, III, II, I, IV

11.
I. The settlers planted Osage oranges all across Middle America, and today long lines and rectangles of Osage orange trees can still be seen on the prairies, running along the former boundaries of farms that no longer exist.
II. After trying sod walls and water-filled ditches with no success, American farmers began to look for a plant that was adaptable to prairie weather, and that could be trimmed into a hedge that was "pig-tight, horse-high, and bull-strong."
III. The tree, so named because it bore a large (but inedible) fruit the size of an orange, was among the sturdiest and hardiest of American trees, and was prized among Native Americans for the strength and flexibility of bows which were made from its wood.
IV. The first people to practice agriculture on the American flatlands were faced with an important problem: what would they use to fence their land in a place that was almost entirely without trees or rocks?
V. Finally, an Illinois farmer brought the settlers a tree that was native to the land between the Red and Arkansas rivers, a tree called the Osage orange.

The BEST order is:
A. II, I, V, III, IV   B. I, II, III, IV, V   C. IV, II, V, III, I   D. IV, II, I, III, V

12.
I. After about ten minutes of such spirited and complicated activity, the head dancer is free to make up his or her own movements while maintaining the interest of the New Year's crowd.
II. The dancer will then perform a series of leg kicks, while at the same time operating the lion's mouth with his own hand and moving the ears and eyes by means of a string which is attached to the dancer's own mouth.
III. The most difficult role of this dance belongs to the one who controls the lion's head; this person must lead all the other "parts" of the lion through the choreographed segments of the dance.
IV. The head dancer begins with a complex series of steps. alternately stepping forward with the head raised, and then retreating a few steps while lowering the head, a movement that is intended to create the impression that the lion is keeping a watchful eye for anything evil.
V. When performing a traditional Chinese New Year's lion dance, several performers must fit themselves inside a large lion costume and work together to enact different parts of the dance.

The BEST order is:
A. V, III, IV, II, I   B. III, IV, II, V, I   C. III, I, V, IV, II   D. IV, II, III, V, I

13.
   I. For many years the shell of the chambered nautilus was treasured in Europe for its beauty and intricacy, but collectors were unaware that they were in possession of the structure that marked a "missing link" in the evolution of marine mollusks.
   II. The nautilus, however, evolved a series of enclosed chambers in its shell, and invented a new use for the structure: the shell began to serve as a buoyancy device.
   III. Equipped with this new flotation device, the nautilus did not need the single, muscular foot of its predecessors, but instead developed flaps, tentacles, and a gentle form of jet propulsion that transformed it into the first mollusk able to take command of its own density and explore a three-dimensional world.
   IV. By pumping and adjusting air pressure into the chambers, the nautilus could spend the day resting on the bottom, and then rise toward the surface at night in search of food.
   V. The nautilus shell looks like a large snail shell, similar to those of its ancestors, who used their shells as protective coverings while they were anchored to the sea floor.

   The BEST order is:
   A. V, II, IV, I, III   B. V, I, II, III, IV   C. I, II, V, III, IV   D. I, V, II, IV, III

   13._____

14.
   I. While France and England battled for control of the region, the Acadiens prospered on the fertile farmland, which was finally secured by England in 1713.
   II. Early in the 17th century, settlers from Western France founded a colony called Acadie in what is now the Canadian province of Nova Scotia.
   III. At this time, English officials feared the presence of spies among the Acadiens who might be loyal to their French homeland, and the Acadiens were deported to spots along the Atlantic and Caribbean shores of America.
   IV. The French settlers remained on this land, under English rule, for around forty years, until the beginning of the French and Indian War, another conflict between France and England.
   V. As the Acadien refugees drifted toward a final home in Southern Louisiana, neighbors shortened their name to "Cadien," and finally "Cajun," the name which the descendants of early Acadiens still call themselves.

   The BEST order is:
   A. I, IV, II, III, V   B. II, I, III, V, IV   C. II, I, IV, III, V   D. V, II, III, IV, I

   14._____

15.
   I. Traditional households in the Eastern and Western regions of Africa serve two meals a day—one at around noon, and the other in the evening.
   II. The starch is then used in the way that Americans might use a spoon, to scoop up a portion of the main dish on the person's plate.
   III. The reason for the starch's inclusion in every meal has to do with taste as well as nutrition; African food can be very spicy, and the starch is known to cool the burning effect of the main dish.
   IV. When serving these meals, the main dish is usually served on individual plates, and the starch is served on a communal plate, from which diners break off a piece of bread or scoop rice or fufu in their fingers.

   15._____

V. The typical meals usually consist of a thick stew or soup as the main course, and an accompanying starch—either bread, rice, or *fufu*, a starchy grain paste similar in consistency to mashed potatoes.
The BEST order is:
A. V, II, III, IV, I   B. V, I, IV, III, II   C. I, IV, V, III, II   D. I, V, IV, II, III

16. I. In the early days of the American Midwest, Indiana settlers sometimes came together to hold an event called an apple peeling, where neighboring settlers gathered at the homestead of a host family to help prepare the hosts' apple crop for cooking, canning, and making apple butter.
II. At the beginning of the event, each peeler sat down in front of a ten- or twenty-gallon stone jar and was given a crock of apples and a paring knife.
III. Once a peeler had finished with a crock, another was placed next to him; if the peeler was an unmarried man, he kept a strict count of the number of apples he had peeled, because the winner was allowed to kiss the girl of his choice.
IV. The peeling usually ended by 9:30 in the evening, when the neighbors gathered in the host family's parlor for a dance social.
V. The apples were peeled, cored, and quartered, and then placed into the jar.
The BEST order is:
A. I, V, III, IV, II   B. II, V, III, IV, I   C. I, II, V, III, IV   D. II, I, V, IV, III

16.____

17. I. If your pet turtle is a land turtle and is native to temperate climates, it will stop eating some time in October, which should be your cue to prepare the turtle for hibernation.
II. The box should then be covered with a wire screen, which will protect the turtle from any rodents or predators that might want to take advantage of a motionless and helpless animal.
III. When your turtle hasn't eaten for a while and appears ready to hibernate, it should be moved to its winter quarters, most likely a cellar or garage, where the temperature should range between 40° and 45°F.
IV. Instead of feeding the turtle, you should bathe it every day in warm water, to encourage the turtle to empty its intestines in preparation for its long winter sleep.
V. Here the turtle should be placed in a well-ventilated box whose bottom is covered with a moisture-absorbing layer of clay beads, and then filled three-fourths full with almost dry peat moss or wood chips, into which the turtle will burrow and sleep for several months.
The BEST order is:
A. I, IV, III, V, II   B. III, IV, II, V, I   C. III, II, IV, I, V   D. IV, V, II, III, I

17.____

18. I. Once he has reached the nest, the hunter uses two sturdy bamboo poles like huge chopsticks to pull the next away from the mountainside, into a large basket that will be lowered to people waiting below.
II. The world's largest honeybees colonize the Nealese mountainsides, building honeycombs as large as a person on sheer rock faces that are often hundreds of feet high.

18.____

III. In the remote mountain country of Nepal, a small band of "honey hunters" carry out a tradition so ancient that 10,000 year-old drawings of the practice have been found in the caves of Nepal.
IV. To harvest the honey and beeswax from these combs, a honey hunter climbs above the nests, lowers a long bamboo-fiber ladder over the cliff, and then climbs down.
V. Throughout this dangerous practice, the hunter is stung repeatedly, and only the veterans, with skin that has been toughened over the years, are able to return from a hunt without the painful swelling caused by stings.

The BEST order is:
A. II, IV, III, V, I   B. II, IV, I, V, III   C. V, III, II, IV, I   D. III, II, IV, I, V

19. I. After the Romans left Britain, there were relentless attacks on the islands from the barbarian tribes of northern Germany—the Angles, Saxons, and Jutes.
II. As the empire weakened, Roman soldiers withdrew from Britain, leaving behind a country that continued to practice the Christian religion that had been introduced by the Romans.
III. Early Latin writings tell of a Christian warrior named Arturius (Arthur, in English) who led the British citizens to defeat these barbarian invades, and brought an extended period of peace to the lands of Britain.
IV. Long ago, the British Isles were part of the far-flung Roman Empire that extended across most of Europe and into Africa and Asia.
V. The romantic legend of King Arthur and his knights of the Round Table, one of the most popular and widespread stories of all time, appears to have some foundation in history.

The BEST order is:
A. V, IV, III, II, I   B. V, IV, II, I, III   C. IV, V, II, III, I   D. IV, III, II, I, V

20. I. The cylinder was allowed to cool until it could stand on its own, and then it was cut from the tube and split down the side with a single straight cut.
II. Nineteenth-century glassmakers, who had not yet discovered the glazier's modern techniques for making panes of glass, had to create a method for converting their blown gas into flat sheets.
III. The bubble was then pierced at the end to make a hole that opened up while the glassmaker gently spun it, creating a cylinder of glass.
IV. Turned on its side and laid on a conveyor belt, the cylinder was strengthened, or tempered, by being heated again and cooled very slowly, eventually flattening out into a single rectangular of glass.
V. To do this, the glassmaker dipped the end of a long tube into melted glass and blew into the other end of the tube, creating an expanding bubble of glass.

The BEST order is:
A. II, V, III, IV, I   B. II, IV, V, III, I   C. III, V, II, IV, I   D. III, I, IV, V, II

21.
   I. The splints are almost always hidden, but horses are occasionally born whose splinted toes project from the leg on either side, just above the hoof.
   II. The second and fourth toes remained, but shrank to thin splints of bone that fused invisibly to the horse's leg bone.
   III. Horses are unique among mammals, having evolved feet that each end in what is essentially a single toe, capped by a large, sturdy hoof.
   IV. Julius Caesar, an emperor of ancient Rome, was said to have owned one of these three-toed horses, and considered it so special that he would not permit anyone else to ride it.
   V. Though the horse's earlier ancestors possessed the traditional mammalian set of five toes on each foot, the horse has retained only its third toe; its first and fifth toes disappeared completely as the horse evolved.
   The BEST order is:
   A. III, V, II, I, IV   B. V, III, II, IV, I   C. III, II, V, I, IV   D. V, II, III, I, IV

21.____

22.
   I. The new building materials—some of which are twenty feet long, and weigh nearly six tons—were transported to Pohnpei on rafts, and were brought into their present position by using hibiscus fiber ropes and leverage to move the stone columns upward along the inclined trunks of coconut palm trees.
   II. The ancestors built great fires to heat the stone, and then poured cool seawater on the columns, which caused the stone to contract and split along natural fracture lines.
   III. The now-abandoned enclave of Nan Madol, a group of 92 man-made islands off the shore of the Micronesian island of Pohnpei, is estimated to have been built around the year 500 A.D.
   IV. The islanders say their ancestors quarried stone columns from a nearby island, where large basalt columns were formed by the cooling of molten lava.
   V. The structures of Nan Madol are remarkable for the sheer size of some of the stone "longs" or columns that were used to create the walls of the offshore community, and today anthropologists can only rely on the information of existing local people for clues about how Nan Madol was built.
   The BEST order is:
   A. V, IV, III, II, I   B. V, III, I, IV, II   C. III, V, IV, II, I   D. III, I, IV, II, V

22.____

23.
   I. One of the most easily manipulated substances on earth, glass can be made into ceramic tiles that are composed of over 90% air.
   II. NASA's space shuttles are the first spacecraft ever designed to leave and re-enter the earth's atmosphere while remaining intact.
   III. These ceramic tiles are such effective insulators that when a tile emerges from the oven in which it was fired, it can be held safely in a person's hand by the edges while its interior still glows at a temperature well over 2000°F.
   IV. Eventually, the engineers were led to a material that is as old as our most ancient civilization.
   V. Because the temperature during atmospheric re-entry is so incredibly hot, it took NASA's engineers some time to find a substance capable of protecting the shuttles.

22.____

The BEST order is:
A. V, II, I, II, IV   B. II, V, IV, I, III   C. II, III, I, IV, V   D. V, IV, III, I, II

24. I. The secret to teaching any parakeet to talk is patience, and the understanding that when a bird talks," it is simply imitating what it hears, rather than putting ideas into words.
    II. You should stay just out of sight of the bird and repeat the phrase you want it to learn, for at least fifteen minutes every morning and evening.
    III. It is important to leave the bird without any words of encouragement or farewell; otherwise it might combine stray remarks or phrases, such as "Good night," with the phrase you are trying to teach it.
    IV. For this reason, to train your bird to imitate your words you should keep it free of any distractions, especially other noises, while you are giving it "lesson."
    V. After your repetition, you should quietly leave the bird alone for a while, to think over what it has just heard.
    The BEST order is:
    A. I, IV, II, V, III   B. I, II, IV, III, V   C. III, II, I, V, IV   D. III, I, V, IV, II

24.____

25. I. As a school approaches, fishermen from neighboring communities join their fishing boats together as a fleet, and string their gill nets together to make a huge fence that is held up by cork floats.
    II. At a signal from the party leaders, or *nakura*, the family members pound the sides of the boats or beat the water with long poles, creating a sudden and deafening noise.
    III. The fishermen work together to drag the trap into a half-circle that may reach 300 yards in diameter, and then the families move their boats to form the other half of the circle around the school of fish.
    IV. The school of fish flee from the commotion into the awaiting trap, where a final wall of net is thrown over the open end of the half-circle, securing the day's haul.
    V. Indonesian people from the area around the Sulu islands live on the sea, in floating villages made of lashed-together or stilted homes, and make much of their living by fishing their home waters for migrating schools of snapper, scad, and other fish.
    The BEST order is:
    A. I, V, III, IV, II   B. I, II, IV, III, V   C. V, I, II, III, IV   D. V, I, III, II, IV

25.____

KEY (CORRECT ANSWERS)

1.	D	11.	C
2.	D	12.	A
3.	B	13.	D
4.	A	14.	C
5.	C	15.	D
6.	C	16.	C
7.	D	17.	A
8.	D	18.	D
9.	A	19.	B
10.	B	20.	A

21. A
22. C
23. B
24. A
25. D

PREPARING WRITTEN MATERIAL
EXAMINATION SECTION
TEST 1

DIRECTIONS: Each short paragraph below is followed by four restatements or summaries of the information contained within it. Select the one that most completely and accurately restates the information given in the paragraph. *PRINT THE LETTER OF THE CORRECT ANSWER IN THE SPACE AT THE RIGHT.*

1. India's night jasmine, or hurshinghar, is different from most flowering plants, in that its flowers are closed during the day, and open after dark. The scientific reason for this is probably that the plant has avoided competing with other flowers for pollinating insects and birds, and relies instead on the service of nocturnal bats that are drawn to the flower's nectar. According to an old Indian legend, however, the flowers sprouted from the funeral ashes of a beautiful young girl who had fallen hopelessly in love with the sun.
    A. Despite the Indian legend that explains why the hurshinghar's flowers open at dusk, scientists believe it has to do with competition for available pollinators.
    B. The Indian hurshinghar's closure of its flowers during the day is due to a lack of available pollinators.
    C. The hurshinghar of India has evolved an unhealthy dependency on nocturnal bats.
    D. Like most myths, the Indian legend of the hurshinghar's night-flowering has been disproved by science.

1.____

2. Charles Lindbergh's trans-Atlantic flight from New York to Paris made him an international hero in 1927, but he lived nearly another fifty years, and by most accounts they weren't terribly happy ones. The two greatest tragedies of his life—the 1932 kidnapping and murder of his oldest son, and an unshakeable reputation as a Nazi sympathizer during World War II—he blamed squarely on the rabid media hounds who stalked his every move.
    A. Despite the fact that Charles Lindbergh had a hand in the two greatest tragedies of his life, he insisted on blaming the media for his problems.
    B. Charles Lindbergh lived a largely unhappy life after the glory of his 1927 trans-Atlantic flight, and he blamed his unhappiness on media attention
    C. Charles Lindbergh's later life was marked by despair and disillusionment.
    D. Because of the rabid media attention sparked by Charles Lindbergh's 1927 trans-Atlantic flight, he would later consider it the last happy event of his life

2.____

3. The United States, one of the world's youngest nations in the early twentieth century, had yet to spread its wings in terms of foreign affairs, preferring to remain isolated and opposed to meddling in the affairs of others. But the fact remained that as a young nation situated on the opposite side of the globe from Europe, Africa, and Asia, the United States had much work to do in

3.____

establishing relations with the rest of the world. So, too, as the European colonial powers continued to battle for influence in North and South America, did the United States come to believe that it was proper for them to keep these nations from encroaching into their sphere of influence.
- A. The roots of the Monroe Doctrine can be traced to the foreign policy shift of the United States during the early nineteenth century.
- B. In the early nineteenth century, the United States shifted its foreign policy to reflect a growing desire to actively protect its interests in the Western Hemisphere.
- C. In the early nineteenth century, the United States was too young and undeveloped to have devised much in the way of foreign policy.
- D. The United States adopted a more aggressive foreign policy in the early nineteenth century in order to become a diplomatic player on the world stage.

4. Hertha Ayrton, a nineteenth-century Englishwoman, pursued a career in science during a time when most women were not given the opportunity to go to college. Her series of successes led to her induction into the Institution of Electrical Engineers in 1899, when she was the first woman to receive this professional honor. Her most noted accomplishment was the research and invention of an anti-gas fan that the British War Office used in the trench warfare of World War I. 4.____
   - A. The British Army's success in World War I can be partly attributed to Hertha Ayrton, a groundbreaking British scientist.
   - B. Hertha Ayrton was the first woman to be inducted into the Institution of Electrical Engineers.
   - C. The injustices of nineteenth-century England were no match for the brilliant mind of Hertha Ayrton.
   - D. Hertha Ayrton defied the restrictions of her society by building a successful scientific career.

5. Scientists studying hyenas in Tanzania's Ngorongoro Crater have observed that hyena clans have evolved a system of territoriality that allows each clan a certain space to hunt within the 100-square-mile area. These territories are not marked by natural boundaries, but by droppings and excretions from the hyenas' scent glands. Usually, the hyenas take these boundary lines very seriously; some hyena clans have been observed abandoning their pursuit of certain prey after the prey has crossed into another territory, even though no members of the neighboring clan are anywhere in sight. 5.____
   - A. The hyenas of Ngorongoro Crater illustrate that the best way to peacefully co-exist within a limited territory is to strictly delineate and defend territorial borders.
   - B. While most territorial boundaries are marked using geographical features, the hyenas of Ngorongoro Crater have devised another method.
   - C. The hyena clans of Ngorongoro Crater, in order to co-exist within a limited hunting territory, have developed a method of marking strict territorial boundaries.
   - D. As with most species, the hyenas of Ngorongoro Crater have proven the age-old motto: "To the victor go the spoils."

6. The flood control policy of the U.S. Army Corps of Engineers has long been an obvious feature of the American landscape—the Corps seeks to contain the nation's rivers with an enormous network of dams and levees, "channelizing" rivers into small, confined routes that will stay clear of settled flood—plains when rivers rise. As a command of the U.S. Army, the Corps seems to have long seen the nation's rivers as an enemy to be fought; one of the agency's early training films speaks of the Corps' "battle" with its adversary, Mother Nature.

    6._____

    A. The dams and levees built by the U.S. Army Corps of Engineers have at least defeated their adversary, Mother Nature.
    B. The flood control policy of the U.S. Army Corps of Engineers has often reflected a military point of view, making the nation's rivers into enemies that must be defeated.
    C. When one realizes that the flood policy of the U.S. Army Corps of Engineers has always relied on a kind of military strategy, it is only possible to view the Corps' efforts as a failure.
    D. By damming and channelizing the nation's rivers, the U.S. Army Corps of Engineers have made America's flood plains safe for farming and development.

7. Frogs with extra legs or missing legs have been showing up with greater frequency over the past decade, and scientists have been baffled by the cause. Some researchers have concluded that pesticide runoff from farms is to blame; others say a common parasite, the trematode, is the culprit. Now, a new study suggests that both these factors in combination have disturbed normal development in many frogs, leading to the abnormalities.

    7._____

    A. Despite several studies, scientists still have no idea what is causing the widespread incidence of deformities among aquatic frogs.
    B. In the debate over what is causing the increase in frog deformities, environmentalists tend to blame pesticide runoff, while others blame a common parasite, the trematode.
    C. A recent study suggests that both pesticide runoff and natural parasites have contributed to the increasing rate of deformities in frogs.
    D. Because of their aquatic habitat, frogs are among the most susceptible organisms to chemical ad environmental change, and this is illustrated by the increasing rate of physical deformities among frog populations.

8. The builders of the Egyptian pyramids, to insure that each massive structure was built on a completely flat surface, began by cutting a network of criss-crossing channels into the pyramid's mapped-out ground space and partly filling the channels with water. Because the channels were all interconnected, the water was distributed evenly throughout the channel system, and all the workers had to do to level their building surface was cut away any rock above the waterline.

    8._____

    A. The modern carpenter's level uses a principle that was actually invented several centuries ago by the builders of the Egyptian pyramids.
    B. The discovery of the ancient Egyptians' sophisticated construction techniques is a quiet argument against the idea that they were built by slaves.

C. The use of water to insure that the pyramids were level mark the Egyptians as one of the most scientifically advanced of the ancient civilizations.
D. The builders of the Egyptian pyramids used a simple but ingenious method for ensuring a level building surface with interconnected channels of water

9. Thunderhead Mountain, a six-hundred-foot-high formation of granite in the Black Hills of South Dakota, is slowly undergoing a transformation that will not be finished for more than a century, when what remains of the mountain will have become the largest sculpture in the world. The statue, begun in 1947 by a Boston Sculptor named Henry Ziolkowski, is still being carved and blasted by his wife and children into the likeness of Crazy Horse, the legendary chief of the Sioux tribe of American natives. The enormity of the sculpture—the planned length of one of the figure's arms is 263 feet—is understandable, given the historical greatness of Crazy Horse.   9.____
    A. Only a hero as great as Crazy Horse could warrant a sculpture so large that it will take morae than a century to complete.
    B. In 1947, sculptor Henry Ziolkowski began work on what he imagined would be the largest sculpture in the world—even though he knew he would not live to see it completed.
    C. The huge Black Hills sculpture of the great Sioux chief Crazy Horse, still being carried out by the family of Henry Ziolkowski, will some day be the largest sculpture in the world.
    D. South Dakota's Thunderhead Mountain will soon be the site of the world's largest sculpture, a statue of the Sioux chief Crazy Horse.

10. Because they were some of the first explorers to venture into the western frontier of North America, the French were responsible for the naming of several native tribes. Some of these names were poorly conceived—the worst of which was perhaps Eskimo, the name for the natives of the far North, which translates roughly as "eaters of raw flesh." The name is incorrect; these people have always cooked their fish and game, and they now call themselves the Inuit, a native term that means "the people."   10.____
    A. The first to explore much of North America's western frontier were the French, and they usually gave improper or poorly-informed names to the native tribes.
    B. The Eskimos of North America have never eaten raw flesh, so it is curious that the French would give them a name that means "eaters of raw flesh."
    C. The Inuit have fought for many years to overcome the impression that they eat raw flesh.
    D. Like many native tribes, the Inuit were once incorrectly named by French explorers, but they have since corrected the mistake themselves.

5 (#1)

11. Of the 30,000 species of spiders worldwide, only a handful are dangerous to human beings, but this doesn't prevent many people from having a powerful fear of all spiders, whether they are venomous or not. The leading scientific theory about arachnophobia, as this fear is known, is that far in our evolutionary past, some species of spider must have presented a serious enough threat to people that the sight of a star-shaped body or an eight-legged walk was coded into our genes as a danger signal.   11.____
    A. Scientists theorize that peoples' widespread fear of spiders can be traced to an ancient spider species that was dangerous enough to trigger this fearful reaction.
    B. The fear known as arachnophobia is triggered by the sight of a star-shaped body or an eight-legged walk.
    C. Because most spiders have a uniquely shaped body that triggers a human fear response, many humans are afflicted with the fear of spiders known as arachnophobia.
    D. Though only a few of the planet's 30,000 spider species are dangerous to people, many people have an unreasonable fear of them.

12. From the 1970s to the 1990s, the percentage of Americans living in the suburbs climbed from 37% to 47%. In the latter part of the 1990s, a movement emerged that questioned the good of such a population shift—or at least, the good of the speed and manner in which this suburban land was being developed. Often, people began to argue, the planning of such growth was flawed, resulting in a phenomenon that has become known as suburban "sprawl," or the growth of suburban orbits around cities at rates faster than infrastructures could support, and in ways that are damaging to the environment   12.____
    A. The term "urban sprawl" was coined in the 1990s, when the movement against unchecked suburban development began to gather momentum.
    B. In the 1980s and 1990s, home builders benefited from a boom in their most favored demographic segment, suburban new home buyers.
    C. Suburban development tends to suffer from poor planning, which can lead to a lower quality of life for residents
    D. The surge in suburban residences in the late twentieth century was criticized by many as "sprawl" that could not be supported by existing resources

13. Medicare, a $200 billion-a-year program, processes 1 billion claims annually, and in the year 2000, the computer system that handles these claims came under criticism. The General Accounting Office branded Medicare's financial management system as outdated and inadequate—one in a series of studies and reports warning that the program is plagued with duplication, overcharges, double billings, and confusion among users.   13.____
    A. The General Accounting Office's 2000 report proves that Medicare is bloated bureaucracy in need of substantial reform.
    B. Medicare's confusing computer network is an example of how the federal government often neglects the programs that mean the most to average American citizens.

C. In the year 2000, the General Accounting Office criticized Medicare's financial accounting network as inefficient and outdated.
D. Because it has to handle so many claims each year, Medicare's financial accounting system often produces redundancies and errors.

14. The earliest known writing materials were thin clay tablets, used in Mesopotamia 14.____
more than 5,000 years ago. Although the tablets were cheap and easy to produce, they had two major disadvantages: they were difficult to store, and once the clay had dried and hardened, a person could not write on them. The ancient Egyptians later discovered a better writing material—the thin bark of the papyrus reed, a plant that grew near the mouth of the Nile River, which could be peeled into long strips, woven into a mat-like layer, pounded flat with heavy mallets, and then dried in the sun.
    A. The Egyptians, after centuries of frustration with clay writing tablets, were finally forced to invent a better writing surface.
    B. With the bark of the papyrus reed, ancient Egyptians made a writing material that overcame the disadvantages of clay tablets.
    C. The Egyptian invention of the papyrus scroll was necessitated in part by a relative lack of available clay.
    D. The word "paper" can be traced to the innovations of the Egyptians, who made the first paper-like writing material from the bark of papyrus plant.

15. In 1850, the German pianomaker Heinrich Steinweg and his family stepped off 15.____
an immigrant ship in New York City, threw themselves into competition with dozens of other established craftsmen, and defeated them all by reinventing the instrument. The company they created commanded the market for nearly the next century and a half, while their competitors—some of the most acclaimed pianomakers in the business—faded into obscurity. And all the while, Steinway & Sons, through their sponsorship and encouragement of the world's most distinguished pianists, helped define the cultural life of the young United States.
    A. The Steinways capitalized on weak competition during the mid-nineteenth century to capture the American piano market.
    B. Because of their technical and cultural innovations, the Steinways had an advantage over other American pianomakers.
    C. Heinrich Steinweg founded the Steinway piano empire in 1850.
    D. From humble immigrant origins, the Steinway family rose to dominate both the pianomaking industry and American musical culture.

16. Feng Shui, the ancient Chinese science of studying the natural environment's 16.____
effect on a person's well-being, has gained new popularity in the design and decoration of buildings. Although a complex area of study, a basic premise of Feng Shui is that each building creates a unique field of energy which affects the inhabitants of that building or home. In recent years, decorators and realtors have begun to offer services which include a diagnosis of a building's Feng Shui, or energy.
    A. Feng Shui, the Chinese science of balancing environmental energies, has been given more aesthetic quality by recent practitioners.

B. Generally, practitioners of Feng Shui work to create balance within a room, carefully arranging sharp and soft surfaces to create a positive environment that suits the room's primary purpose.
C. The idea behind the Chinese "science" of Feng Sui objects give off certain energies that affect a building's inhabitants has been a difficult one for most Westerners to accept, but it is gaining in popularity.
D. The ancient Chinese science of Feng Shui, which studies the balance of energies in a person's environment, has become popular among those who design and decorate buildings.

17. Because the harsh seasonal variations of the Kansas plains make survival difficult for most plant life, the area is dominated by tall, sturdy grasses. The only tree that has been able to survive and prosper throughout the wide expanse of prairie is the cottonwood, which can take root and grow in the most extreme climatic conditions. Sometimes a storm will shear off a living branch and carry it downstream, where it may snag along a sandbar and take root.
    A. Among the plant life of the Kansas plains, the only tree is the cottonwood.
    B. The only prosperous tree on the Kansas plains is the cottonwood, which can take root and grow in a wide range of conditions.
    C. Only the cottonwood, whose branches can grow after being broken off and washed down a river, is capable of surviving the climatic extremes of the Kansas plains.
    D. Because it is the most widespread and hardiest tree on the Kansas plains, the cottonwood had become a symbol of pioneer grit and fortitude.

17.____

18. In the twenty-first century, it's easy to see the automobile as the keystone of American popular culture. Subtract linen dusters, driving goggles, and women's *crepe de chine* veils from our history, and you've taken the Roaring out of the Twenties. Take away the ducktail haircuts, pegged pants, and upturned collars from the teen Car Cult of the Fifties, and the decade isn't nearly as Fabulous. Were the chromed and tailfinned muscle cars of the automobile' Golden Age modeled after us, or were we mimicking them?
    A. Ever since its invention, the automobile has shaped American culture.
    B. Many of the familiar names we give historical era, such as "Roaring Twenties" and "Fabulous Fifties," were given because of the predominance of the automobile.
    C. Americans' tastes in clothing have been determined primarily by the cars they drive.
    D. Teenagers have had a fascination for automobiles ever since the motorcar was first invented.

18.____

19. Since the 1960s, an important issue for Canada has been the status of minority French-speaking Canadians, especially in the province of Quebec, whose inhabitants make up 30% of the Canadian population and trace their ancestry back to a Canada that preceded British influence. In response to pressure from Quebec nationalists, the government in 1982 added a Charter of Rights to the constitution, restoring important rights that dated back to the time of aboriginal treaties. Separatism is still a prominent issue, though successive

19.____

8 (#1)

referendums and constitutional inquiries have not resulted in any realistic progress toward Quebec's independence.
    A. Despite the fact that Quebec's inhabitants have their roots in Canada's original settlers, they have been constantly oppressed by the descendants of those who came later, the British.
    B. It seems unavoidable that Quebec's linguistic and cultural differences with the rest of Canada will some day lead to its secession.
    C. French-speaking Quebec's activism over the last several decades has led to concessions by the Canadian government, but it seems that Quebec will remain a part of the country for some time.
    D. The inhabitants of Quebec are an aboriginal culture that has been exploited by the Canadian government for years, but they are gradually winning back their rights.

20. For years, musicians and scientists have tried to discover what it is about an eighteenth-century Stradivarius violin—which may sell for more than $1 million on today's market—that gives it its unique sound. In 1977, American scientist Joseph Nagyvary discovered that the Stradivarius is made of a spruce wood that came from Venice, where timber was stored beneath the sea, and unlike the dry-seasoned wood from which other violins were made, this spruce contains microscopic holes which add resonance to the violin's sound. Nagyvary also found the varnish used on the Stradivarius to be equally unique, containing tiny mineral crystals that appear to have come from ground-up gemstones, which would filter out high-pitched tones and give the violin a smoother sound.

20.____

    A. After carefully studying Stradivarius violins to discover the source of their unique sound, an American scientist discovered two qualities in the construction of them that set them apart from other instruments: the wood from which they were made, and the varnish used to coat the wood.
    B. The two qualities that give the Stradivarius violin such a unique sound are the wood, which adds resonance, and the finish, which filters out high-pitched tones.
    C. The Stradivarius violin, because of the unique wood and finish used in its construction, is widely regarded as the finest string instrument ever manufactured in the world.
    D. A close study of the Stradivarius violin has revealed that the best wood for making violins is Venetian spruce, stored underwater.

21. People who watch the display of fireflies on a clear summer evening are actually witnessing a complex chemical reaction called "bioluminescence," which turns certain organisms into living light bulbs. Organisms that produce this light undergo a reaction in which oxygen combines with a chemical called lucerfin and an enzyme called luciferase. Depending on the organism, the light produced from this reaction can range from the light green of the firefly to the bright red spots of a railroad worm.

21.____

    A. Although the function of most displays of bioluminescence is to attract mates, as is the case with fireflies, other species rely on bioluminescence for different purposes.

9 (#1)

B. Bioluminescence, a phenomenon produced by several organisms, is the result of a chemical reaction that takes place within the body of the organism.
C. Of all the organisms in the world, only insects are capable of displaying bioluminescence.
D. Despite the fact that some organisms display bioluminescence, these reactions produce almost no heat, which is why the light they create is sometimes referred to as cold light.

22. The first of America's "log cabin" presidents, Andrew Jackson rose from humble backcountry origins to become a U.S. congressman and senator, a renowned military hero, and the seventh president of the United States. Among many Americans, especially those of the western frontier, he was acclaimed as a symbol of the "new" American: self-made, strong through closeness to nature, and endowed with a powerful moral courage.   22.____
    A. Andrew Jackson was the first American president to rise from modest origins.
    B. Because he was born poor, President Andrew Jackson was more popular among Americans of the western frontier.
    C. Andrew Jackson's humble background, along with his outstanding achievements, made him into a symbol of American strength and self-sufficiency.
    D. Andrew Jackson achieved success as a legislator, soldier, and president because he was born humbly and had to work for every honor he ever received.

23. In the past few decades, while much of the world's imagination has focused on the possibilities of outer space, some scientists have been exploring a different frontier—the ocean floor. Although ships have been sailing the oceans for centuries, only recently have scientists developed vehicles strong enough to sustain the pressure of deep-sea exploration and observation. These fiberglass vehicles, called submersibles, are usually just big enough to take two or three people to the deepest parts of the oceans' floors.   23.____
    A. Modern submersible vehicles, thanks to recent technological innovations, are now exploring underwater cliffs, crevices, and mountain ranges that were once unreachable.
    B. While most people tend to fantasize about exploring outer space, they should be turning toward a more accessible realm—the depths of the earth's oceans.
    C. Because of the necessarily small size of submersible vehicles, exploration of the deep ocean is not a widespread activity.
    D. Recent technological developments have helped scientists to turn their attention from deep space to the deep ocean.

24. The panda—a native of the remote mountainous regions of China—subsists almost entirely on the tender shoots of the bamboo plant. This restrictive diet has allowed the panda to evolve an anatomical structure that is completely different from that of other bears, whose paws are aligned for running, stabbing, and scratching. The panda's paw has an over-developed wrist bone that juts out below the other claws like a thumb, and the panda uses this "thumb" to grip bamboo shoots while it strips them of their leaves.
    A. The panda is the only bear-like animal that feeds on vegetation, and it has a kind of thumb to help it grip bamboo shoots.
    B. The panda's limited diet of bamboo has led it to evolve a thumb-like appendage for grasping bamboo shoots.
    C. The panda's thumb-like appendage is a factor that limits its diet to the shoots of the bamboo plant.
    D. Because bamboo shoots must be held tightly while eaten, the panda's thumb-like appendage ensure that it is the only bear-like animal that eats bamboo.

25. The stability and security of the Balkan region remains a primary concern for Greece in post-Cold War Europe, and Greece's active participation in peacekeeping and humanitarian operations in Georgia, Albania, and Bosnia are substantial examples of this commitment. Due to its geopolitical position, Greece believes it necessary to maintain, at least for now, a more nationalized defense force than other European nations. It is Greece's hope that the new spirit of integration and cooperation will help establish a common European foreign affairs and defense policy that might ease some of these regional tensions, and allow a greater level of Greek participation in NATO's integrated military structure.
    A. Greece's proximity to the unstable Balkan region has led it to keep a more nationalized military, though it hopes to become more involved in a common European defense force.
    B. The Balkan states present a greater threat to Greece than any other European nation, and Greece has adopted a highly nationalist military force as a result.
    C. Greece, the only Balkan state to belong to NATO, has an isolationist approach to defense, but hopes to achieve greater integration in the organization's combined forces.
    D. Greece's failure to become more militarily integrated with the rest of Europe can be attributed to the failure to establish a common European defense policy.

KEY (CORRECT ANSWERS)

1.	A	11.	A
2.	B	12.	D
3.	B	13.	C
4.	D	14.	B
5.	C	15.	D
6.	B	16.	D
7.	C	17.	B
8.	D	18.	A
9.	C	19.	C
10.	D	20.	A

21. B
22. C
23. D
24. B
25. A

EXAMINATION SECTION
TEST 1

DIRECTIONS: The questions that follow the paragraphs below are designed to test your appreciation of correctness and effectiveness of expression in English. The paragraphs are presented first in full so that you may read it through for sense. Disregard the errors you find as you will be asked to correct them in the questions that follow. The paragraphs are then presented sentence by sentence with portions underlined and numbered. At the end of this material, you will find numbers corresponding to those below the underlined portions, each followed by five alternatives lettered A, B, C, D, and E. In every case, the usage in the alternative lettered A is the same as that in the original paragraph and is followed by four possible usages. Choose the usage that you consider BEST in each case. *PRINT THE LETTER OF THE CORRECT ANSWER IN THE SPACE AT THE RIGHT.*

    The use of the machine produced up to the present time outstanding changes in our modern world. One of the most significant of these changes have been the marked decreases in the length of the working day and the working week. The fourteen-hour day not only has been reduced to one of ten hours but also, in some lines of work, to one of eight or even six. The trend toward a decrease is further evidenced in the longer weekend already given to employees in many business establishment. There seems also to be a trend toward shorter working weeks and longer summer vacations. An important feature of this development is that leisure is no longer the privilege of the wealthy few,—it has become the common right of most people. Using it wisely, leisure promotes health, efficiency and happiness, for there is time for each individual to live their own "more abundant life" and having opportunities for needed recreation.

    Recreation, like the name implies, is a process of revitalization. In giving expression to the play instincts of the human race, new vigor and effectiveness are afforded by recreation to the body and to the mind. Of course not all forms of amusement, by no means constitute recreation. Furthermore, an activity that provides recreation for one person may prove exhausting for another. Today, however, play among adults, as well as children, is regarded as a vital necessity of modern life. Play being recognized as an important factor in improving mental and physical health and thereby reducing human misery and poverty.

    Among the most important form of amusement available at the present time are the automobile, the moving picture, the radio, television, and organized sports. The automobile, especially, has been a boon to the American people, since it has been the chief means of them getting out into the open. The motion picture, the radio and television have tremendous opportunities to supply whole-some recreation and to promote cultural advancement. A criticism often leveled against organized sports as a means of recreation is because they make passive spectators of too many people. It has been said "that the American public is afflicted with "spectatoritis," but there is some recreational advantages to be gained even from being a spectator at organized games. Such sports afford a release from the monotony of daily toil, get people outdoors and also provide an exhilaration that is tonic in its effect.

2 (#1)

The chief concern, of course, should be to eliminate those forms of amusement that are socially undesirable. There are, however, far too many people who, we know, do not use their leisure to the best advantage. Sometime leisure leads to idleness, and idleness may lead to demoralization. The value of leisure both to the individual and to society will depend on the uses made of it.

The use of the machine <u>produced</u> up to the
                               1

1.   A. produced   B. produces   C. has produced   1.____
      D. had produced   E. will have produced

present time many outstanding changes in our modern world. One of the most significant of these changes <u>have been</u> the marked
                                                            2

2.   A. have been   B. was   C. were   2.____
      D. has been   E. will be

decreases in the length of the working day and the working week. <u>The fourteen-hour day not only has been reduced</u> to one of ten hours but also, in some lines of work, to one of eight or
                              3

even six.

3.   A. The fourteen-hour day not only has been reduced   3.____
      B. Not only the fourteen-hour day has been reduced
      C. Not the fourteen-hour day only has been reduced
      D. The fourteen-hour day has not only been reduced

The trend toward a decrease is further evidenced in the longer week-end <u>already</u> given

4.   A. already   B. all ready   C. allready   4.____
      D. ready   E. all in all

to employees in many business establishments. There seems also to be a trend toward shorter working weeks and longer summer vacations. An important feature of this development is that leisure is no longer the privilege of the wealthy few<u>, —it</u> has become the common right of most people.

5.   A. , —it   B. : it   C. ; it   5.____
      D. …it   E. omit punctuation

<u>Using it wisely,</u> leisure promotes health, efficiency, and happiness, for there is time for each
         6
individual to live <u>their</u> own "more abundant life" and <u>having</u> opportunities for needed recreation
                     7   8

6.   A. Using it wisely   B. If used wisely   6.____
      C. Having used it wisely   D. Because of its wise use
      E. Because of usefulness

3 (#1)

7. A. their   B. his   C. its   D. our   E. your   7.____

8. A. having   B. having had   C. to have   8.____
   D. to have had   E. had

Recreation, <u>like</u> the name implies, is a
           9

9. A. like   B. since   C. through   D. for   E. as   9.____

process of revitalization. In giving expression to the play instincts of the human race, <u>new vigor and effectiveness are afforded by creation to the body and to the mind.</u>
                                                                                           10

10. A. new vigor and effectiveness are afforded by recreation to the body and to the mind   10.____
    B. recreation affords new vigor and effectiveness to the body and to the mind
    C. there are afforded new vigor and effectiveness to the body and to the mind
    D. by recreation the body and mind are afforded new vigor and effectiveness
    E. the body and the mind afford new vigor and effectiveness to themselves by recreation

Of course not all forms of amusement, <u>by no means,</u> constitute recreation. Furthermore, an
                                           11
activity that provides recreation for one person may prove exhausting for another. Today, however, play among adults, as well as children is regarded as a vital necessity of modern life.

11. A. by no means   B. by those means   C. by some means   11.____
    D. by every means   E. by any means

<u>Play being recognized</u> as an important factor in improving mental and physical health and
       12
thereby reducing human misery and poverty.

12. A. . Play being recognized as   B. , by their recognizing play as   12.____
    C. . They recognizing play as   D. . Recognition of it being
    E. , for play is recognized as

Among the most important forms of amusement available at the present time are the automobile, the moving picture, the radio, television, and organized sports. The automobile, especially, has been a boon to the American people, since it has been the chief means of <u>them</u>
                                                                                                                    13
getting out into the open. The motion picture, the radio and television have tremendous opportunities to supply wholesome recreation and to promote cultural advancement. A criticism often leveled against organized

13. A. them   B. their   C. his   D. our   E. the people   13.____

141

sports as a means of recreation is <u>because</u> they make passive spectators of too many people.
                                        14

14. A. because   B. since   C. as   D. that   E. why   14.____

it has been said <u>"that</u> the American public is afflicted with "spectatoritis," but there <u>is</u> some
                    15   16
recreational advantages to be gained even from being a spectator at organized games.

15. A. "that   B. "that"   C. that"   D. 'that   E. that   15.____

16. A. is   B. was   C. are   D. were   E. will be   16.____

Such sports afford a release from the monotony of daily toil, get people outdoors and also provide an exhilaration that is tonic in its effect. The chief concern, of course, should be to eliminate those forms of amusement that are socially undesirable. There are, however, far too many people <u>who,</u> we know, do not use their leisure to the best advantage. Sometimes leisure
                    17
leads to idleness, and idleness may lead to demoralization. The value of leisure both to the individual and to society will depend on the uses made of it.

17. A. who   B. whom   C. which   D. such as   E. that which   17.____

KEY (CORRECT ANSWERS)

1.	C	11.	E
2.	D	12.	E
3.	E	13.	B
4.	A	14.	D
5.	C	15.	E
6.	B	16.	C
7.	B	17.	A
8.	C		
9.	E		
10.	B		

TEST 2

DIRECTIONS: The questions that follow the paragraphs below are designed to test your appreciation of correctness and effectiveness of expression in English. The paragraphs are presented first in full so that you may read it through for sense. Disregard the errors you find as you will be asked to correct them in the questions that follow. The paragraphs are then presented sentence by sentence with portions underlined and numbered. At the end of this material, you will find numbers corresponding to those below the underlined portions, each followed by five alternatives lettered A, B, C, D, and E. In every case, the usage in the alternative lettered A is the same as that in the original paragraph and is followed by four possible usages. Choose the usage that you consider BEST in each case. *PRINT THE LETTER OF THE CORRECT ANSWER IN THE SPACE AT THE RIGHT.*

    When this war is over, no nation will either be isolated in war or peace. Each will be within trading distance of all the others and will be able to strike them. Every nation will be most as dependent on the rest for the maintainance of peace as is any of our own American states on all the others. The world that we have known was a world made up of individual nations, each of which had the privilege of doing about as they pleased without being embarassed by outside interference. The world has dissolved before the impact of an invention, the airplane has done to our world what gunpowder did to the feudal world. Whether the coming century will be a period of further tragedy or one of peace and progress depend very largely on the wisdom and skill with which the present generation adjusts their thinking to the problems immediately at hand. Examining the principal movements sweeping through the world, it can be seen that they are being accelerated by the war. There is undoubtedly many of these whose courses will be affected for good or ill by the settlements that will follow the war. The United States will share the responsibility of these settlements with Russia, England and China. The influence of the United States, however, will be great. This country is likely to emerge from the war stronger than any other nation. Having benefitted by the absence of actual hostilities on our own soil, we shall probably be less exhausted that our allies and better able than them to help restore the devastated areas. However many mistakes have been made in our past, the tradition of America, not only the champion of freedom but also fair play, still lives among millions who can see light and hope scarcely nowhere else.

When this war is over, no nation will <u>either be isolated in war or peace.</u>
                                                      1

1. A. either be isolated in war or peace
   B. be either isolated in war or peace
   C. be isolated in neither war nor peace
   D. be isolated either in war or in peace
   E. be isolated neither in war or peace

1.____

<u>Each</u> will be
 2

2. A. Each   B. It   C. Some   D. They   E. A nation

2.____

2 (#2)

<u>within trading distance of all others and will be able to strike them.</u>
                     3

3.   A. within trading distance of all the others and will be able to strike them   3.____
     B. near enough to trade with and strike all the others
     C. trading and striking the others
     D. within trading and striking distance of all the others
     E. able to strike and trade with all the others

Every nation will be <u>most</u> as dependent on

4.   A. most   B. wholly   C. much   D. mostly   E. almost   4.____

the rest for the <u>maintainance</u> of peace as is
                    5

5.   A. maintainance   B. maintainence   C. maintenence   5.____
     D. maintenance   E. maintanence

any of our own American states on all the others. The world that we have known as a world made up of individual <u>nations, each</u>
                               6

6.   A. nations, each   B. nations. Each   C. nations: each   6.____
     D. nations; each   E. nations each

of which had the <u>priviledge</u> of doing about as
                 7

7.   A. priviledge   B. priveledge   C. privelege   7.____
     D. privalege   E. privilege

<u>they</u> pleased without being
 8

8.   A. they   B. it   C. they individually   8.____
     D. he   E. the nations

<u>embarassed</u> by outside interference. That
    9

9.   A. embarassed   B. embarrassed   C. embaressed   9.____
     D. embarrased   E. embarrashed

world has dissolved before the impact of an <u>invention, the</u> airplane has done to our world what
                                                   10

gunpowder did to the feudal world. Whether the coming century will be a period of further tragedy or one of peace and

3 (#2)

10. A. invention, the   B. invention but the   C. invention: the   10.____
     D. invention. The   E. invention and the

progress <u>depend</u> very largely on the wisdom and skill with which the present generation
         11

11. A. depend   B. will have depended   C. depends   11.____
     D. depended   E. shall depend

<u>adjusts their</u> thinking to the problems immediately at hand.
    12

12. A. adjusts their   B. adjusts there   C. adjusts its   12.____
     D. adjust our   E. adjust it's

<u>Examining the principal movements sweeping through the world, it can be seen</u>
                                    13

13. A. Examining the principal movements sweeping through the world, it can be   13.____
        seen
     B. Having examined the principal movements sweeping through the world, it
        can be seen
     C. Examining the principal movements sweeping through the world can be
        seen
     D. Examining the principal movements sweeping through the world, we can
        see
     E. It can be seen examining the principal movements sweeping through the
        world

that they are being <u>accelerated</u> by the war.
                         14

14. A. accelerated   B. acelerated   C. accelerated   14.____
     D. acellerated   E. accelerated

There <u>is</u> undoubtedly many of these whose courses will be affected for good or ill by the
       15
settlements that will follow the war. The United States will share the responsibility of these
settlements with Russia, England and China. The influence of the United

15. A. is   B. were   C. was   D. are   E. might be

States, <u>however</u>, will be great. This country is likely to emerge from the war stronger than any
           16
other nation.

16. A. , however,   B. however,   C. , however   16.____
     D. however   E. ; however,

145

4 (#2)

Having <u>benefitted</u> by the absence of actual hostilities on our own soil, we shall probably be
      17
less exhausted

17. A. benefitted   B. beniffited   C. benefited   17.____
      D. benifited   E. benafitted

than our allies and better able than <u>them</u> to help restore the devastated areas. However many
                                      18
mistakes have been made in our past, the tradition of America,

18. A. them   B. themselves   C. they   18.____
      D. the world   E. the nations

<u>not only the champion of freedom but also fair play,</u> still lives among millions who can
                 19

19. A. not only the champion of freedom but also fair play,   19.____
      B. the champion of not only freedom but also of fair play,
      C. the champion not only of freedom but also of fair play,
      D. not only the champion but also freedom and fair play,
      E. not the champion of freedom only, but also fair play,

see light and hope <u>scarcely nowhere else.</u>
              20

20. A. scarcely nowhere else   B. elsewhere   20.____
      C. nowhere   D. scarcely anywhere else
      E. anywhere

KEY (CORRECT ANSWERS)

1.	D	11.	C
2.	A	12.	C
3.	D	13.	D
4.	E	14.	A
5.	D	15.	D
6.	A	16.	A
7.	E	17.	C
8.	B	18.	C
9.	B	19.	C
10.	D	20.	D

WRITTEN ENGLISH EXPRESSION
EXAMINATION SECTION
TEST 1

DIRECTIONS: The questions that follow the paragraph below are designed to test your appreciation of correctness and effectiveness of expression in English. The paragraph is presented first in full so that you may read it through for sense. Disregard the errors you find, as you will be asked to correct them in the questions that follow. The paragraph is then presented sentence by sentence with portions underlined and numbered. At the end of this material, you will find numbers corresponding to those below the underlined portions, each followed by five alternatives lettered A to E. In every case, the usage in the alternative lettered A is the same as that in the original paragraph and is followed by four possible usages. Choose the usage you consider BEST in each case. *PRINT THE LETTER OF THE CORRECT ANSWER IN THE SPACE AT THE RIGHT.*

When this war is over, no nation will either be isolated in war or peace. Each will be within trading distance of all the others and will be able to strike them. Every nation will be most as dependent on the rest for the maintainance of peace as is any of our own American states on all the others. The world that we have known was a world made up of individual nations, each of which has the priviledge of doing about as they pleased without being embarassed by outside interference. The world has dissolved before the impact of an invention, the airplane has done to our world what gunpowder did to the feudal world. Whether the coming century will be a period of further tragedy or one of peace and progress depend very largely on the wisdom and skill with which the present generation adjusts their thinking to the problems immediately at hand. Examining the principal movements sweeping through the world, it can be seen that they are being accelerated by the war. There is undoubtedly many of these whose courses will be affected for good or ill by the settlement that will follow the war. The United States will share the responsibility of these settlements with Russia, England and China. The influence of the United States, however, will be great. This country is likely to emerge from the war stronger than any other nation. Having benefitted by the absence of actual hostilities on our own soil, we shall probably be less exhausted than our allies and better able to help restore the devastated areas. However many mistakes have been made in our past, the tradition of America, not only the champion of freedom but also fair play, still lives among millions who can see light and hope scarcely nowhere else.

1. When this war is over, no nation will either be isolated in war or peace.   1.____
   - A. either be isolated in war or peace
   - B. be either isolated in war or peace
   - C. be isolated in neither war nor peace
   - D. be isolated either in war or in peace
   - E. be isolated neither in war or peace

2. Each   2.____
   - A. Each   B. It   C. Some   D. They   E. A nation

3. within trading distance of all the others and will be able to strike them.   3.____
   A. within trading distance of all the others and will be able to strike them.
   B. near enough to trade with and strike all the others.
   C. trading and striking the others.
   D. within trading and striking distance of all the others.
   E. able to strike and trade with all the others,

4. Every nation will be most as dependent on   4.____
   A. most   B. wholly   C. much   D. mostly   E. almost

5. the rest for the maintainance of peace as is   5.____
   A. maintainance   B. maintainence   C. maintenence
   D. maintenance   E. maintanence

6. any of our own American states on all the others. The world that we have   6.____
   known was a world made up of individual nations, each
   A. nations, each   B. nations. Each   C. nations: each
   D. nations; each   E. nations each

7. of which had the priviledge of doing about as   7.____
   A. priviledge   B. priveledge   C. privelege
   D. privalege   E. privilege

8. they pleased without being   8.____
   A. they   B. it   C. they individually
   D. he   E. the nations

9. embarassed by outside interference. That   9.____
   A. embarassed   B. embarrassed   C. embaressed
   D. embarrased   E. embarressed

10. world has dissolved before the impact of an invention, the airplane has done   10.____
    to our world what gunpowder did to the feudal world. Whether the coming
    century will be a period of further tragedy or one of peace and
    A. invention, the   B. invention but the   C. invention: the
    D. invention. The   E. invention and the

11. progress depend very largely on the wisdom and skill with which the present   11.____
    generation
    A. depend   B. will have depended   C. depends
    D. depended   E. shall depend

12. adjusts their thinking to the problems immediately at hand.   12.____
    A. adjusts their   B. adjusts there   C. adjusts its
    D. adjust our   E. adjust it's

3 (#1)

13. Examining the principal movements sweeping through the world, it can be seen
    A. Examining the principal movements sweeping through the world, it can be seen
    B. Having examined the principal movements sweeping through the world, it can be seen
    C. Examining the principal movements sweeping through the world can be seen
    D. Examining the principal movements sweeping through the world, we can see
    E. It can be seen examining the principal movements sweeping through the world

14. that they are being accelerated by the war.
    A. accelerated   B. acelerated   C. accelerated
    D. acellerated   E. acelerrated

15. There is undoubtedly many of these whose courses will be affected for good or ill by the settlements that will follow the war. The United States will share the responsibility of these settlements with Russia, England and China. The influence of the United
    A. is   B. were   C. was   D. are   E. might be

16. States, however, will be great. This country is likely to emerge from the war stronger than any other nation.
    A. , however,   B. however,   C. , however
    D. however   E. ; however

17. Having benefitted by the absence of actual hostilities on our own soil, we shall probably be less exhausted
    A. benefitted   B. benifitted   C. benefited
    D. benifited   E. benafitted

18. than our allies and better able than them to help restore the devastated areas. However many mistakes have been made in our past, the tradition of American,
    A. them   B. themselves   C. they
    D. the world   E. the nations

19. not only the champion of freedom but also fair play, still lives among millions who can
    A. not only the champion of freedom but also fair play,
    B. the champion of not only freedom but also of fair play,
    C. the champion not only of freedom but also of fair play,
    D. not only the champion but also freedom and fair play,
    E. not the champion of freedom only, but also fair play,

20. see light and hope <u>scarcely nowhere else.</u>   20._____
    A. scarcely nowhere else
    B. elsewhere
    C. nowhere
    D. scarcely anywhere else
    E. anywhere

KEY (CORRECT ANSWERS)

1.	D	11.	C
2.	A	12.	C
3.	D	13.	D
4.	E	14.	A
5.	D	15.	D
6.	A	16.	A
7.	E	17.	C
8.	B	18.	C
9.	B	19.	C
10.	D	20.	D

TEST 2

DIRECTIONS: The questions that follow the paragraph below are designed to test your appreciation of correctness and effectiveness of expression in English. The paragraph is presented first in full so that you may read it through for sense. Disregard the errors you find, as you will be asked to correct them in the questions that follow. The paragraph is then presented sentence by sentence with portions underlined and numbered. At the end of this material, you will find numbers corresponding to those below the underlined portions, each followed by five alternatives lettered A to E. In every case, the usage in the alternative lettered A is the same as that in the original paragraph and is followed by four possible usages. Choose the usage you consider BEST in each case. *PRINT THE LETTER OF THE CORRECT ANSWER IN THE SPACE AT THE RIGHT.*

    The use of the machine produced up to the present time outstanding changes in our modern world. One of the most significant of these changes have been the marked decreases in the length of the working day and the working week. The fourteen-hour day not only has been reduced to one of ten hours but also, in some lines of work, to one of eight or even six. The trend toward a decrease is further evidenced in the longer weekend already given to employees in many business establishments. There seems also to be a trend toward shorter working weeks and longer summer vacations. An important feature of this development is that leisure is no longer the privilege of the wealthy few,—it has become the common right of most people. Using it wisely, leisure promotes health, efficiency, and happiness, for there is time for each individual to live their own "more abundant life" and having opportunities for needed recreation.

    Recreation, like the name implies, is a process of revitalization. In giving expression to the play instincts of the human race, new vigor and effectiveness are afforded by recreation to the body and to the mind. Of course not all forms of amusement, by no means, constitute recreation. Furthermore, an activity that provides recreation for one person may prove exhausting for another. Today, however, play among adults, as well as children, is regarded as a vital necessity of modern life. Play being recognized as an important factor in improving mental and physical health and thereby reducing human misery and poverty,

    Among the most important forms of amusement available at the present time are the automobile, the moving picture, the radio, television, and organized sports. The automobile, especially, has been a boon to the American people, since it has been the chief means of them getting out into the open. The motion picture, the radio and television have tremendous opportunities to supply wholesome recreation and to promote cultural advancement. A criticism often leveled against organized sports as a means of recreation is because they make passive spectators of too many people. It has been said "that the American public is afflicted with "spectatoritis," but there is some recreational advantages to be gained even from being a spectator at organized games. Such sports afford a release from the monotony of daily toil, get people outdoors and also provide an exhilaration that is tonic in its effect.

    The chief concern, of course, should be to eliminate those forms of amusement that are socially undesirable. There are, however, far too many people who, we know, do not use their leisure to the best advantage. Sometimes leisure leads to idleness, and idleness may lead to demoralization. The value of leisure both to the individual and to society will depend on the uses made of it.

2 (#2)

1. The use of the machine produced up to the   1.____
   A. produced   B. produces   C. has produced
   D. had produced   E. will have produced

2. present time many outstanding changes in our modern world. One of the most   2.____
   significant of these changes have been the marked
   A. have been   B. was   C. were
   D. has been   E. will be

3. decreases in the length of the working day and the working week. The fourteen-   3.____
   hour day not only has been reduced to one of ten hour but also, in some line of work, to
   one of eight or even six.
   A. The fourteen-hour day not only has been reduced
   B. Not only the fourteen-hour day has been reduced
   C. Not the fourteen-hour day only has been reduced
   D. The fourteen-hour day has not only been reduced
   E. The fourteen-hour day has been reduced not only

4. The trend toward a decrease is further evidenced in the longer week end already   4.____
   given
   A. already   B. all ready   C. allready   D. ready   E. all in all

5. to employees in many business establishments. There seems also to be a trend   5.____
   toward shorter working weeks and longer summer vacations. An important
   feature of this development is that leisure is no longer the privilege of the
   wealthy few,—it has become the common right of people.
   A. , —it   B. : it   C. ; it
   D. ...it   E. omit punctuation

6. Using it wisely, leisure promotes health, efficiency, and happiness, for there is   6.____
   time for
   A. Using it wisely   B. If used wisely
   C. Having used it widely   D. Because of its wise use
   E. Because of usefulness

7. each individual to live their own "more abundant life"   7.____
   A. their   B. his   C. its   D. our   E. your

8. and having opportunities for needed recreation.   8.____
   A. having   B. having had   C. to have
   D. to have had   E. had

9. Recreation, like the name implies, is a   9.____
   A. like   B. since   C. through   D. for   E. as

152

10. process of revitalization. In giving expression to the play instincts of the human race, <u>new vigor and effectiveness are afforded by recreation to the body and to the mind.</u>
    A. new vigor and effectiveness are afforded by recreation to the body and to the mind.
    B. recreation affords new vigor and effectiveness to the body and to the mind.
    C. there are afforded new vigor and effectiveness to the body and to the mind.
    D. by recreation the body and mind are afforded new vigor and effectiveness.
    E. the body and the mind afford new vigor and effectiveness to themselves by recreation.

11. Of course not all forms of amusement, <u>by no means,</u> constitute recreation. Furthermore, an activity that provides recreation for one person may prove exhausting for another. Today, however, play among adults, as well as children, is regarded as a vital necessity of modern life.
    A. by no means   B. by those means   C. by some means
    D. by every means   E. by any means

12. <u>Play being recognized</u> as an important factor in improving mental and physical health and thereby reducing human misery and poverty.
    A. . Play being recognized as   B. . by their recognizing play as
    C. . They recognizing play as   D. . Recognition of it being
    E. , for play is recognized as

13. Among the most important forms of amusement available at the present time are the automobile, the moving picture, the radio, television, and organized sports. The automobile, especially, has been a boon to the American people, since it has been the chief means of <u>them</u> getting out into the open. The motion picture, the radio, and television have tremendous opportunities to supply wholesome recreation and to promote cultural advancement. A criticism often leveled against organized
    A. them   B. their   C. his   D. our   E. the people

14. sports as a means of recreation is <u>because</u> they make passive spectators of too many people
    A. because   B. since   C. as   D. that   E. why

15. It has been said "<u>that</u> the American public is afflicted with "spectatoritis,"
    A. "that   B. "that"   C. that"   D. 'that   E. that

16. but there <u>is</u> some recreational advantages to be gained even from being a spectator at organized games
    A. is   B. was   C. are   D. were   E. will be

17. Such sports afford a release from the monotony of daily toil, get people outdoors and also provide an exhilaration that is tonic in its effect. The chief concern, of course, should be to eliminate those forms of amusement that are socially undesirable. There are, however, far too many people who, we know, do not use their leisure to the best advantage. Sometimes leisure leads to idleness, and idleness may lead to demoralization. The value of leisure both to the individual and to society will depend on the uses made of it.
    A. who   B. whom   C. which   D. such as   E. that which

17.____

KEY (CORRECT ANSWERS)

1. C   11. E
2. D   12. E
3. E   13. B
4. A   14. D
5. C   15. E

6. B   16. C
7. B   17. A
8. C
9. E
10. B

TEST 3

DIRECTIONS: The questions that follow the paragraph below are designed to test your appreciation of correctness and effectiveness of expression in English. The paragraph is presented first in full so that you may read it through for sense. Disregard the errors you find, as you will be asked to correct them in the questions that follow. The paragraph is then presented sentence by sentence with portions underlined and numbered. At the end of this material, you will find numbers corresponding to those below the underlined portions, each followed by five alternatives lettered A to E. In every case, the usage in the alternative lettered A is the same as that in the original paragraph and is followed by four possible usages. Choose the usage you consider BEST in each case. *PRINT THE LETTER OF THE CORRECT ANSWER IN THE SPACE AT THE RIGHT.*

    The process by which the community influence the actions of its members is known as social control. Imitation which takes place when the action of one individual awakens the impulse in each other to attempt the same thing, is one of the means by which society gains this control. When the child acts as other members of his group acts, he receives their approval. There is also adults who seem almost equally imitative. Advertisers of luxuries are careful to convey the idea that important persons use and indorse the merchandise concerned, for most folk will do their utmost to follow the example of those whom they think are the best people.
    Akin to imitation as a means of social control is suggestion. The child is taught to think and feel as do the adults of his community. He is neither encouraged to be critical or to examine all the evidence for his opinion. To be sure, there would be scarcely no time left for other things if school children would have been expected to have considered all sides of every matter on which they hold opinions. It is possible, however and probably very desirable, for pupils of high school age to learn that the point of view accepted in their community is not the only one, and that many widely held opinions may be mistaken. The way in which suggestion operates is illustrated by advertising methods. Depending on skillful suggestion, argument is seldom used in advertising. The words accompanying the picture do not seek to convince the reason but only to intensify the suggestion.
    Some persons are more susceptible to suggestion than others. The ignorant person is more easily moved to action by suggestion than he who is well educated, education developing the habit of criticizing what is read and heard. Whoever would think clearly, freeing himself from emotion and prejudice, must beware of the influence of the crowd or mob. A crowd is a group of people in a highly suggestible condition, each stimulating the feelings of the others until an intense uniform emotion has control of the group. Such a crowd may become irresponsible and anonymous, and whose activity may lead in any direction. The educated person ought to be beyond reach of this kind of appeal, no one may be said to have a real individuality who, at the mercy of the suggestions of others, allow themselves to succumb to "crowd-mindedness."

1. The process by which the community <u>influence the action of its members</u> is known as social control.
    A. influence the actions of its members
    B. influences the actions of its members
    C. had influenced the actions of its members
    D. influences the actions of their members
    E. will influence the actions of its members

1._____

2. Imitation which takes place when the action
   A. which   B. , which   C. —which   D. that   E. what

3. of one individual awakens the impulse in each other to attempt the same thing, is one of the means by which society gains this control.
   A. each other   B. some other   C. one other
   D. another   E. one another

4. When the child acts as other members of his group acts, he receives their approval
   A. acts   B. act   C. has acted
   D. will act   E. will have acted

5. There is also adults who seem almost equally imitative.
   A. is   B. are   C. was   D. were   E. will be

6. Advertisers of luxuries are careful to convey the idea that important persons use and indorse the merchandise concerned, for most folk will do their utmost to follow the example of those whom they think are the best people.
   A. whom   B. what   C. which
   D. who   E. that which

7. Akin to imitation as a means of social control is suggestion. The child is taught to think and feel as do the adults of his community.
   A. do   B. does   C. had   D. may   E. might

8. He is neither encouraged to be critical or to examine all the evidence for his opinions.
   A. neither encouraged to be critical or to examine
   B. neither encouraged to be critical nor to examine
   C. either encouraged to be critical or to examine
   D. encouraged either to be critical nor to examine
   E. not encouraged either to be critical or to examine

9. To be sure, there would be scarcely no time left for other things.
   A. scarcely no   B. hardly no   C. scarcely any
   D. enough   E. but only

10. if school children would have been expected
    A. would have been   B. should have been   C. would have
    D. were   E. will be

11. to have considered all sides of every matter on which they hold opinions
    A. to have considered   B. to be considered
    C. to consider   D. to have been considered
    E. and have considered

12. It is possible, <u>however</u> and probably very desirable, for pupils of high school age to learn that the point of view accepted in their community is not the only one, and that many widely held opinions may be mistaken. The way in which suggestion operates is illustrated by advertising methods.
    A. , however
    B. however,
    C. ; however,
    D. however
    E. , however,

12.____

13. <u>Depending on skillful suggestion, argument is seldom used in advertising.</u> The words accompanying the picture do not seek to convince the reason but only to intensify the suggestion.
    A. Depending on skillful suggestion, argument is seldom used in advertising.
    B. Argument is seldom used by advertisers, who depend instead on skillful suggestion.
    C. Skillful suggestion is depended on by advertisers instead of argument.
    D. Suggestion, which is more skillful, is used in place of argument by advertisers.
    E. Instead of suggestion, depending on argument is used by skillful advertisers.

13.____

14. Some persons are more susceptible to suggestion than others. The ignorant person is more easily moved to action by suggestion than he who is well educated, <u>education developing</u> the habit of criticizing what is read and heard. Whoever would think clearly, freeing himself from emotion and prejudice, must beware of the influence of the crowd or mob.
    A. , education developing
    B. , education developed by
    C. , for education develops
    D. . Education will develop
    E. . Education developing

14.____

15. A crowd is a group of people in a highly suggestible condition, each stimulating the feelings of the others until an intense uniform emotion has control of the group. Such a crowd may become irresponsible and anonymous, <u>and whose</u> activity may lead in any direction. The educated person ought to be beyond reach of this kind of appeal,
    A. and whose
    B. whose
    C. and its
    D. and the
    E. and the crowd's

15.____

16. <u>no</u> one may be said to have a real individuality who,
    A. , no
    B. : no
    C. —no
    D. . No
    E. omit punctuation

16.____

17. at the mercy of the suggestions of others, <u>allow themselves</u> to succumb to "crowd-mindedness."
    A. allow themselves
    B. allows themselves
    C. allow himself
    D. allows himself
    E. allow ourselves

17.____

KEY (CORRECT ANSWERS)

1.	B	11.	C
2.	B	12.	E
3.	D	13.	B
4.	B	14.	C
5.	B	15.	C
6.	D	16.	D
7.	A	17.	D
8.	E		
9.	C		
10.	D		

TEST 4

DIRECTIONS: The questions that follow are designed to test your appreciation of correctness and effectiveness of expression in English. In each statement, you will find underlined portions. In some cases, the usage in the underlined portion is correct. In other cases, it requires correction. Five (5) alternatives lettered A to E are presented. In every case, the usage in the alternative lettered A (No Change) is the same as that in the original statement and is followed by four (4) other possible usages. Choose the usage you consider BEST in each case. *PRINT THE LETTER OF THE CORRECT ANSWER IN THE SPACE AT THE RIGHT.*

Sample Questions and Answers

Questions
1. John ran home.
   A. No change
   D. runed
   B. run
   E. None right
   C. runned

2. John aint here.
   A. No change
   D. arre'nt
   B. ain't
   E. None right
   C. am not

Answers
1. A
   (The sentence is obviously correctly written. Therefore, the correct answer is A. No change.)

2. E
   (word aint is unacceptable in usage today. The correct answer should be is not or isn't. Since the alternatives offered in A, B, C, and D are all incorrect, the correct answer is, therefore, E. None right.)

1. It takes study to become a lawyer.
   A. No change
   C. in becoming
   E. None right
   B. before you can become
   D. for becoming

2. His novels never concern old people who wished to be young.
   A. No change
   B. concerned old people who wish
   C. concerned old people who had wished
   D. concern old people who wish
   E. None right

3. You people like we boys as much as we. boys like you.
   A. No change
   C. us boys as much as us
   E. None right
   B. we boys as much as us
   D. us boys as much as we

4. Jane and Mary are more poised than he, but Bill is the brighter of all three. 4._____
   A. No change
   B. more poised than he, but Bill is the brightest
   C. more poised than him, but Bill is the brightest
   D. more poised than him, but Bill is the brighter
   E. None right

5. It is a thing of joy, beauty, and containing terror. 5._____
   A. No change
   B. and abounding in
   C. and of
   D. and contains
   E. None right

6. If he was able, he would demand that she return home. 6._____
   A. No change
   B. were able, he would demand that she return
   C. was able, he would demand that she returns
   D. were able, he would demand that she returns
   E. None right

7. He use to visit when he was supposed to. 7._____
   A. No change
   B. use to visit when he was suppose to.
   C. used to visit when he was suppose to.
   D. used to visit when he was supposed to.
   E. None right

8. I saw the seamstress and asked her for a needle, hook and eye, and thimble. 8._____
   A. No change
   B. seamstress, and asked her for a needle, hook and eye
   C. seamstress and asked her for a needle, hook and eye
   D. seamstress, and asked her for a needle, hook and eye
   E. None right

9. A tall, young, man threw the heavy, soggy, ball. 9._____
   A. No change
   B. , young man threw the heavy, soggy
   C. young man threw the heavy, soggy
   D. , young man threw the heavy soggy
   E. None right

10. The week before my sister, thinking of other matters, thrust her hand into the fire. 10._____
    A. No change
    B. before, my sister thinking of other matters
    C. before my sister thinking of other matters
    D. before my sister, thinking of other matters
    E. None right

11. We seldom eat a roast at our house. My wife being a vegetarian. 11._____
    A. No change
    B. my
    C. , my
    D. ; my
    E. None right

3 (#4)

12. I have only one request. That you leave at once. 12.____
    A. No change   B. that   C. ; that
    D. : that   E. None right

13. I admire stimulating conversation and appreciative listening, therefore I talk 13.____
    to myself.
    A. No change   B. , therefore,   C. therefore
    D. therefore,   E. None right

14. The battle-scarred veteran was as bald as a newlaid egg. 14.____
    A. No change
    B. battlescarred veteran was as bald as a new-laid egg.
    C. battle-scarred veteran was as bald as a new-laid egg.
    D. battle scarred veteran was as bald as a new laid egg.
    E. None right

15. The President's proclamation opened with the following statement: "The 15.____
    intention of the government is, to make the people aware of one of the greatest
    dangers to the safety of the country."
    A. No change
    B. , "The intention of the government is
    C. : "The intention of the government is:
    D. : "The intention of the government is
    E. None right

16. I get only a week vacation after two years work. 16.____
    A. No change
    B. week's vacation after two years work.
    C. week's vacation after two years' work.
    D. weeks vacation after two years work.
    E. None right

17. You first wash your brush in turpentine. Then hang it up to dry. 17.____
    A. No change   B. First you   C. First you should
    D. First   E. None right

18. The teacher insisted that you and he were responsible for the mistakes of 18.____
    Joe and me.
    A. No change
    B. him were responsible for the mistakes of Joe and me.
    C. he were responsible for the mistakes of Joe and I.
    D. him were responsible for the mistakes of Joe and I.
    E. None right

19. He sometimes in a generous mood gave the flowers to others that he had grown 19.____
    in his garden.
    A. No change
    B. He in a generous mood sometimes gave to others the flowers
    C. In a generous mood he sometimes gave the flowers to others

161

4 (#4)

D. Sometimes in a generous mood he gave to others the flowers
E. None right

20. He is attending college since September.
    A. No change
    B. has attended
    C. was attending
    D. attended
    E. None right

21. He enjoys me hearing him singing.
    A. No change
    B. my hearing him sing
    C. me hearing him sing
    D. me hearing his singing
    E. None right

22. Even patients of anxious temperament occasionally feel an element of primitive pleasure.
    A. No change
    B. temperament occassionally feel an element of primitive
    C. temperment occasionally feel an element of primitive
    D. temperament occasionally feel an element of primitive
    E. None right

23. Undoubtedly even the loneliest patient feels tranquill.
    A. No change
    B. Undoubtably even the loneliest patient feels tranquill.
    C. Undoubtedly even the loneliest patient feels tranquil.
    D. Undouvtably even the loneliest patient feels tranquil.
    E. None right

24. Sophmores taking behavioral psychology must pay a labratory fee.
    A. No change
    B. Sophmores taking behavioral psychology must pay a laboratory
    C. Sophmores taking behavioral psychology must pay a laboratory
    D. Sophomores taking behavioral psychology must pay a labratory
    E. None right

25. Atheletic heroes often find their studies an unnecessary hinderance.
    A. No change
    B. Athletic heroes often find their studies an unnecessary hinderance.
    C. Athletic heros often find their studies an unnecessary hindrance.
    D. Athletic heroes often find their studies an unnecessary hindrance.
    E. None right

KEY (CORRECT ANSWERS)

1. A
2. D
3. D
4. B
5. E

6. B
7. D
8. D
9. C
10. E

11. C
12. D
13. E
14. C
15. D

16. C
17. D
18. A
19. D
20. B

21. B
22. A
23. E
24. C
25. D

TEST 5

DIRECTIONS: The questions that follow are designed to test your appreciation of correctness and effectiveness of expression in English. In each statement, you will find underlined portions. In some cases, the usage in the underlined portion is correct. In other cases, it requires correction. Five (5) alternatives lettered A to E are presented. In every case, the usage in the alternative lettered A (No Change) is the same as that in the original statement and is followed by four (4) other possible usages. Choose the usage you consider BEST in each case. *PRINT THE LETTER OF THE CORRECT ANSWER IN THE SPACE AT THE RIGHT.*

1. Many of the childrens' games were supervised by students who's interests lay in teaching.
   A. No change
   B. children's games were supervised by students who's
   C. childrens' games were supervised by students whose
   D. children's games were supervised by students whose
   E. None right

   1.____

2. I told father that a college president was invited to speak.
   A. No change
   B. Father that a college president
   C. father that a College President
   D. Father that a College president
   E. None right

   2.____

3. One should either be able to read German or French.
   A. No change
   B. be able either to read
   C. be able to either read
   D. be able to read either
   E. None right

   3.____

4. Twirling around on my piano stool, my head begins to swim.
   A. No change
   B. My head begins to swim, twirling around on my piano stool.
   C. Twirling around on my piano stool, a dizzy spell ensues.
   D. Twirling around on my piano stool, I begin to feel dizzy.
   E. None right

   4.____

5. As the reverberations of my deep bass voice increase, one of my dogs starts to howl.
   A. No change
   B. increase, one of my dogs start
   C. increases, one of my dogs start
   D. increases, one of my dogs starts
   E. None right

   5.____

6. Roy bellows at Eve that it is her, not he who shouts.
   A. No change   B. her, not him   C. she, not him
   D. she, not he   E. None right

   6.____

164

7. The only man who I think will knock out whoever he fights is Roy. 7._____
   A. No change
   B. who I think will knock out whomever
   C. whom I think will knock out whomever
   D. whom I think will knock out whoever
   E. None right

8. The more prettier of my eyes is the glass one. 8._____
   A. No change   B. most pretty   C. prettier
   D. prettiest   E. None right

9. When a good actress cries, she feels real sad. 9._____
   A. No change   B. feels real sadly
   C. feels really sadly   D. really feels sad
   E. None right

10. I asked the instructor what I should do with this examina-paper. Can you imagine what he said? 10._____
    A. No change   B. ? Can you imagine what he said.
    C. ? Can you imagine what he said?   D. . Can you imagine what he said.
    E. None right

11. Not wishing to hurt my friend's feeling, I tell him that I am leaving, because I have a previous engagement. 11._____
    A. No change   B. I tell him that I am leaving
    C. , I tell him that I am leaving D. I tell him that I am leaving,
    E. None right

12. I remember Utopia College where I studied, while I lived abroad, when the world was at peace. 12._____
    A. No change
    B. College where I studied, while I lived abroad
    C. College, where I studied while I lived abroad
    D. College, where I studied, while I lived abroad
    E. None right

13. Would Robinson Crusoe have survived if he was less unimaginative? 13._____
    A. No change   B. were   C. had been
    D. would have been E. None right

14. Neither time nor tide delay either the traveler or the stay-at-home from his pastime. 14._____
    A. No change
    B. delays either the traveler or the stay-at-home from his
    C. delay either the traveler or the stay-at-home from their
    D. delays either the traveler or the stay-at-home from their
    E. None right

15. When the committee reports its findings somebody will lose their composure.
    A. No change
    B. their findings somebody will lose their
    C. their findings somebody will lose his
    D. its findings somebody will lose his
    E. None right

16. The worst one of the problems which is confronting me concern money.
    A. No change
    B. are confronting me concern
    C. is confronting me concerns
    D. are confronting me concerns
    E. None right

17. Far in the distance rumble the motors of the convoy, but there's no signs of it yet.
    A. No change
    B. rumbles the motors of the convoy, but there is
    C. rumbles the motors of the convoy, but there are
    D. rumble the motors of the convoy, but there are
    E. None right

18. Neither of the patients believe that Hansel or Gretel are alive.
    A. No change
    B. believes that Hansel or Gretel are
    C. believe that Hansel or Gretel is
    D. believes that Hansel or Gretel is
    E. None right

19. Its in untried emergencies that a man's native metal receives its ultimate test.
    A. No change
    B. It's in untried emergencies that a man's native metal receives its
    C. It's in untried emergencies that a man's native metal receives its
    D. It's in untried emergencies that a man's native metal receives its'
    E. None right

20. Expecting my friends to be on time, their tardiness seemed almost an insult.
    A. No change
    B. it seemed that their tardiness was almost an insult.
    C. resentment at their tardiness grew in my mind.
    D. only an accident on the way could account for their tardiness.
    E. None right

21. On first reading "The Wasteland" seems obscure.
    A. No change
    B. On first reading it, "The Wasteland" seems obscure.
    C. "The Wasteland" seems an obscure poem on first reading it.
    D. On first reading "The Wasteland," it seems an obscure poem.
    E. None right

22. A special light will be required to inspect the engine. 22.____
    A. No change
    B. To inspect the engine, a special light will be required.
    C. To inspect the engine, you will require a special light.
    D. To inspect the engine, your light must be special.
    E. None right

23. When mixing it, the cake batter must be thoroughly beaten. 23.____
    A. No change   B. mixing   C. being mixed
    D. being mix   E. None right

24. What you say may be different from me. 24.____
    A. No change   B. from what I say   C. than me
    D. than mine   E. None right

25. Trumping is playing a trump when another suit has been led. 25.____
    A. No change   B. to play   C. if you play
    D. where one plays E. None right

KEY (CORRECT ANSWERS)

1.	D		11.	C
2.	A		12.	C
3.	D		13.	C
4.	D		14.	B
5.	A		15.	D
6.	D		16.	D
7.	B		17.	D
8.	C		18.	D
9.	D		19.	B
10.	A		20.	E

21. B
22. B
23. C
24. B
25. A

ENGLISH GRAMMAR AND USAGE
EXAMINATION SECTION
TEST 1

DIRECTIONS: In the passages that follow, certain words and phrases are underlined and numbered. In each question, you will find alternatives for each underlined part. You are to choose the one that BEST expresses the idea, makes the statement appropriate for standard written English, or is worded MOST consistently with the style and tone of the passage as a whole. Choose the alternative you consider BEST and write the letter in the space at the right. If you think the original version is BEST, choose NO CHANGE. Read each passage through once before you begin to answer the questions that accompany it. You cannot determine most answers without reading several sentences beyond the phrase in question. Be sure that you have read far enough ahead each time you choose an alternative.

Questions 1-14.

DIRECTIONS: Questions 1 through 14 are based on the following passage.

Modern filmmaking <u>had began</u> in Paris in 1895 with the work of the Lumiere brothers.
   1
Using their <u>invention, the Cinématographe,</u> the Lumières were able to photograph, print,
         2
and project moving pictures onto a screen. Their films showed <u>actual occurrences. A</u> train
                                                                            3
approaching a station, people a factory, workers demolishing a wall.

These early films had neither plot nor sound. But another Frenchman, Georges Méliès,
soon incorporated plot lines <u>into</u> his films. And with his attempts to draw upon the potential of
                               4
film to create fantasy <u>worlds</u>. Méliès also <u>was an early pioneer from</u> special film effects. Edwin
                         5   6
Porter, an American filmmaker, took Méliès emphasis on narrative one step further. Believing
<u>that, continuity of shots</u> was of primary importance in filmmaking, Porter connected
      7
<u>images to present,</u> a sustained action. His GREAT TRAIN ROBBERY of 1903 opened a new
      8
era in film.

<u>Because</u> film was still considered <u>as</u> low entertainment in early twentieth century America,
    9   10
it was on its way to becoming a respected art form. Beginning in 1908, the American director

D.W. Griffith discovered and explored techniques to make film a more expressive medium.

169

With his technical contributions, as well as his attempts to develop the intellectual and moral
                                11
potential of film, Griffith helped build a solid foundation for the industry.

   Thirty years after the Lumière brothers' first show, sound had yet been added to the
   12   13
movies. Finally, in 1927, Hollywood produced its first *talkie*, THE JAZZ SINGER. With sound,

modern film coming of age.
             14

1. A. NO CHANGE   B. begun   1.____
    C. began   D. had some beginnings

2. A. NO CHANGE   B. invention—the Cinématographe   2.____
    C. invention, the Cinématgraphe—   D. invention, the Cinématographe

3. A. NO CHANGE   B. actually occurrences, a   3.____
    C. actually occurrences—a   D. actual occurrences: a

4. A. NO CHANGE   B. about   4.____
    C. with   D. to

5. A. NO CHANGE   B. worlds   5.____
    C. worlds' and   D. worlds and

6. A. NO CHANGE   B. pioneered   6.____
    C. pioneered the beginnings of   D. pioneered the early beginnings of

7. A. NO CHANGE   B. that continuity of shots   7.____
    C. that, continuity of shots,   D. that continuity of shots

8. A. NO CHANGE   B. images to present   8.____
    C. that, continuity of shots   D. that continuity of shots

9. A. NO CHANGE   9.____
    B. (Begin new paragraph) in view of the fact that
    C. (Begin new paragraph) Although
    D. Do NOT begin new paragraph) Since

10. A. NO CHANGE   B. as if it were   10.____
    C. like it was   D. OMIT the underlined portion

11. A. NO CHANGE   B. similar to   11.____
    C. similar with   D. like with

170

3 (#1)

12. A. NO CHANGE
    B. (Begin new paragraph) Consequently, thirty
    C. (Do NOT begin new paragraph) Therefore, thirty
    D. (Do NOT begin new paragraph) As a consequence, thirty

    12.____

13. A. NO CHANGE
    B. (Begin new paragraph) Consequently, thirty
    C. (No NOT begin new paragraph) Therefore, thirty
    D. (Do NOT begin new paragraph As a consequence, thirty

    13.____

14. A. NO CHANGE   B. comes
    C. came   D. had came

    14.____

Questions 15-22.

DIRECTIONS: Questions 15 through 22 are based on the following passage.

One of the most awesome forces in nature is the tsunami, or tidal wave. A

tsunami—the word is Japanese for harbor wave, can generate the destructive power of many
                    15
atomic bombs.

Tsunamis usually appear in a series of four or five waves about fifteen minutes apart.
       16
They begin deep in the ocean, gather remarkable speed as they travel, and cover great

instances. The wave triggered by the explosion of Krakatoa in 1883 circled the world in three

days.

Tsunamis being known to sink large ships at sea, they are most dangerous when they
       17
reach land. Close to shore, an oncoming tsunami is forced upward and skyward, perhaps as
                                                            18
high as 100 feet. This combination of height and speed accounts for the tsunami's great power.

That *tsunami* is a Japanese word is no accident, due to the fact that no nation
                                                 19
frequently has been so visited by giant waves as Japan. Tsunamis reach that country regularly,
   20   21
and with devastating consequences. One Japanese tsunami flattened several towns in

1896, also killed 27,000 people. The 2011 tsunami caused similar loss of life as well as untold
        22
damage from nuclear radiation.

171

15. A. NO CHANGE
     B. tsunami, the word is Japanese for harbor wave—
     C. tsunami—the word is Japanese for harbor wave—
     D. tsunami—the word being Japanese for harbor wave,

16. A. NO CHANGE
     B. (Begin new paragraph) Consequently, tsunamis
     C. (Do NOT begin new paragraph) Tsunamis consequently
     D. (Do NOT begin new paragraph) Yet, tsunamis

17. A. NO CHANGE   B. Because tsunamis have been
     C. Although tsunamis have been   D. Tsunamis have been

18. A. NO CHANGE   B. upward to the sky,
     C. upward in the sky   D. upward,

19. A. NO CHANGE
     B. when one takes into consideration the fact that
     C. seeing as how
     D. for

20. A. NO CHANGE   B. (Place after *has*)
     C. (Place after *so*)   D. (Place after *visited*)

21. A. NO CHANGE   B. Moreover, tsunamis
     C. However, tsunamis   D. Because tsunamis

22. A. NO CHANGE   B. 1896 and killed 27,000 people
     C. 1896 and killing 27,000 people   D. 1896, and 27,000 people as well

Questions 23-33.

DIRECTIONS: Questions 23 through 33 are based on the following passage.

I was <u>married one</u> August on a farm in Maine. The <u>ceremony, itself, taking</u> place in an
           23   24
arbor of pine boughs <u>we had built and constructed</u> in the yard next to the house. On the morning
               25
of the wedding day, we parked the tractors behind the shed, <u>have tied</u> the dogs to an oak tree to
             26
keep them from chasing the guests, and put the cows out to pasture. <u>Thus</u> we had thought of
             27
everything, it seemed. we had forgotten how interested a cow can be in what is going on

<u>around them.</u> During the ceremony, my sister <u>(who has taken several years of lessons)</u> was to
  28   29
play a flute solo. We were all listening intently when she <u>had began</u> to play. As the first notes
                                                   30
reached us, we were surprised to hear a bass line under the flute's treble melody. Looking

around, the source was quickly discovered. There was Star, my pet Guernsey, her head hanging
                31
over the pasture fence, mooing along with the delicate strains of Bach.

Star took our laughter as being like a compliment, and we took her contribution that way,
                                    32
too. It was a sign of approval—the kind you would find only at a farm wedding.

23. A. NO CHANGE
    B. married, one
    C. married on an
    D. married, in an

24. A. NO CHANGE
    B. ceremony itself taking
    C. ceremony itself took
    D. ceremony, itself took

25. A. NO CHANGE
    B. which had been built and constructed
    C. we had built and constructed it
    D. we had built

26. A. NO CHANGE
    B. tie
    C. tied
    D. tying

27. A. NO CHANGE
    B. (Do NOT begin new paragraph) And
    C. (Begin new paragraph) But
    D. (Begin new paragraph (Moreover,

28. A. NO CHANGE
    B. around her
    C. in her own vicinity
    D. in their immediate area

29. A. NO CHANGE
    B. (whom has taken many years of lessons)
    C. (who has been trained in music)
    D. OMIT the underlined portion

30. A. NO CHANGE
    B. begun
    C. began
    D. would begin

31. A. NO CHANGE
    B. the discovery of the source was quick
    C. the discovery of the source was quickly made.
    D. we quickly discovered the source.

32. A. NO CHANGE
    A. as
    C. just as
    D. as if

33. A. NO CHANGE B Yet it was 33.____
    C. But it was D. Being

Questions 34-42.

DIRECTIONS: Questions 34 through 42 are based on the following passage,

Riding a bicycle in Great Britain is not the same as riding a bicycle in the United States. Americans bicycling in Britain will find some <u>basic fundamental</u> differences in the rules of the
                                                                               34
road and in the attitudes of motorists.

<u>Probably</u> most difficult for the American cyclist is adjusting <u>with</u> British traffic patterns.
     35   36
<u>Knowing that traffic</u> in Britain moves on the left-hand side of the road, bicycling <u>once</u> there is the
       37   38
mirror image of what it is in the United States.

The problem of adjusting to traffic patterns is somewhat lessened, <u>however</u> by the respect
                                                                        39
with which British motorists treat bicyclists. A cyclist in a traffic circle, for example, is given the same right-of-way <u>with</u> the driver of any other vehicle. However, the cyclist is expected to obey
                         40
the rules of the road. <u>This difference in the American and British attitudes toward bicyclists</u> may
                                                     41
stem from differing attitudes toward the bicycle itself. Whereas Americans frequently view bicycles as <u>toys, but</u> the British treat them primarily as vehicles.
                    42

34. A. NO CHANGE B basic and fundamental 34.____
    C. basically fundamental D. basic

35. A. NO CHANGE B. Even so, probably 35.____
    C. Therefore, probably D. As a result, probably

36. A. NO CHANGE B. upon 36.____
    C. on D. to

37. A. NO CHANGE B. Seeing that traffic 37.____
    C. Because traffic D. Traffic

38. A. NO CHANGE B. once you are 38.____
    C. once one is D. OMIT the underlined portion

7 (#1)

39. A. NO CHANGE   B. also,   39.____
    C. moreover,   D. therefore,

40. A. NO CHANGE   B. as   40.____
    C. as if   D. as with

41. A. NO CHANGE   41.____
    B. difference in the American and British attitudes toward bicyclists
    C. difference, in the American and British attitudes toward bicyclists
    D. difference in the American, and British, attitudes toward bicyclists

42. A. NO CHANGE   B. toy;   42.____
    C. toys,   D. toys; but

Questions 43-51.

DIRECTIONS: Questions 43 through 51 are based on the following passage.

People have always believed that supernatural powers <u>tend toward some influence on</u>
                                                                                     43

lives for good or for ill. Superstition originated with the idea that individuals <u>could in turn,</u> exert
                                                                                                                                                                                     44

influence <u>at</u> spirits. Certain superstitions are <u>so deeply embedded</u> in our culture that intelligent
          45   46

people sometimes act in accordance with them.

One common superstitious act is knocking on wood after boasting of good fortune. People once believed that gods inhabited trees and, therefore, were present in the wood used to build houses. Fearing that speaking of good luck within the gods' hearing might anger <u>them, people</u>
   47

knocked on wood to deafen the gods and avoid their displeasure.

Another superstitious <u>custom and practice</u> is throwing salt over the left shoulder.
                                         48

<u>Considering</u> salt was once considered sacred, people thought that spilling it brought bad
  49

luck. Since right and left represented good and evil, the believers used their right hands, which symbolized good, to throw a pinch of salt over their left shoulders into the eyes of the evil gods. <u>Because of this</u>, people attempted to avert misfortune.
     50

Without realizing the origin of superstitions, many people exhibit superstitious behavior. <u>Others avoid</u> walking under ladders and stepping on cracks in sidewalks, without having any
  51
idea why they are doing so.

175

43. A. NO CHANGE
     C. tend to influence on
     C. can influence
     D. are having some influence on

44. A. NO CHANGE.
     C. could, in turn
     B. could, turning
     D. could, in turn,

45. A. NO CHANGE
     C. toward
     C. of
     D. on

46. A. NO CHANGE
     C. deepest embedded
     B. deepest embedded
     D. embedded deepest

47. A. NO CHANGE
     C. them: some people
     B. them; some people
     D. them, they

48. A. NO CHANGE
     C   traditional custom
     B. Custom
     D. customary habit

49. A. NO CHANGE
     C. Because
     B. Although
     D. Keeping in mind that

50. A. NO CHANGE
     C. Consequently
     B. As a result of this,
     D. In this way,

51. A. NO CHANGE
     C. Avoiding
     B. Often avoiding
     D. They avoid

Questions 52-66.

DIRECTIONS: Questions 52 through 65 are based on the following passage.

In the 1920s, the Y.M.C.A. sponsored one of the first programs <u>in order to promote</u>
                                                                        52
more enlightened public opinion on racial matters; the organization started special university

classes <u>in which</u> young people could study race relations. Among the guest speakers invited to
         53
conduct the sessions, one of the most popular was George Washington Carver, the scientist

from Tuskegee Institute.

As a student, Carver himself had been active in the Y.M.C.A. <u>He shared</u> its evangelical
                                                                54
and educational philosophy. However, in <u>1923,</u> the Y.M.C.A. arranged <u>Carver's first initial</u>
                                          55   56
speaking tour, the scientist accepted with apprehension. He was to speak at several white

colleges, most of whose students had never seen, let alone heard, an educated black man.

9 (#1)

Although Carver's appearances did sometimes cause occasional controversy, but
                                    57   58
his quiet dedication prevailed, and his humor quickly won over his audiences. Nevertheless, for
                                                                                59
the next decade, Carver toured the Northeast, Midwest, and South under Y.M.C.A.

sponsorship. Speaking at places never before open to blacks. On these tours Carver
       60
befriended thousands of students, many of whom subsequently corresponded with his
                                            61
afterwards. The tours, unfortunately were not without discomfort for Carver. There were
  62   63
the indignities of *Jim Crow* accommodations and racial insults from strangers. As a result,
                                                                                   64
the scientist's enthusiasm never faltered. Avoiding any discussion of the political and social
                                              65
aspects of racial injustice; instead, Carver conducted his whole life as an indirect attack to
                                                                                            66
prejudice. This, as much as his science, is his legacy to humankind.

52. A. NO CHANGE   to promote   52.____
    C. for the promoting of what is   D. for the promotion of what are

53. A. NO CHANGE   C. from which   53.____
    C. that   D. by which

54. A. NO CHANGE   B. Sharing.   54.____
    C. Having Shared   D. Because He Shared

55. A. NO CHANGE   B. 1923   55.____
    C. 1923, and   D. 1923, when

56. A. NO CHANGE   B. Carvers' first, initial   56.____
    C. Carvers first initial   D. Carver's first

57. A. NO CHANGE   B. sometimes did   57.____
    C. did   D. OMIT the underlined portion

58. A. NO CHANGE   B. controversy and   58.____
    C. controversy   D. controversy, however

59. A. NO CHANGE   B. However, for   59.____
    C. However, from   D. For

60. A. NO CHANGE   B. sponsorship and spoke   60.____
    C. sponsorship; and spoke   D. sponsorship, and speaking

177

10 (#1)

61. A. NO CHANGE
    B. who
    C. them
    D. those

    61.____

62. A. NO CHANGE
    B. later
    C. sometimes later.
    D. OMIT the underlined portion and end the sentence with a period

    62.____

63. A. NO CHANGE
    B. tours, unfortunately, were
    C. tours unfortunately, were
    D. tours, unfortunately, are

    63.____

64. A. NO CHANGE
    B. So
    C. But
    D. Therefore,

    64.____

65. A. NO CHANGE
    B. He avoided discussing
    C. Having avoided discussing
    D. Upon avoiding the discussion of

    65.____

66. A. NO CHANGE
    B. over
    C. on
    D. of

    66.____

Questions 67-75.

DIRECTIONS: Questions 67 through 75 are based on the following passage.

Shooting rapids is not the only way to experience the thrill of canoeing. An ordinary-
                                                                                    67
looking stream, innocent of rocks and white water, can provide adventure, as long as it has

three essential features; a swift current, close banks, and has plenty of twists and turns.
                  68   69
    A powerful current causes tension, for canoeists know they will have only seconds for
    70
executing the maneuvers necessary to prevent crashing into the threes lining the narrow

streams banks. Of course, the narrowness, itself, being crucial in creating the tension. On a
    71   72
broad stream, canoeists can pause frequently, catch their breath, and get their bearings.

However to a narrow stream, where every minute you run the risk of being knocked down by a
         73   74
low-hanging tree limb, they be constantly alert. Yet even the fast current and close banks would

be manageable if the stream were fairly straight. The expenditure of energy required to paddle

furiously, first on one side of the canoe and then on the other, wearies both the nerves as well
                                                                              75
as the body.

11 (#1)

67. A. NO CHANGE
    C. Many finding that an
    B. They say that for adventure an
    D. The old saying that an
    67.____

68. A. NO CHANGE
    C. features,
    B. features
    D. features; these being
    68.____

69. A. NO CHANGE
    C. with
    B. there must be
    D. OMIT the underlined portion
    69.____

70. A. NO CHANGE
    C. Therefore, a
    B. Thus, a
    D. Furthermore, a
    70.____

71. A. NO CHANGE
    C. streams bank's
    B. stream's banks.
    D. banks of the streams
    71.____

72. A. NO CHANGE
    C. narrowness itself is
    B. narrowness, itself is
    D. narrowness in itself being
    72.____

73. A. NO CHANGE
    C. on
    B. near
    D. with
    73.____

74. A. NO CHANGE
    C. one runs
    B. the canoer runs
    D. they run
    74.____

75. A. NO CHANGE
    B. the nerves as well as the body
    C. the nerves, also, as well as the body
    D. not only the body but also the nerves as well
    75.____

KEY (CORRECT ANSWERS)

1.	C	21.	A	41.	A	61.	A
2.	A	22.	B	42.	C	62.	D
3.	D	23.	A	43.	B	63.	B
4.	A	24.	C	44.	C	64.	C
5.	B	25.	D	45.	D	65.	B
6.	B	26.	C	46.	A	66.	C
7.	D	27.	C	47.	A	67.	A
8.	B	28.	B	48.	B	68.	B
9.	C	29.	D	49.	C	69.	D
10.	D	30.	C	50.	D	70.	A
11.	A	31.	D	51.	D	71.	B
12.	A	32.	B	52.	B	72.	C
13.	B	33.	A	53.	A	73.	C
14.	C	34.	D	54.	A	74.	D
15.	C	35.	A	55.	D	75.	B
16.	A	36.	D	56.	D		
17.	C	37.	C	57.	C		
18.	D	38.	D	58.	C		
19.	D	39.	A	59.	D		
20.	C	40.	B	60.	B		

READING COMPREHENSION
UNDERSTANDING AND INTERPRETING WRITTEN MATERIAL
EXAMINATION SECTION
TEST 1

DIRECTIONS: Each question or incomplete statement is followed by several suggested answers or completions. Select the one that BEST answers the question or completes the statement. *PRINT THE LETTER OF THE CORRECT ANSWER IN THE SPACE AT THE RIGHT.*

Questions 1-5.

DIRECTIONS: Questions 1 through 5 are to be answered SOLELY on the basis of the following passage.

The most effective control mechanism to prevent gross incompetence on the part of public employees is a good personnel program. The personnel officer in the line departments and the central personnel agency should exert positive leadership to raise levels of performance. Although the key factor is the quality of the personnel recruited, staff members other than personnel officers can make important contributions to efficiency. Administrative analysts, now employed in many agencies, make detailed studies of organization and procedures, with the purpose of eliminating delays, waste, and other inefficiencies. Efficiency is, however, more than a question of good organization and procedures; it is also the product of the attitudes and value of the public employees. Personal motivation can provide the will to be efficient. The best management studies will not result in substantial improvement of the performance of those employees who feel no great urge to wok up to their abilities.

1. The above passage indicates that the KEY factor in preventing gross incompetence of public employees is the
   A. hiring of administrative analysts to assist personnel people
   B. utilization of effective management studies
   C. overlapping of responsibility
   D. quality of the employees hired

1.____

2. According to the above passage, the central personnel agency staff SHOULD
   A. work more closely with administrative analysts in the line departments than with personnel officers
   B. make a serious effort to avoid jurisdictional conflicts with personnel officers in line departments
   C. contribute to improving the quality of work of public employees
   D. engage in a comprehensive program to change the public's negative image of public employees

2.____

3. The above passage indicates that efficiency in an organization can BEST be brought about by
   A. eliminating ineffective control mechanisms
   B. instituting sound organizational procedures
   C. promoting competent personnel
   D. recruiting people with desire to do good work

4. According to the above passage, the purpose of administrative analysts in a public agency is to
   A. prevent injustice to the public employee
   B. promote the efficiency of the agency
   C. protect the interests of the public
   D. ensure the observance of procedural due process

5. The above passage implies that a considerable rise in the quality of work of public employees can be brought about by
   A. encouraging positive employee attitudes toward work
   B. controlling personnel officers who exceed their powers
   C. creating warm personal associations among public employees in an agency
   D. closing loopholes in personnel organization and procedures

Questions 6-8.

DIRECTIONS: Questions 6 through 8 are to be answered SOLELY on the basis of the following passage.

EMPLOYEE NEEDS

The greatest waste in industry and in government may be that of human resources. This waste usually derives not from employees' unwillingness or inability, but from management's ineptness to meet the maintenance and motivational needs of employees. Maintenance needs refer to such needs as providing employees with safe places to work, written work rules, job security, adequate salary, employer-sponsored social activities, and with knowledge of their role in the overall framework of the organization. However, of greatest significance to employees are the motivational needs of job growth, achievement, responsibility, and recognition.

Although employee dissatisfaction may stem from either poor maintenance or poor motivation factors, the outward manifestation of the dissatisfaction may be very much like, i.e., negativism, complaints, deterioration of performance, and so forth. The improvement in the lighting of an employee's work area or raising his level of ay won't do much good if the source of the dissatisfaction is the absence of a meaningful assignment. By the same token, if an employee is dissatisfied with what he considers inequitable pay, the introduction of additional challenge in his work may simply make matters worse.

It is relatively easy for an employee to express frustration by complaining about pay, washroom conditions, fringe benefits, and so forth; but most people cannot easily express resentment in terms of the more abstract concepts concerning job growth, responsibility, and achievement.

It would be wrong to assume that there is no interaction between maintenance and motivational needs of employee. For example, conditions of high motivation often overshadow poor maintenance conditions. If an organization is in a period of strong growth and expansion, opportunities for job growth, responsibility, recognition, and achievement are usually abundant, but the rapid growth may have outrun the upkeep of maintenance factors. In this situation, motivation may be high, but only if employees recognize the poor maintenance conditions as unavoidable and temporary. The subordination of maintenance factors cannot go on indefinitely, even with the highest motivation.

Both maintenance and motivation factors influence the behavior of all employees, but employees are not identical and, furthermore, the needs of any individual do not remain orientation toward maintenance factors and those with greater sensitivity toward motivation factors.

A highly maintenance-oriented individual, preoccupied with the factors peripheral to his job rather than the job itself, is more concerned with comfort than challenge. He does not get deeply involved with his work but does with the condition of his work area, toilet facilities, and his time for going to lunch. By contrast, a strongly motivation-oriented employee is usually relatively indifferent to his surroundings and is caught up in the pursuit of work goals.

Fortunately, there are few people who are either exclusively maintenance-oriented or purely motivation-oriented. The former would be deadwood in an organization, while the latter might trample on those around him in his pursuit to achieve his goals.

6. With respect to employee motivational and maintenance needs, the management policies of an organization which is growing rapidly will probably result
    A. more in meeting motivational needs rather than maintenance needs
    B. more in meeting maintenance needs rather than motivational needs
    C. in meeting both of these needs equally
    D. in increased effort to define the motivational and maintenance needs of its employees

7. In accordance with the above passage, which of the following CANNOT be considered as an example of an employee maintenance need for railroad clerks?
    A. Providing more relief periods
    B. Providing fair salary increases at periodic intervals
    C. Increasing job responsibilities
    D. Increasing health insurance benefits

8. Most employees in an organization may be categorized as being interested in
    A. maintenance needs only
    B. motivational needs only
    C. both motivational and maintenance needs
    D. money only, to the exclusion of all other needs

Questions 9-11.

DIRECTIONS: Questions 9 through 11 are to be answered SOLELY on the basis of the following passage.

GOOD EMPLOYEE PRACTICES

As a city employee, you will be expected to take an interest in you work and perform the duties of your job to the best of your ability and in a spirit of cooperation. Nothing shows an interest in your work more than coming to work on time, not only at the start of the day but also when returning from lunch. If it is necessary for you to keep a personal appointment at lunch hour which might cause a delay in getting back to work on time, you should explain the situation to your supervisor and get his approval to come back a little late before you leave for lunch.

You should do everything that is asked of you willingly and consider important even the small jobs that your supervisor gives you. Although these jobs may seem unimportant, if you forget to do them or if you don't do them right, trouble may develop later.

Getting along well with your fellow workers will add much to the enjoyment of your work. You should respect your fellow workers and try to see their side when a disagreement arises. The better you get along with your fellow workers and your supervisor, the better you will like your job and the better you will be able to do it.

9. According to the above passage, in your job as a city employee, you are expected to
    A. show a willingness to cooperate on the job
    B. get your supervisor's approval before keeping any personal appointments at lunch hour
    C. avoid doing small jobs that seem unimportant
    D. do the easier jobs at the start of the day and the more difficult ones later on

9.____

10. According to the above passage, getting to work on time shows that you
    A. need the job
    B. have an interest in your work
    C. get along well with your fellow workers
    D. like your supervisor

10.____

11. According to the above passage, the one of the following statements that is NOT true is:
    A. If you do a small job wrong, trouble may develop
    B. You should respect your fellow workers
    C. If you disagree with a fellow worker, you should try to see his side of the story
    D. The less you get along with your supervisor, the better you will be able to do your job

11.____

Questions 12-15.

DIRECTIONS: Questions 12 through 15 are to be answered SOLELY on the basis of the following passage.

EMPLOYEE SUGGESTIONS

To increase the effectiveness of the city government, the city asks its employees to offer suggestions when they feel an improvement could be made in some government operation. The Employees' Suggestions Program was started to encourage city employees to do this. Through this Program, which is only for city employees, cash awards may be given to those whose suggestions are submitted and approved. Suggestions are looked for not only from supervisors but from all city employees as any city employee may get an idea which might be approved and contribute greatly to the solution of some problem of city government.

Therefore, all suggestions for improvement are welcome, whether they be suggestions on how to improve working conditions, or on how to increase the speed with which work is done, or on how to reduce or eliminate such things as waste, time losses, accidents or fire hazards. There are, however, a few types of suggestions for which cash awards cannot be given. An example of this type would be a suggestion to increase salaries or a suggestion to change the regulations about annual leave or about sick leave. The number of suggestions sent in has increased sharply during the past few years. It is hoped that it will keep increasing in the future in order to meet the city's needs for more ideas for improved ways of doing things.

12. According to the above passage, the MAIN reason why the city asks its employees for suggestions about government operations is to
    A. increase the effectiveness of the city government
    B. show that the Employees' Suggestion Program is working well
    C. show that everybody helps run the city government
    D. have the employee win a prize

12.____

13. According to the above passage, the Employees' Suggestion Program can approve awards ONLY for those suggestions that come from
    A. city employees
    B. city employees who are supervisors
    C. city employees who are not supervisors
    D. experienced employee of the city

13.____

14. According to the above passage, a cash award cannot be given through the Employees' Suggestion Program for a suggestion about
    A. getting work done faster
    B. helping prevent accidents on the job
    C. increasing the amount of annual leave for city employees
    D. reducing the chance of fire where city employees work

14.____

15. According to the above passage, the suggestions sent in during the past few years have
    A. all been approved
    B. generally been well written
    C. been mostly about reducing or eliminating waste
    D. been greater in number than before

15.____

Questions 16-18.

DIRECTIONS: Questions 16 through 18 are to be answered SOLELY on the basis of the following passage.

The supervisor will gain the respect of the members of his staff and increase his influence over them by controlling his temper and avoiding criticizing anyone publicly. When a mistake is made, the good supervisor will take it over with the employee quietly and privately. The supervisor will listen to the employee's story, suggest the better way of doing the job, and offer help so the mistake won't happen again. Before closing the discussion, the supervisor should try to find something good to say about other parts of the employee's work. Some praise and appreciation, along with instruction, is more likely to encourage an employee to improve in those areas where he is weakest.

16. A good title that would show the meaning of the above passage would be
    A. How to Correct Employee Errors
    B. How to Praise Employees
    C. Mistakes are Preventable
    D. The Weak Employee

16.____

17. According to the above passage, the work of an employee who has made a mistake is more likely to improve if the supervisor
    A. avoids criticizing him
    B. gives him a chance to suggest a better way of doing the work
    C. listens to the employee's excuses to see if he is right
    D. praises good work at the same time he corrects the mistake

17.____

18. According to the above passage, when a supervisor needs to correct an employee's mistake, it is important that he
    A. allow some time to go by after the mistake is made
    B. do so when other employee are not present
    C. show his influence with his tone of voice
    D. tell other employee to avoid the same mistake

18.____

Questions 19-23.

DIRECTIONS: Questions 19 through 23 are to be answered SOLELY on the basis of the following passage.

In studying the relationships of people to the organizational structure, it is absolutely necessary to identify and recognize the informal organizational structure. These relationships are necessary when coordination of a plan is attempted. They may be with *the boss*, line supervisors, staff personnel, or other representatives of the formal organization's hierarchy, and they may include the *liaison men* who serve as the leaders of the informal organization. An acquaintanceship with the people serving in these roles in the organization, and its formal counterpart, permits a supervisor to recognize sensitive areas in which it is simple to get conflict reaction. Avoidance of such areas, plus conscious efforts to inform other people of his own objectives for various plans, will usually enlist their aid and support. Planning *without* people can lead to disaster because the individuals who must act together to make any plan a success are more important than the plans themselves.

19. Of the following titles, the one that MOST clearly describes the above passage is
    A. Coordination of a Function
    B. Avoidance of Conflict
    C. Planning With People
    D. Planning Objectives

20. According to the above passage, attempts at coordinating plans may fail unless
    A. the plan's objectives are clearly set forth
    B. conflict between groups is resolved
    C. the plans themselves are worthwhile
    D. informal relationships are recognized

21. According to the above passage, conflict
    A. may, in some cases, be desirable to secure results
    B. produces more heat than light
    C. should be avoided at all costs
    D. possibilities can be predicted by a sensitive supervisor

22. The above passage implies that
    A. informal relationships are more important than formal structure
    B. the weakness of a formal structure depends upon informal relationships
    C. liaison men are the key people to consult when taking formal and informal structures into account
    D. individuals in a group are at least as important as the plans for the group

23. The above passage suggests that
    A. some planning can be disastrous
    B. certain people in sensitive areas should be avoided
    C. the supervisor should discourage acquaintanceships in the organization
    D. organizational relationships should be consciously limited

Questions 24-25.

DIRECTIONS: Questions 24 and 25 are to be answered SOLELY on the basis of the following passage.

Good personnel relations of an organization depend upon mutual confidence, trust, and good will. The basis of confidence is understanding. Most troubles start with people who do not understand each other. When the organization's intentions or motives are misunderstood, or when reasons for actions, practices, or policies are misconstrued, complete cooperation from individuals is not forthcoming. If management expects full cooperation from employees, it has a responsibility of sharing with them the information which is the foundation of proper understanding, confidence, and trust. Personnel management has long since outgrown the days when it was the vogue to *treat them rough and tell them nothing*. Up-to-date personnel management provides all possible information about the activities, aims, and purposes of the organization. It seems altogether creditable that a desire should exist among employees for such information which the best-intentioned executive might think would not interest them and which the worst-intentioned would think was none of their business.

24. The above passage implies that one of the causes of the difficulty which an organization might have with its personnel relations is that its employees
    A. have not expressed interest in the activities, aims, and purposes of the organization
    B. do not believe in the good faith of the organization
    C. have not been able to give full cooperation to the organization
    D. do not recommend improvements in the practices and policies of the organization

25. According to the above passage, in order for an organization to have good personnel relations, it is NOT essential that
    A. employees have confidence in the organization
    B. the purposes of the organization be understood by the employees
    C. employees have a desire for information about the organization
    D. information about the organization be communicated to employees

KEY (CORRECT ANSWERS)

1.	D		11.	D
2.	C		12.	A
3.	D		13.	A
4.	B		14.	C
5.	A		15.	D
6.	A		16.	A
7.	C		17.	D
8.	C		18.	B
9.	A		19.	C
10.	B		20.	D

21. D
22. D
23. A
24. B
25. C

TEST 2

DIRECTIONS: Each question or incomplete statement is followed by several suggested answers or completions. Select the one that BEST answers the question or completes the statement. *PRINT THE LETTER OF THE CORRECT ANSWER IN THE SPACE AT THE RIGHT.*

Questions 1-8.

DIRECTIONS: Questions 1 through 8 are to be answered SOLELY on the basis of the following passage.

    Important figures in education and in public affairs have recommended development of a private organization sponsored in part by various private foundations which would offer installment payment plans to full-time matriculated students in accredited colleges and universities in the United States and Canada. Contracts would be drawn to cover either tuition and fees, or tuition, fees, room and board in college facilities, from one year up to and including six years. A special charge, which would vary with the length of the contract, would be added to the gross repayable amount. This would be in addition to interest at a rate which would vary with the income of the parents. There would be a 3% annual interest charge for families with total income, before income taxes, of $50,000 or less. The rate would increase by 1/10 of 1% for every $1,000 of additional net income in excess of $50,000 up to a maximum of 10% interest. Contracts would carry an insurance provision on the life of the parent or guardian who signs the contract; all contracts must have the signature of a parent or guardian. Payment would be scheduled in equal monthly installments.

1. Which of the following students would be eligible for the payment plan described in the above passage? A
   A. matriculated student taking six semester hours toward a graduate degree
   B. matriculated student taking seventeen semester hours toward an undergraduate degree
   C. graduate matriculated at the University of Mexico taking eighteen semester hours toward a graduate degree
   D. student taking eighteen semester hours in a special pre-matriculation program

1.____

2. According to the above passage, the organization described would be sponsored in part by
   A. private foundations   B. colleges and universities
   C. persons in the field of education   D. persons in public life

2.____

3. Which of the following expenses could NOT be covered by a contract with the organization described in the above passage?
   A. Tuition amounting to $20,000 per year
   B. Registration and laboratory fees
   C. Meals at restaurants near the college
   D. Rent for an apartment in a college dormitory

3.____

4. The total amount to be paid would include ONLY the
   A. principal
   B. principal and interest
   C. principal, interest, and special charge
   D. principal, interest, special charge, and fee

4.____

5. The contract would carry insurance on the
   A. life of the student
   B. life of the student's parents
   C. income of the parents of the student
   D. life of the parent who signed the contract

5.____

6. The interest rate for an annual loan of $25,000 from the organization described in the above passage for a student whose family's net income was $55,000 should be
   A. 3%   B. 3.5%   C. 4%   D. 4.5%

6.____

7. The interest rate for an annual loan of $35,000 from the organization described in the above passage for a student whose family's net income was $100,000 should be
   A. 5%   B. 8%   C. 9%   D. 10%

7.____

8. John Lee has submitted an application for the installment payment plan described in the above passage. John's mother and father have a store which grossed $500,000 last year, but the income which the family received from the store was $90,000 before taxes. They also had $5,000 income from stock dividends. They paid $10,000 in income taxes.
   The amount of income upon which the interest should be based is
   A. $85,000   B. $90,000   C. $95,000   D. $105,000

8.____

Questions 9-13.

DIRECTIONS: Questions 9 through 13 are to be answered SOLELY on the basis of the following passage.

Since the organization chart is pictorial in nature, there is a tendency for it to be drawn in an artistically balanced and appealing fashion, regardless of the realities of actual organizational structure. In addition to being subject to this distortion, there is the difficulty of communicating in any organization chart the relative importance or the relative size of various component parts of an organizational structure. Furthermore, because of the need for simplicity of design, an organization chart can never indicate the full extent of the interrelationships among the component parts of an organization.

These interrelationships are often just as vital as the specifications which an organization chart endeavors to indicate. Yet, if an organization chart were to be drawn with all the wide variety of criss-crossing communication and cooperation networks existent within a typical organization, the chart would probably be much more confusing than informative. It is also obvious that no organization chart as such can prove or disprove that the organizational structure it represents is effective in realizing the objectives of the organization. At best, an organization chart can only illustrate some of the various factors to be taken into consideration in understanding, devising, or altering organizational arrangements.

9. According to the above passage, an organization chart can be expected to portray the
   A. structure of the organization along somewhat ideal lines
   B. relative size of the organizational units quite accurately
   C. channels of information distribution within the organization graphically
   D. extent of the obligation of each unit to meet the organizational objectives

10. According to the above passage, those aspects of internal functioning which are NOT shown on an organization chart
    A. can be considered to have little practical application in the operations of the organization
    B. might well be considered to be as important as the structural relationships which a chart does present
    C. could be the cause of considerable confusion in the operations of an organization which is quite large
    D. would be most likely to provide the information needed to determine the overall effectiveness of an organization

11. In the above passage, the one of the following conditions which is NOT implied as being a defect of an organization chart is that an organization chart may
    A. present a picture of the organizational structure which is different from the structure that actually exists
    B. fail to indicate the comparative size of various organizational units
    C. be limited in its ability to convey some of the meaningful aspects of organizational relationships
    D. become less useful over a period of time during which the organizational facts which it illustrated have changed

12. The one of the following which is the MOST suitable title for the above passage is
    A. The Design and Construction of an Organization Chart
    B. The Informal Aspects of an Organization Chart
    C. The Inherent Deficiencies of an Organization Chart
    D. The Utilization of a Typical Organization Chart

13. It can be inferred from the above passage that the function of an organization chart is to
    A. contribute to the comprehension of the organization form and arrangements
    B. establish the capabilities of the organization to operate effectively
    C. provide a balanced picture of the operations of the organization
    D. eliminate the need for complexity in the organization's structure

Questions 14-16.

DIRECTIONS: Questions 14 through 16 are to be answered SOLELY on the basis of the following passage.

In dealing with visitors to the school office, the school secretary must use initiative, tact, and good judgment. All visitors should be greeted promptly and courteously. The nature of their business should be determined quickly and handled expeditiously. Frequently, the secretary should be able to handle requests, deliveries, or passes herself. Her judgment should determine when a visitor should see members of the staff or the principal. Serious problems or doubtful cases should be referred to a supervisor.

14. In general, visitors should be handled by the 14.____
    A. school secretary
    B. principal
    C. appropriate supervisor
    D. person who is free

15. It is wise to obtain the following information from visitors: 15.____
    A. Name
    B. Nature of business
    C. Address
    D. Problems they have

16. All visitors who wish to see members of the staff should 16.____
    A. be permitted to do so
    B. produce identification
    C. do so for valid reasons only
    D. be processed by a supervisor

Questions 17-19.

DIRECTIONS: Questions 17 through 19 are to be answered SOLELY on the basis of the following passage.

Information regarding payroll status, salary differentials, promotional salary increments, deductions, and pension payments should be given to all members of the staff who have questions regarding these items. On occasion, if the secretary is uncertain regarding the information, the staff member should be referred to the principal or the appropriate agency. No question by a staff member regarding payroll status should be brushed aside as immaterial or irrelevant. The school secretary must always try to handle the question or pass it on to the person who can handle it.

17. If a teacher is dissatisfied with information regarding her salary status, as given 17.____
    by the school secretary, the matter should be
    A. dropped
    B. passed on to the principal
    C. passed on by the secretary to proper agency or the principal
    D. made a basis for grievance procedures

18. The following is an adequate summary of the above passage: 18.____
    A. The secretary must handle all payroll matters
    B. The secretary must handle all payroll matter or know who can handle them
    C. The secretary or the principal must handle all payroll matters
    D. Payroll matter too difficult to handle must be followed up until they are solved

19. The above passage implies that
    A. many teachers ask immaterial questions regarding payroll status
    B. few teachers ask irrelevant pension questions
    C. no teachers ask immaterial salary questions
    D. no question regarding salary should be considered irrelevant

19.____

Questions 20-22.

DIRECTIONS: Questions 20 through 22 are to be answered SOLELY on the basis of the following passage.

The necessity for good speech on the part of the school secretary cannot be overstated. The school secretary must deal with the general public, the pupils, the members of the staff, and the school supervisors. In every situation which involves the general public, the secretary serves as a representative of the school. In dealing with pupils, the secretary's speech must serve as a model from which students may guide themselves. Slang, colloquialisms, malapropisms, and local dialects must be avoided.

20. The above passage implies that the speech pattern of the secretary must be
    A. perfect
    B. very good
    C. average
    D. on a level with that of the pupils

20.____

21. The last sentence indicates that slang
    A. is acceptable
    B. occurs in all speech
    C. might be used occasionally
    D. should be shunned

21.____

22. The above passage implies that the speech of pupils
    A. may be influenced
    B. does not change readily
    C. is generally good
    D. is generally poor

22.____

Questions 23-25.

DIRECTIONS: Questions 23 through 25 are to be answered SOLELY on the basis of the following passage.

The school secretary who is engaged in the task of filing records and correspondence should follow a general set of rules. Items which are filed should be available to other secretaries or to supervisors quickly and easily by means of the application of a modicum of common sense and good judgment. Items which, by their nature, may be difficult to find should be cross-indexed. Folders and drawers should be neatly and accurately labeled. There should never be a large accumulation of papers which have not been filed.

23. A good general rule to follow in filing is that materials should be
    A. placed in folders quickly
    B. neatly stored
    C. readily available
    D. cross-indexed

23.____

24. Items that are filed should be available to
    A. the secretary charged with the task of filing
    B. secretaries and supervisors
    C. school personnel
    D. the principal

    24._____

25. A modicum of common sense means _____ common sense.
    A. an average amount of   B. a great deal of
    C. a little   D. no

    25._____

KEY (CORRECT ANSWERS)

1.	B	11.	D
2.	A	12.	C
3.	C	13.	A
4.	C	14.	A
5.	D	15.	B
6.	B	16.	C
7.	B	17.	C
8.	C	18.	B
9.	A	19.	D
10.	B	20.	B

21. D
22. A
23. C
24. B
25. C

TEST 3

DIRECTIONS: Each question or incomplete statement is followed by several suggested answers or completions. Select the one that BEST answers the question or completes the statement. *PRINT THE LETTER OF THE CORRECT ANSWER IN THE SPACE AT THE RIGHT.*

Questions 1-4.

DIRECTIONS: Questions 1 through 4 are to be answered SOLELY on the basis of the following passage.

The proposition that administrative activity is essentially the same in all organizations appears to underlie some of the practices in the administration of private higher education. Although the practice is unusual in public education, there are numerous instances of industrial, governmental, or military administrators being assigned to private institutions of higher education and, to a lesser extent, of college and university presidents assuming administrative positions in other types of organizations. To test this theory that administrators are interchangeable, there is a need for systematic observation and classification. The myth that an educational administrator must first have experience in the teaching profession is firmly rooted in a long tradition that has historical prestige. The myth is bound up in the expectations of the public and personnel surrounding the administrator. Since administrative success depends significantly on how well an administrator meets the expectations others have of him, the myth may be more powerful than the special experience in helping the administrator attain organizational and educational objectives. Educational administrators who have risen through the teaching profession have often expressed nostalgia for the life of a teacher or scholar, but there is no evidence that this nostalgia contributes to administrative success.

1. Which of the following statements as completed is MOST consistent with the above passage?
   The greatest number of administrators has moved from
   A. industry and the military to government and universities
   B. government and universities to industry and the military
   C. government, the armed forces, and industry to colleges and universities
   D. colleges and universities to government, the armed forces, and industry

1.____

2. Of the following, the MOST reasonable inference from the above passage is that a specific area requiring further research is the
   A. place of myth in the tradition and history of the educational profession
   B. relative effectiveness of educational administrators from inside and outside the teaching profession
   C. performance of administrators in the administration of public colleges
   D. degree of reality behind the nostalgia for scholarly pursuits often expressed by educational administrators

2.____

3. According to the above passage, the value to an educational administrator of experience in the teaching profession
   A. lies in the first-hand knowledge he has acquired of immediate educational problems
   B. may lie in the belief of his colleagues, subordinates, and the public that such experience is necessary
   C. has been supported by evidence that the experience contributes to administrative success in educational fields
   D. would be greater if the administrator were able to free himself from nostalgia for his former duties

3._____

4. Of the following, the MOST suitable title for the above passage is
   A. Educational Administration, Its Problems
   B. The Experience Needed For Educational Administration
   C. Administration in Higher Education
   D. Evaluating Administrative Experience

4._____

Questions 5-6.

DIRECTIONS: Questions 5 and 6 are to be answered SOLELY on the basis of the following passage.

Management by objectives (MBO) may be defined as the process by which the superior and the subordinate managers of an organization jointly define its common goals, define each individual's major areas of responsibility in terms of the results expected of him and use these measure as guides for operating the unit and assessing the contribution of each of its members.

The MBO approach requires that after organizational goals are established and communicated, targets must be set for each individual position which are congruent with organizational goals. Periodic performance reviews and a final review using the objectives set as criteria are also basic to this approach.

Recent studies have shown that MBO programs are influenced by attitudes and perceptions of the boss, the company, the reward-punishment system, and the program itself. In addition, the manner in which the MBO program is carried out can influence the success of the program. A study done in the late sixties indicates that the best results are obtained when the manager sets goals which deal with significant problem areas in the organizational unit, or with the subordinate's personal deficiencies. These goals must be clear with regard to what is expected of the subordinate. The frequency of feedback is also important in the success of a management-by-objectives program. Generally, the greater the amount of feedback, the more successful the MBO program.

5. According to the above passage, the expected output for individual employees should be determined
   A. after a number of reviews of work performance
   B. after common organizational goals are defined
   C. before common organizational goals are defined
   D. on the basis of an employee's personal qualities

5._____

6. According to the above passage, the management-by-objectives approach requires
    A. less feedback than other types of management programs
    B. little review of on-the-job performance after the initial setting of goals
    C. general conformance between individual goals and organizational goals
    D. the setting of goals which deal with minor problem areas in the organization

6._____

Questions 7-10.

DIRECTIONS: Questions 7 through 10 are to be answered SOLELY on the basis of the following passage.

Management, which is the function of executive leadership, has as its principal phases the planning, organizing, and controlling of the activities of subordinate groups in the accomplishment of organizational objectives. Planning specifies the kind and extent of the factors, forces, and effects, and the relationships among them, that will be required for satisfactory accomplishment. The nature of the objectives and their requirements must be known before determinations can be made as to what must be done, how it must be done and why, where actions should take place, who should be responsible, and similar programs pertaining to the formulation of a plan. Organizing, which creates the conditions that must be present before the execution of the plan can be undertaken successfully, cannot be done intelligently without knowledge of the organizational objectives. Control, which has to do with the constraint and regulation of activities entering into the execution of the plan, must be exercised in accordance with the characteristics and requirements of the activities demanded by the plan.

7. The one of the following which is the MOST suitable title for the above passage is
    A. The Nature of Successful Organization
    B. The Planning of Management Functions
    C. The Importance of Organizational Functions
    D. The Principle Aspects of Management

7._____

8. It can be inferred from the above passage that the one of the following functions whose existence is essential to the existence of the other three is the
    A. regulation of the work needed to carry out a plan
    B. understanding of what the organization intends to accomplish
    C. securing of information of the factors necessary for accomplishment of objectives
    D. establishment of the conditions required for successful action

8._____

9. The one of the following which would NOT be included within any of the principal phases of the function of executive leadership as defined in the above passage is
    A. determination of manpower requirements
    B. procurement of required material
    C. establishment of organizational objectives
    D. scheduling of production

9._____

10. The conclusion which can MOST reasonably be drawn from the above passage is that the control phase of managing is most directly concerned with the
    A. influencing of policy determinations
    B. administering of suggestion systems
    C. acquisition of staff for the organization
    D. implementation of performance standards

10.____

Questions 11-12.

DIRECTIONS: Questions 11 and 12 are to be answered SOLELY on the basis of the following passage.

Under an open-and-above-board policy, it is to be expected that some supervisors will gloss over known shortcomings of subordinates rather than face the task of discussing team face-to-face. It is also to be expected that at least some employees whose job performance is below par will reject the supervisor's appraisal as biased and unfair. Be that as it may, these are inescapable aspects of any performance appraisal system in which human beings are involved. The supervisor who shies away from calling a spade a spade, as well as the employee with a chip on his shoulder, will each in his own way eventually be revealed in his true light—to the benefit of the organization as a whole.

11. The BEST of the following interpretations of the above passage is that
    A. the method of rating employee performance requires immediate revision to improve employee acceptance
    B. substandard performance ratings should be discussed with employees even if satisfactory ratings are not
    C. supervisors run the risk of being called unfair by the subordinates even though their appraisals are accurate
    D. any system of employee performance rating is satisfactory if used properly

11.____

12. The BEST of the following interpretations of the above passage is that
    A. supervisors generally are not open-and-above-board with their subordinates
    B. it is necessary for supervisors to tell employees objectively how they are performing
    C. employees complain when their supervisor does not keep them informed
    D. supervisors are afraid to tell subordinates their weaknesses

12.____

Questions 13-15.

DIRECTIONS: Questions 13 through 15 are to be answered SOLELY on the basis of the following passage.

During the last decade, a great deal of interest has been generated around the phenomenon of *organizational development,* or the process of developing human resources through conscious organization effort. Organizational development (OD) stresses improving interpersonal relationships and organizational skills, such as communication, to a much greater degree than individual training ever did. The kind of training that an organization should emphasize depends upon the present and future structure of the organization. If future organizations are to be unstable, shifting coalitions, then individual skills and abilities, particularly those emphasizing innovativeness, creativity, flexibility, and the latest technological knowledge, are crucial and individual training is most appropriate.

But if there is to be little change in organizational structure, then the main thrust of training should be group-oriented or organizational development. This approach seems better designed for overcoming hierarchical barriers, for developing a degree of interpersonal relationships which make communication along the chain of command possible, and for retaining a modicum of innovation and/or flexibility.

13. According to the above passage, group-oriented training is MOST useful in in
    A. developing a communications system that will facilitate understanding through the chain of command
    B. highly flexible and mobile organizations
    C. preventing the crossing of hierarchical barriers within an organization
    D. saving energy otherwise wasted on developing methods of dealing with rigid hierarchies

14. The one of the following conclusions which can be drawn MOST appropriately from the above passage is that
    A. behavioral research supports the use of organizational development training methods rather than individualized training
    B. it is easier to provide individualized training in specific skills than to set up sensitivity training programs
    C. organizational development eliminates innovative or flexible activity
    D. the nature of an organization greatly influences which training methods will be most effective

15. According to the above passage, the one of the following which is LEAST important for large-scale organizations geared to rapid and abrupt change is
    A. current technological information
    B. development of a high degree of interpersonal relationships
    C. development of individual skills and abilities
    D. emphasis on creativity

Questions 16-18.

DIRECTIONS: Questions 16 through 18 are to be answered SOLELY on the basis of the following passage.

The increase in the extent to which each individual is personally responsible to others is most noticeable in a large bureaucracy. No one person *decides* anything; each decision of any importance, is the product of an intricate process of brokerage involving individuals inside and outside the organization who feel some reason to be affected by the decision, or two have special knowledge to contribute to it. The more varied the organization's constituency, the more inside *veto-groups* will need to be taken into account. But even if no outside consultations were involved, sheer size would produce a complex process of decision. For a large organization is a deliberately created system of tensions into which each individual is expected to bring workways, viewpoints, and outside relationships markedly different from those of his colleagues. It is the administrator's task to draw from these disparate forces the elements of wise action from day to day, consistent with the purposes of the organization as a whole.

16. The above passage is essentially a description of decision-making as 16.____
    A. an organization process
    B. the key responsibility of the administrator
    C. the one best position among many
    D. a complex of individual decisions

17. Which one of the following statements BEST describes the responsibilities of an administrator? 17.____
    A. He modifies decisions and goals in accordance with pressures from within and outside the organization.
    B. He creates problem-solving mechanisms that rely on the varied interests of his staff and *veto-groups*.
    C. He makes determinations that will lead to attainment of his agency's objectives.
    D. He obtains agreement among varying viewpoints and interests

18. In the context of the operations of a central public personnel agency, a *veto-group* would LEAST likely consist of 18.____
    A. employee organizations
    B. professional personnel societies
    C. using agencies
    D. civil service newspapers

Questions 19-25.

DIRECTIONS: Questions 19 through 25 are to be answered SOLELY on the basis of the following passage, which is an extract from a report prepared for Department X, which outlines the procedure to be followed in the case of transfers of employees.

Every transfer, regardless of the reason therefore, requires completion of the record of transfer, Form DT411. To denote consent to the transfer, DT411 should contain the signatures of the transferee and the personnel officer(s) concerned, except that, in the case of an involuntary transfer, the signatures of the transferee's present and prospective supervisors shall be entered in Boxes 8A and 8B, respectively, since the transferee does not consent. Only a permanent employee may request a transfer; in such cases, the employee's attendance record shall be duly considered with regard to absences, latenesses, and accrued overtime balances. In the case of an inter-district transfer, the employee's attendance record must be included in Section 8A of the transfer request, Form DT410, by the personnel officer of the district from which the transfer is requested. The personnel officer of the district to which the employee requested transfer may refuse to accept accrued overtime balances in excess of ten days.

An employee on probation shall be eligible for transfer. If such employee is involuntarily transferred, he shall be credited for the period of time already served on probation. However, if such transfer is voluntary, the employee shall be required to serve the entire period of his probation in the new position. An employee who has occurred a disability which prevents him from performing his normal duties may be transferred during the period of such disability to other appropriate duties. A disability transfer requires the completion of either DT414 if the disability is job-connected, or Form DT415 if it is not a job-connected disability. In either case, the personnel officer of the district from which the transfer is made signs in Box 6A of the first two copies and the personnel officer of the district to which the transfer is made signs in Box 6B of the last two copies, or, in the case of an intra-district disability transfer, the personnel officer must sign in Box 6A of the first two copies and Box 6B of the last two copies.

19. When a personnel officer consents to an employee's request for transfer from his district, this procedure requires that the personnel officer sign Forms
    A. DT411
    B. DT410 and DT411
    C. DT411 and either Form DT414 or DT415
    D. DT410 and DT411, and either Form DT414 or DT415

20. With respect to the time record of an employee transferred against his wishes during his probationary period, this procedure requires that
    A. he serve the entire period of his probation in his present office
    B. he lose his accrued overtime balance
    C. his attendance record be considered with regard to absences and latenesses
    D. he be given credit for the period of time he has already served on probation

21. Assume you are a supervisor and an employee must be transferred into your office against his wishes.
    According to this procedure, the box you must sign on the record of transfer is
    A. 6A   B. 8A   C. 6B   D. 8B

22. Under this procedure, in the case of a disability transfer, when must Box 6A on Forms DT414 and DT415 be signed by the personnel officer of the district to which the transfer is being made?
    A. In all cases when either Form DT414 or Form DT415 is used
    B. In all cases when Form DT414 is used and only under certain circumstances when Form DT415 is used
    C. In all cases when Form DT415 is used and only under certain circumstances when Form DT414 is used
    D. Only under certain circumstances when either Form DT414 or Form DT415 is used

23. From the above passage, it may be inferred MOST correctly that the number of copies of Form DT414 is
    A. no more than 2
    B. at least 3
    C. at least 5
    D. more than the number of copies of Form DT415

23.____

24. A change in punctuation and capitalization only which would change one sentence into two and possibly contribute to somewhat greater ease of reading this report extract would be MOST appropriate in the
    A. 2nd sentence, 1st paragraph
    B. 3rd sentence, 1st paragraph
    C. next to the last sentence, 2nd paragraph
    D. 2nd sentence, 2nd paragraph

24.____

25. In the second paragraph, a word that is INCORRECTLY used is
    A. *shall* in the 1st sentence
    B. *voluntary* in the 3rd sentence
    C. *occurred* in the 4th sentence
    D. *intra-district* in the last sentence

25.____

KEY (CORRECT ANSWERS)

1.	C	11.	C
2.	B	12.	B
3.	B	13.	A
4.	B	14.	D
5.	B	15.	B
6.	C	16.	A
7.	D	17.	C
8.	B	18.	B
9.	C	19.	A
10.	D	20.	D

21.	D
22.	D
23.	B
24.	B
25.	C

READING COMPREHENSION
UNDERSTANDING AND INTERPRETING WRITTEN MATERIAL
EXAMINATION SECTION
TEST 1

DIRECTIONS: Each question or incomplete statement is followed by several suggested answers or completions. Select the one that BEST answers the question or completes the statement. *PRINT THE LETTER OF THE CORRECT ANSWER IN THE SPACE AT THE RIGHT.*

1. Most managers make the mistake of using absolutes as signals of trouble or its absence. A quality problem emerges—that means trouble; a test is passed—we have no problems. Outside of routine organizations, there are always going to be such signals of trouble or success, but they are not very meaningful. Many times everything looks good, but the roof is about to cave in because something no one thought about and for which there is no rule, procedure, or test has been neglected. The specifics of such problems cannot be predicted, but they are often signaled in advance by changes in the organizational system: Managers spend less time on the project; minor problems proliferate; friction in the relationships between adjacent work groups or departments increases; verbal progress reports become overly glib, or overly reticent; change occur in the rate at which certain events happen, not in whether or not they happen. And they are monitored by random probes into the organization—seeing how things are going.
   According to the above paragraph,
   A. managers do not spend enough time managing
   B. managers have a tendency to become overly glib when writing reports
   C. managers should be aware that problems that exist in the organization may not exhibit predictable signals of trouble
   D. managers should attempt to alleviate friction in the relationship between adjacent work groups by monitoring random probes into the organization's problems

   1.____

2. *Lack of challenge* and *excessive zeal* are opposite villains. You cannot do your best on a problem unless you are motivated. Professional problem solvers learn to be motivated somewhat by money and future work that may come their way if they succeed. However, challenge must be present for at least some of the time, or the process ceases to be rewarding. On the other hand, an excessive motivation to succeed, especially to succeed quickly, can inhibit the creative process. The tortoise-and-the-hare phenomenon is often apparent in problem solving. The person who thinks up the simple elegant solution, although he or she may take longer in doing so, often wins. As in the race, the tortoise depends upon an inconsistent performance from the rabbit. And if the rabbit spends so little time on conceptualization that the rabbit merely chooses the first answers that occur, such inconsistency is almost guaranteed.

   2.____

According to the above paragraph,
- A. excessive motivation to succeed can be harmful in problem solving
- B. it is best to spend a long time on solving problems
- C. motivation is the most important component in problem solving
- D. choosing the first solution that occurs is a valid method of problem solving

3. Virginia Woolf's approach to the question of women and fiction, about which she wrote extensively, polemically, and in a profoundly feminist way, was grounded in a general theory of literature. She argued that the writer was the product of her or his historical circumstances and that material conditions were of crucial importance. Secondly, she claimed that these material circumstances had a profound effect on the psychological aspects of writing, and that they could be seen to influence the nature of the creative work itself. According to this paragraph,   3.____
   - A. the material conditions and historical circumstances in which male and female writers find themselves greatly influence their work
   - B. a woman must have an independent income to succeed as a writer
   - C. Virginia Woolf preferred the writings of female authors, as their experiences more clearly reflected hers
   - D. male writers are less likely than women writers to be influenced by material circumstances

4. A young person's first manager is likely to be the most influential person in his or her career. If this manager is unable or unwilling to develop the skills the young employee needs to perform effectively, the latter will set lower personal standards than he or she is capable of achieving, that person's self-image will be impaired, and he or she will develop negative attitudes toward the job, the employer—in all probability—his or her career. Since the chances of building a successful career with the employer will decline rapidly, he or she will leave, if that person has high aspirations, in hope of finding a better opportunity. If, on the other hand, the manager helps the employee to achieve maximum potential, he or she will build a foundation for a successful career.   4.____
   According to the above paragraph,
   - A. If an employee has negative attitudes towards his or her job, the manager is to blame
   - B. managers of young people often have a great influence upon their careers
   - C. good employees will leave a job they like if they are not given a chance to develop their skills
   - D. managers should develop the full potential of their young employees

5. The reason for these difference is not that the Greeks had a superior sense of form or an inferior imagination or joy in life, but that they thought differently. Perhaps an illustration will make this clear. With the historical plays of Shakespeare in mind, let the reader contemplate the only extant Greek play on a historical subject, the Persians of Aeschylus, a play written less than ten years after the event which it deals with, and performed before the Athenian people who had played so notable a part in the struggle—incidentally,   5.____

immediately below the Acropolis which the Persians had sacked and defiled. Any Elizabethan dramatist would have given us a panorama of the whole war, its moments of despair, hope, and triumph; we should see on the stage the leaders who planned and some of the soldiers who won the victory. In the Persians we see nothing of the sort. The scene is laid in the Persian capital, one action is seen only through Persian eyes, the course of the war is simplified so much that the naval battle of Artemisium is not mentioned, nor even the heroic defense of Thermopylae, and not a single Greek is mentioned by name. The contrast could hardly be more complete.
Which sentence is BEST supported by the above paragraph?
- A. Greek plays are more interesting than Elizabethan plays.
- B. Elizabethan dramatists were more talented than Greek dramatists.
- C. If early Greek dramatists had the same historical material as Shakespeare had, the final form the Greek work would take would be very different from the Elizabethan work.
- D. Greeks were historically more inaccurate than Elizabethans.

6. The problem with present planning systems, public or private, is that accountability is weak. Private planning systems in the global corporations operate on a set of narrow incentives that frustrate sensible public policies such as full employment, environmental protection, and price stability. Public planning is Olympian and confused because there is neither a clear consensus on social values nor political priorities. To accomplish anything, explicit choices must be made, but these choices can be made effectively only with the active participation of the people most directly involved. This, not nostalgia for small-town times gone forever, is the reason that devolution of political power to local communities is a political necessity. The power to plan locally is a precondition for sensible integration of cities, regions, and countries into the world economy.
According to the author,
   - A. people most directly affected by issues should participate in deciding those issues
   - B. private planning systems are preferable to public planning systems
   - C. there is no good system of government
   - D. county governments are more effective than state governments

6.____

Questions 7-11.

DIRECTIONS: Questions 7 through 11 are to be answered SOLELY on the basis of the following passage.

The ideal relationship for the interview is one of mutual confidence. To try to pretend, to put on a front of cordiality and friendship is extremely unwise for the interviewer because he will certainly convey, by subtle means, his real feelings. It is the interviewer's responsibility to take the lead in establishing a relationship of mutual confidence.

As the interviewer, you should help the interviewee to feel at ease and ready to talk. One of the best ways to do this is to be at ease yourself. If you are, it will probably be evident; if you are not, it will almost certainly be apparent to the interviewee. Begin the interview with topics for discussion which are easy to talk about and non-menacing. This interchange can be like the conversation of people when they are waiting for a bus, at the ballgame, or discussing the weather. However, do not prolong this warm-up too long since the interviewee knows as well as you do that these are not the things he came to discuss. Delaying too long in betting down too business may suggest to him that you are reluctant to deal with the topic.

Once you get onto the main topics, do all that you can to get the interviewee to talk freely with a little prodding from you as possible. This will probably require that you give him some idea of the area and of ways of looking at it. Avoid, however, prejudicing or coloring his remarks by what you say; especially, do not in any way indicate that there are certain things you want to hear, others which you do not want to hear. It is essential that he feel free to express his own ideas unhampered by your ideas, your values and preconceptions.

Do not appear to dominate the interview, nor have even the suggestion of a patronizing attitude. Ask some questions which will enable the interviewee to take pride in his knowledge. Take the attitude that the interviewee sincerely wants the interview to achieve its purpose. This creates a warm, permissive atmosphere that is most important in all interviews.

7. Of the following, the BEST title for the above passage is　　　　　　　　　　　　　　　7._____
   A. PERMISSIVENESS IN INTERVIEWING
   B. INTERVIEW TECHNIQUES
   C. THE FACTOR OF PRETENSE IN THE INTERVIEW
   D. THE CORDIAL INTERVIEW

8. Which of the following recommendations on the conduct of an interview is made　　　　8._____
   by the above passage?
   A. Conduct the interview as if it were an interchange between people discussing the weather.
   B. The interview should be conducted in a highly impersonal manner.
   C. Allow enough time for the interview so that the interviewee does not feel rushed.
   D. Start the interview with topics which are not threatening to the interviewee.

9. The above passage indicates that the interviewer should　　　　　　　　　　　　　　9._____
   A. feel free to express his opinions
   B. patronize the interviewee and display a permissive attitude
   C. permit the interviewee to give the needed information in his own fashion
   D. provide for privacy when conducting the interview

10. The meaning of the word *unhampered*, as it is used in the last sentence of the　　　　10._____
    fourth paragraph of the above passage, is MOST NEARLY
    A. unheeded　　　B. unobstructed　　C. hindered　　D. aided

11. It can be INFERRED from the above passage that　　　　　　　　　　　　　　　　11._____
    A. interviewers, while generally mature, lack confidence
    B. certain methods in interviewing are more successful than others in obtaining information
    C. there is usually a reluctance on the part of interviewers to deal with unpleasant topics
    D. it is best for the interviewer not to waiver from the use of hard and fast rules when dealing with clients

Questions 12-19.

DIRECTIONS: Questions 12 through 19 are to be answered SOLELY on the basis of the following passage.

Disabled cars pose a great danger to bridge traffic at any time, but during rush hours it is especially important that such vehicles be promptly detected and removed. The term *disable car* is an all-inclusive label referring to cars stalled due to a flat tire, mechanical failure, an accident, or locked bumpers. Flat tires are the most common reason why cars become disabled. The presence of disabled vehicles caused 68% of all traffic accidents last year. Of these, 75% were serious enough to require hospitalization of at least one of the vehicle's occupants.

The basic problem in the removal of disabled vehicles is detection of the car. Several methods have been proposed to aid detection. At a 1980 meeting of traffic experts and engineers, the idea of sinking electronic eyes into roadways was first suggested. Such *eyes* let officers know when traffic falls below normal speed and becomes congested. The basic argument against this approach is the high cost of installation of these eyes. One Midwestern state has, since 1978, employed closed circuit television to detect the existence and locations of stalled vehicles. When stalled vehicles are seen on the closed circuit television screen, the information is immediately communicated by radio to units stationed along the roadway, thus enabling the prompt removal of these obstructions to traffic. However, many cities lack the necessary manpower and equipment to use this approach. For the past five years, several east-coast cities have used the method known as *safety chains*, consisting of mobile units which represent the links at the *safety chain*. These mobile units are stationed as posts one or two miles apart along roadways to detect disabled cars. Standard procedure is for the units in the *safety chain* to have roof blinker lights turned on to full rotation. The officer, upon spotting a disabled car, at once assumes a post that gives him the most control in directing traffic around the obstruction. Only after gaining such control does he investigate and decide what action should be taken.

12. From the above passage, The PERCENTAGE of accidents caused by disabled cars in which hospitalization was required by at least one of the occupants of a vehicle last year was
    A. 17%   B. 51%   C. 68%   D. 75%

13. According to the above passage, vehicles are MOST frequently disabled because of
    A. flat tires
    B. locked bumpers
    C. brake failure
    D. overheated motors

14. According to the above passage, in the electronic eye method of detection, the *eyes* are placed
    A. on lights along the roadway
    B. on patrol cars stationed along the roadway
    C. in booths spaced two miles apart
    D. into the roadway

15. According to the above passage, the factor COMMON to both the *safety chain* method and the *closed circuit television* method of detecting disabled vehicles is that both
    A. require the use of *electronic eyes*
    B. may be used where there is a shortage of officers
    C. employ units that are stationed along the highway
    D. require the use of trucks to move the heavy equipment used

15.____

16. The one of the following which is NOT discussed in the above passage as a method that may be used to detect disabled vehicles is
    A. closed circuit television   B. radar
    C. electronic eyes   D. safety chains

16.____

17. One DRAWBACK mentioned by the above passage to the use of the closed circuit television method for detection of disabled cars is that this technique
    A. cannot be used during bad weather
    B. does not provide for actual removal of the cars
    C. must be operated by a highly skilled staff of traffic engineers
    D. requires a large amount of manpower and equipment

17.____

18. The NEWEST of the methods discussed in the above passage for detection of disabled vehicles is
    A. electronic eyes   B. the mobile unit
    C. the safety chain   D. closed circuit television

18.____

19. When the *safety chain* method is being used, an officer who spots a disabled vehicle should FIRST
    A. turn off his roof blinker lights
    B. direct traffic around the disabled vehicle
    C. send a ratio message to the nearest mobile unit
    D. conduct an investigation

19.____

20. The universe is 15 billion years old, and the geological underpinnings of the earth were formed long before the first sea creature slithered out of the slime. But it is only in the last 6,000 years or so that men have descended into mines to chop and scratch at the earth's crust. Human history is, as Carl Sagan has put it, the equivalent of a few seconds in the 15 billion year life of the earth. What alarms those who keep track of the earth's crust is that since 1950 human beings have managed to consume more minerals than were mined in all previous history, a splurge of a millisecond in geologic time that cannot be long repeated without using up the finite riches of the earth.
Of the following, the MAIN idea of this paragraph is:
    A. There is true cause for concern at the escalating consumption of the earth's minerals in recent years.
    B. Human history is the equivalent of a few seconds in the 15 billion year life of the earth
    C. The earth will soon run out of vital mineral resources

20.____

21. The authors of the Economic Report of the President are collectively aware, despite their vision of the asset-rich household, of the real economy in which millions of Americans live. There are glimpses, throughout the Report, of the underworld in which about 23 million people do not have public or private health insurance; in which the number of people receiving unemployment compensation was 41 percent of the total unemployed, in which the average dole for the compensated unemployed is about one-half of take-home pay. The authors understand, for example, that a worker may become physically disabled and that individuals generally do not like the risk of losing their ability to earn income. But such realities justify no more than the most limited interference in the (imperfect) market for disability insurance. There is only, as far as I can tell, one moment of genuine emotion in the entire Report when the authors' passions are stirred beyond market principles. They are discussing the leasing provisions of the 1981 Tax Act (conditions which so reduce tax revenues that they are apparently opposed in their present form by the Business Roundtable, the American Business Conference, and the National Association of Manufacturers).

    In the dark days before the 1981 ACT, according to the Report, (*firms with temporary tax losses* (a condition especially characteristic of new enterprises) were often unable to take advantage of investment tax incentives. The reason was that temporarily unprofitable companies had no taxable income against which to apply the investment tax deduction. It was a piteous contingency for the truly needy entrepreneur. But all was made right with the Tax Act. Social Security for the disabled incompetent corporation: the compassionate soul of Reagan's new economy.

    According to the above passage,
    - A. the National Association of Manufacturers and those companies that are temporarily unprofitable oppose the leasing provisions of the 1981 Tax Act
    - B. the authors of the Report are willing to ignore market principles in order to assist corporations unable to take advantage of tax incentives
    - C. the authors of the Report feel the National Association of Manufacturers and the Business Roundtable are wrong in opposing the leasing provisions of the 1981 Tax Act
    - D. the authors of the Report have more compassion for incompetent corporations than for disabled workers

21.____

22. Much of the lore of management in the West regards ambiguity as a symptom of a variety of organizational ills whose cure is larger doses of rationality, specificity, and decisiveness. But is ambiguity sometimes desirable? Ambiguity may be thought of as a shroud of the unknown surrounding certain events. The Japanese have a word for it, *ma*, for which there is no English translation. The word is valuable because it gives an explicit place to the unknowable aspect of things. In English, we may refer to an empty space between the chair and the table; the Japanese don't say the space is empty but *full of nothing*. However amusing the illustration, it goes to the core of the issue. Westerners speak of what is unknown primarily in reference to what is known (like the space between the chair and the table, while most eastern languages give honor to the unknown in its own right.

22.____

Of course, there are many situations that a manager finds himself in where being explicit and decisive is not only helpful but necessary. There is considerable advantage, however, in having a dual frame of reference—recognizing the value of both the clear and the ambiguous. The point to bear in mind is that in certain situations, ambiguity may serve better than absolute clarity.

Which sentence is BEST supported by the above passage?
- A. We should cultivate the art of being ambiguous.
- B. Ambiguity may sometimes be an effective managerial tool,
- C. Westerners do not have a dual frame of reference.
- D. It is important to recognize the ambiguous aspects of all situations.

23. Everyone ought to accustom himself to grasp in his thought at the same time facts that are at once so few and so simple, that he shall never believe that he has knowledge of anything which he does not mentally behold with a distinctiveness equal to that of the objects which he knows most distinctly of all. It is true that some people are born with a much greater aptitude for such discernment than others, but the mind can be made much more expert at such work by art and exercise. But there is one fact which I should here emphasize above all others; and that is everyone should firmly persuade himself that none of the sciences, however abstruse, is to be deduced from lofty and obscure matters, but that they all proceed only from what is easy and more readily understood.

    According to the author,
    - A. people should concentrate primarily on simple facts
    - B. intellectually gifted people have a great advantage over others
    - C. even difficult material and theories proceed from what is readily understood
    - D. if a scientist cannot grasp a simple theory, he or she is destined to fail

23.____

24. Goethe's casual observations about language contain a profound truth. Every word in every language is a part of a system of thinking unlike any other. Speakers of different languages live in different worlds; or rather, they live in the same world but can't help looking at it in different ways. Words stand for patterns of experience. As one generation hand its language down to the next, it also hands down a fixed pattern of thinking, seeing, and feeling. When we go from one language to another, nothing stays put; different peoples carry different nerve patterns in their brains, and there's no point where they fully match.

    According to the above passage,
    - A. language differences and their ramifications are a major cause of tensions between nations
    - B. it is not a good use of one's time to read novels that have been translated from another language because of the tremendous differences in interpretation
    - C. differences in languages reflect the different experiences of people the world over
    - D. language students should be especially careful to retain awareness of the subtleties of their native language

24.____

Questions 25-27.

DIRECTIONS: Questions 25 through 27 are to be answered SOLELY on the basis of the following passage.

The context of all education is twofold—individual and social. Its business is to make us more and more ourselves, too cultivate in each of us our own distinctive genius, however modest it may be, while showing us how this genius may be reconciled with the needs and claims of the society of which we are a part. Thought it is not education's aim to cultivate eccentrics, that society is richest, most flexible, and most humane that best uses and most tolerates eccentricity. Conformity beyond a point breeds sterile minds and, therefore, a sterile society.

The function of secondary—and still more of higher education is to affect the environment. Teachers are not, and should not be, social reformers. But they should be the catalytic agents by means of which young minds are influenced to desire and execute reform. To aspire to better things is a logical and desirable part of mental and spiritual growth.

25. Of the following, the MOST suitable title for the above passage is 25.____
 A. EDUCATION'S FUNCTION IN CREATING INDIVIDUAL DIFFERENCES
 B. THE NEED FOR EDUCATION TO ACQUAINT US WITH OUR SOCIAL ENVIRONMENT
 C. THE RESPONSIBILITY OF EDUCATION TOWARD THE INDIVIDUAL AND SOCIETY
 D. THE ROLE OF EDUCATION IN EXPLAINIING THE NEEDS OF SOCIETY

26. On the basis of the above passage, it may be inferred that 26.____
 A. conformity is one of the forerunners of totalitarianism
 B. education should be designed to create at least a modest amount of genius in everyone
 C. tolerance of individual differences tends to give society opportunities for improvement
 D. reforms are usually initiated by people who are somewhat eccentric

27. On the basis of the above passage, it may be inferred that 27.____
 A. genius is likely to be accompanied by a desire for social reform
 B. nonconformity is an indication of the inquiring mind
 C. people who are not high school or college graduates are not able to affect the environment
 D. teachers may or may not be social reformers

Questions 28-30.

DIRECTIONS: Questions 28 through 30 are to be answered SOLELY on the basis of the following passage.

Disregard for odds and complete confidence in one's self have produced many of our great successes. But every young man who wants to go into business for himself should appraise himself as a candidate for the one percent to survive. What has he to offer that is new or better? Has he special talents, special know-how, a new invention or service, or more capital than the average competitor? Has he the most important qualification of all, a willingness to work harder than anyone else? A man who is working for himself without limitation of hours or personal sacrifice can run circles around any operation that relies on paid help. But he must forget the eight-hour day, the forty-hour week, and the annual vacation. When he stops work, his income stops unless he hires a substitute. Most small operations have their busiest day on Saturday, and the owner uses Sunday to catch up on his correspondence, bookkeeping, inventorying, and maintenance chores. The successful self-employed man invariably works harder and worries more than the man on a salary. His wife and children make corresponding sacrifices of family unity and continuity; they never know whether their man will be home or in a mood to enjoy family activities.

28. The title that BEST expresses the ideas of the above passage is 28._____
    A. OVERCOMING OBSTACLES
    B. RUNNING ONE'S OWN BUSINESS
    C. HOW TO BECOME A SUCCESS
    D. WHY SMALL BUSINESSES FAIL

29. The above passage suggests that 29._____
    A. small businesses are the ones that last
    B. salaried workers are untrustworthy
    C. a willingness to work will overcome loss of income
    D. working for one's self may lead to success

30. The author of the above passage would MOST likely believe in 30._____
    A. individual initiative   B. socialism
    C. corporations   D. government aid to small business

KEY (CORRECT ANSWERS)

1.	C	11.	B	21.	D
2.	A	12.	B	22.	B
3.	A	13.	A	23.	C
4.	B	14.	D	24.	C
5.	C	15.	C	25.	C
6.	A	16.	B	26.	D
7.	B	17.	D	27.	D
8.	D	18.	A	28.	B
9.	C	19.	B	29.	D
10.	B	20.	A	30.	A